Unwin Education Books: 37

PATTERNS OF EDUCATION
IN THE BRITISH ISLES

Unwin Education Books

Series Editor: Ivor Morrish, BD, BA, Dip.Ed (London), BA (Bristol)

1 Education Since 1800 IVOR MORRISH
2 Moral Development WILLIAM KAY
3 Physical Education for Teaching BARBARA CHURCHER
4 The Background of Immigrant Children IVOR MORRISH
5 Organising and Integrating the Infant Day JOY TAYLOR
6 The Philosophy of Education: An Introduction HARRY SCHOFIELD
7 Assessment and Testing: An Introduction HARRY SCHOFIELD
8 Education: Its Nature and Purpose M. V. C. JEFFREYS
9 Learning in the Primary School KENNETH HASLAM
10 The Sociology of Education: An Introduction IVOR MORRISH
11 Fifty Years of Freedom RAY HEMMINGS
12 Developing a Curriculum AUDREY and HOWARD NICHOLLS
13 Teacher Education and Cultural Change H. DUDLEY PLUNKETT and JAMES LYNCH
14 Reading and Writing in the First School JOY TAYLOR
15 Approaches to Drama DAVID A. MALE
16 Aspects of Learning BRIAN O'CONNELL
17 Focus on Meaning JOAN TOUGH
18 Moral Education WILLIAM KAY
19 Concepts in Primary Education JOHN E. SADLER
20 Moral Philosophy for Education ROBIN BARROW
21 Beyond Control? PAUL FRANCIS
22 Principles of Classroom Learning and Perception RICHARD J. MUELLER
23 Education and Community ERIC MIDWINTER
24 Creative Teaching AUDREY and HOWARD NICHOLLS
25 Preachers of Culture MARGARET MATHIESON
26 Mental Handicap: An Introduction DAVID EDEN
27 Aspects of Educational Change IVOR MORRISH
28 Beyond Initial Reading JOHN POTTS
29 The Foundations of Maths in the Infant School JOY TAYLOR
30 Common Sense and the Curriculum ROBIN BARROW
31 The Second 'R' WILLIAM HARPIN
32 The Diploma Disease RONALD DORE
33 The Development of Meaning JOAN TOUGH
34 The Countesthorpe Experience JOHN WATTS
35 The Place of Commonsense in Educational Thought LIONEL ELVIN
36 Language in Teaching and Learning HAZEL FRANCIS
37 Patterns of Education in the British Isles ROBERT BELL and NIGEL GRANT

Unwin Education Books: 37

Series Editor: Ivor Morrish

Patterns of Education in the British Isles

ROBERT BELL
Senior Lecturer in Educational Studies, Open University

NIGEL GRANT
Reader in Educational Studies, University of Edinburgh

London
GEORGE ALLEN & UNWIN
Boston Sydney

First published in 1977

ISBN 0 04 370082 9 hardback
0 04 370083 7 paperback

Photoset in 10 on 11 point English Times
by Red Lion Setters,
Holborn, London
Printed in Great Britain
by Biddles Ltd, Guildford, Surrey

Foreword

This book is an attempt to examine a group of educational systems that have had to develop in frequent interaction with one another, and to look more closely at the process of that interaction. At the present time, two political developments — probably the most important in these islands for two centuries—make the examination of this topic particularly pressing. As we argue in the text, the entry of the United Kingdom and the Republic of Ireland into the European Economic Community raises wider questions about inter-relations of educational systems that cannot be ignored. At the same time, the growing pressure from the smaller nations for greater control over their own affairs and assertion of their own identities, a pressure that has made devolution part of the policy of every major political party in the United Kingdom, emphasises the need for a greater awareness of the various systems in these islands. With international and internal events highlighting the need to come to terms with the existence of pluralism, we feel that a study of all the educational systems of the north-western European archipelago—more conveniently, if less accurately, termed the British Isles—is one way of trying to do this. Accordingly, we include the systems of England, Wales, Scotland, Northern Ireland, the Irish Republic, the Isle of Man and those of the several Channel Islands in this study.

Since anyone's judgements and interests are likely to be formed in part by his own background and experiences, it may be useful if we declare here those features of our own that seem relevant to the subject of this study. The reader will then be better placed to make his own allowances if they seem necessary.

Robert Bell is an Englishman, but he was born and went to school in Carlisle on the Scottish border. There he mixed with many pupils who were the children of Scottish immigrants. At Cambridge he studied the early cultures of the British Isles, sampling Old Norse, Welsh and Irish in addition to Old French and Old English. He then trained as a teacher at Trinity College, Dublin, and taught for two years in the Irish Republic; this was followed by seven years at a 'Royal' School in Northern Ireland, before he left for the University of Edinburgh. He can therefore claim to have a not too easily paralleled acquaintance with the national cultures of the British Isles. He is now a Senior Lecturer in Educational Studies at that uniquely pan-British educational institution the Open University, and his work in course planning and broadcasting has taken him all over the British Isles as well as to France, Germany and the Nordic countries. He has also been a parliamentary candidate in both Scotland and

England. He is co-editor (with G. Fowler and K. Little) of the sourcebook *Education in Great Britain and Ireland* and co-author (with N. Grant) of *A Mythology of British Education*. He is also editor of the journal *Scottish Educational Studies*.

Nigel Grant is a Scot. Born in Glasgow of mixed parentage (Gaelic-speaking Highland father, Gallowegian mother, both journalists), he went to school in Inverness, and from there proceeded to Glasgow University, where he took an MA in English literature and language, returning later to take an M.Ed and PhD. After teaching in Glasgow secondary schools and in Jordanhill College of Education, he joined the staff of the University of Edinburgh, where he is now Reader in Educational Studies. His professional interests are mainly in comparative education, which has taken him on major lecturing commitments in the United States and Ireland, to the Soviet Union and all the Eastern European countries (Albania excepted), and to most of the Western European countries as well. His publications include two books on education in the USSR and Eastern Europe, articles on various aspects of comparative education (including the problems of cultural and linguistic minorities) and more recently on the educational implications of Scottish devolution; he is also Editor of the journal *Comparative Education* and currently Chairman of the British Section of the Comparative Education Society in Europe, and of the Scottish Educational Research Association.

While working on this book we have, together or separately, visited many places in these islands from Galway to Essex and from Jersey to Shetland. We have talked to and picked the brains of a great many people—administrators, teachers, academics, pupils, researchers, politicians, students, journalists. There are too many to be thanked individually; but some have to be singled out for special thanks for having given generously of their time and having proved of particular help, occasionally more than they could know themselves.

In Ireland, the thanks of the authors are due in special measure to Richard Burke, TD, then Minister for Education of the Republic of Ireland, for sparing a great deal of time at a particularly busy period; Senator John Horgan, a member of Seanad Eireann; Dr D. F. Cregan, CM, President, Dr S. Clyne, Bursar, Michael Clarke, Head of the Department of Education, and all the other staff of St Patrick's College of Education, Dublin, for information, advice, encouragement and help over many years; Dr T. Kellaghan, Director, Educational Research Unit, Dublin; as well as many other helpers on both sides of the Irish border—especially Peppy Barlow, Vincent McGeown, Michael McKeown and John Macnamara.

In Wales to Dr R. M. Jones, University College, Aberystwyth; J. D.

Williams, Dyfed Education Authority; Ieuan Hughes, Coleg Harlech and Gwyn Pritchard of the BBC.

In Scotland to George Foulkes, Chairman, Lothian Region Education Committee; John Nisbet, University of Aberdeen; Stanley Nisbet and Malcolm McKenzie of the University of Glasgow; John McQueen and the staff of the School of Scottish Studies, and Andrew McPherson of the Centre for Educational Sociology, University of Edinburgh. Gordon Brown, formerly Rector of the University of Edinburgh; George Davie, Neil McCormick, University of Edinburgh; Harry Reid, Educational Correspondent, *The Scotsman*; Colin McLean and Iain Thorburn, *Times Educational Supplement Scotland*; Dr T. R. Bone, Principal, and Brian Peck, Lecturer, Jordanhill College of Education; Ethel Rennie, formerly Principal, Craigie College of Education, Ayr; Farquhar McIntosh, Rector, Royal High School, Edinburgh; J. D. Macdonald, Principal Teacher of Gaelic, Portree High School; Alex Bain, Orkney Director of Education; R. A. B. Barnes, Shetland Director of Education; and the headmasters and teachers of Kirkwall Grammar School and Lerwick Primary School.

There are many others who are not so easily assigned to specific countries, such as Margaret Sutherland, a Scotswoman who came from Belfast to Leeds to be an English Professor of Education, the Manxwoman Margot Cameron-Jones, at work in Edinburgh, the Highlander Kenneth Mackinnon, at work in Essex and the Irishman Owen Dudley Edwards, at work in Edinburgh—all of whom are walking embodiments of the essential mobility of modern life in Britain and Ireland.

We are indebted also to very many colleagues in their respective institutions, but at a practical level, we are especially indebted to Miss Sheila Dale, a librarian at the Open University; to the staffs of the National Library of Scotland and the London Library; and to Alex Menzies, Jenny Reeve and Pauline Carney for their patience, application and accuracy in rendering our manuscripts into legible typescript.

Nevertheless, it is only fair to state as clearly as we can that responsibility for the use made of any information or ideas, for the interpretation of these, and for the value judgements made in the following pages, is entirely and unequivocally our own.

Robert Bell
Nigel Grant
Aberystwyth, December 1975

Contents

Now it is this sensation of stemming a stream, of ten thousand things all pouring one way, labels, titles, monuments, metaphors, modes of address, assumptions in controversy, that make an Englishman in Ireland know that he is in a strange land. Nor is he merely bewildered, as among a medley of strange things. On the contrary, if he has any sense, he soon finds them unified and simplified to a single impression, as if he were talking to a strange person. He cannot define it, because nobody can define a person, and nobody can define a nation. He can only see it, smell it, hear it, handle it, bump into it, fall over it, kill it, be killed for it, or be damned for doing it wrong. He must be content with these mere hints of its existence; but he cannot define it, because it is like a person, and no book of logic will undertake to define Aunt Jane or Uncle William. We can only say, with more or less mournful conviction, that if Aunt Jane is not a person, there is no such thing as a person. And I say with equal conviction that if Ireland is not a nation, there is no such thing as a nation.

G. K. Chesterton, *Irish Impressions*
(London, Collins, 1919, pp. 204-5)

Chapter 1

The Disunited Islands

Nobody in Ireland of any intelligence likes nationalism any more than a man with a broken arm likes having it set. A healthy nation is as unconscious of its nationality as a healthy man is of his bones. But if you break a nation's nationality, it will think of nothing else but getting it set again. It will listen to no reformer, no philosopher, to no preacher until the demand of a nationalist is granted. It will attend to no business, however vital, except the business of unification and liberation. Like democracy, national self-government is not for the good of the people, it is for the satisfaction of the people.

Bernard Shaw, Preface to *John Bull's Other Island*

British comparative educationalists are sometimes so busy taking the distant view that they ignore a wealth of material under their noses. The United Kingdom has long been one of the major producers of scholars in comparative studies, many of them leading world figures in that chosen area; yet, with a few exceptions, they have not paid much attention to the educational and cultural pluralism of their own islands. Their training makes them, perhaps, a little less inclined than most to fall back on the tiresome equation of British and English but usually only a little.

This is doubly unfortunate. For one thing, scholars in other countries are inclined to take their cue from British work, assuming that it is accurate—hence the large number of American comparativists who labour under the delusion that there is such a thing as a *British* educational system. For another, they are missing a rich field of study, and one which could actually benefit from their insights and expertise. In the British Isles (if the Irish will forgive the term), there are five distinct major systems to consider, leaving aside for the moment minor island systems, independent legally but dependent in practice, namely Man, Jersey, Guernsey, Alderney and Sark.[1] To add to the interest, no two systems enjoy (if that is the word) the same relationship. The Irish Republic, a country outside even the Commonwealth let alone the United Kingdom, has its own independent system, but is profoundly influenced by a British-ruled past and a constant mobility to and from Britain in the present. Northern Ireland has its own autonomous system, yet for historical reasons has become in some ways more English than the English, while in other ways has remained unmistakably Irish. Wales, though now exercising control over its own primary and secondary schools, is administratively a semi-detached part of the English system, while remaining culturally distinctive. Scotland has an autonomous system, thanks largely to having laid its foundations before the Act of Union of 1707 and having retained a distinctive national church and legal system ever since. Interestingly enough, such governmental and economic pressures as have led to convergence since the beginning of the nineteenth century have at the same time been accompanied by other governmental and economic pressures leading to even greater divergence. Thus for anyone concerned with the interplay of national systems, and the problems of single systems in a multinational complex, Europe's offshore islands offer unique opportunities for their study in microcosm. What follows then is a study of educational variety in the north-west European archipelago.

By this time many English readers will doubtless be bracing themselves for what they see as yet another of those tedious nationalist lectures, oozing with Scottish arrogance and Welsh sour grapes, to which they have become all too accustomed during the devolution debate. They are quite willing to agree that there *are* national differences within the British Isles; they do not happen to think that they are quite as important as ambitious 'regional' politicians have recently suggested. But they are willing to concede that such differences exist if that is necessary to keep the peace. They therefore grin magnanimously whenever they are mentioned.

It may seem unfair to discern such attitudes beneath the indulgent smiles of English readers now groaning under the weight of devolution, but they do depressingly represent the sort of thing that one has heard at a great many national and international conferences within the past ten years when the resurgence of nationalism in Scotland and Wales has at last brought such issues back into English public consciousness. Nevertheless, despite this recent bombardment, the English, on the whole, remain remarkably muddled over the issues involved. For example, although the vast majority of them are well aware (perhaps only too well aware in view of events in Northern Ireland) that the Irish Republic has been an independent state for over fifty years, when they are asked to break down the United Kingdom into its constituent parts they still rhyme off, as their grandparents were taught at school, 'England, Scotland, Ireland, Wales!'

And such parrot learning is, of course, for ever being reinforced. The newspapers continually refer to England, Scotland, Ireland and Wales as the 'home' countries in football competitions and although the less slovenly journalist may sometimes begin his piece by accurately referring to the Lions rugby team, for example, as the 'British Isles' team or the 'British and Irish' team it has usually become the 'British' team by the end of the first paragraph, despite continual but forlorn Irish protest. The continued presence of Northern Ireland within the British state has of course given a certain plausibility to the notion that all Ireland is still in some sense part of a single entity, just as Northern Ireland is often thought of as a part of Great Britain, though a quick glance at the front cover of a United Kingdom passport is enough to remind us that this is not so.

Such solecisms are not a new phenomenon. They are as old as the United Kingdom itself. Indeed it is only recently that they have come to be so often remarked upon.

The first signs of possibly militant change were already being manifested at the time of the present queen's succession when pillarboxes were blown up in Scotland because they were inscribed with the letters E II R in a country where, technically, she was Elizabeth I and not Elizabeth II.[2] Protests over such issues have gradually become more commonplace and we have now moved into a period where more exactitude is normally demanded. But if we now demand greater respect for national sensibilities within the United Kingdom we must remember that this is largely a modern phenomenon. It is doubtful whether all the seventeenth-century inhabitants of these islands had just as clear a notion of England and Scotland as entirely separate countries once their crowns had been united under James VI and I. The English and Scottish parliaments were not united until 1707, when the United Kingdom was first born, but most people in England already thought of Scotland as part of their own country and had been considerably incensed by the Scottish parliament's disastrous attempts in the late seventeenth century to establish a separate colonial empire at Darien in the Panama Isthmus. In a similar way most English people at the end of the eighteenth century already thought of Ireland as part of their own kingdom long before the actual union of Britain and Ireland took place in 1801.

And it has not just been the English who have slurred over such national differences. The natives of Boston or New York regularly referred to themselves as true-born Englishmen before the War of Independence, while even in the mid-twentieth century one of the most famous and most Welsh of Welshmen, Aneurin Bevan, regularly scattered through his speeches such phrases as 'We English' in the style of Lloyd George before him. Significantly the clock-tower commemorating the Irish-born Duke of Wellington in Bevan's Welsh birthplace, Tredegar, still refers to him as 'England's hero'!

And such ambiguities of consciousness remain. When anything

unpleasant happens, when bombs are placed in Birmingham by Irish terrorists, the English are only too ready to suggest that the Irish should be 'sent home' or equally that 'Scotch football hooligans' should be sent back to 'their own country' and away from 'ours'. Yet when a little Irish Republican team, Athlone Town, manages to force a draw with the mighty AC Milan or when (Glasgow) Celtic beats Benfica in some European cup, they are immediately seized upon by English journalists as 'our' successful teams.[3] Similarly, an English stained-glass window will readily be described as the most magnificent in Europe or a Welsh factory described as the largest producer of sausage meat in Europe. Nevertheless the debate on whether to join the European Economic Community was thought of as a debate about 'going into Europe' just as journeys to what was once 'the Continent' are now regularly described as journeys to a 'Europe' from which the British Isles are seen as being distinct.

Such are the simple and largely harmless manifestations of a strong and highly complex English nationalism, rarely discerned until the Empire had disappeared; for while it continued, the terms 'English' and 'imperial' were for most people readily synonymous throughout the British Isles, however painful it now is for modern Scottish, Irish or Welsh nationalists to acknowledge this. The orange banners of Northern Ireland bore pictures of Queen Victoria presenting bibles to African chiefs and beneath them was the universal inscription 'The Secret of England's Greatness', while even Irish nationalist writers (of non-Republican persuasion) regularly spoke of maintaining loyalty to the throne of England rather than (more cumbersomely) to the throne of the United Kingdom. Even those Irish and Scottish unionists[4] who were unwilling to think of themselves as specifically English described themselves as 'West British' or 'North British' without ever expecting the English to call themselves South (or East) Britons.

Certainly the over-arching and muddled rhetoric of imperialism made it easier for English people to be eclectic in deciding whether to dissociate themselves from or associate themselves with the actions of their fellow islanders. When boasting of military prowess, the English regularly regarded the kilted Scots as 'our' regiments but when deciding which parliamentary debates to attend, English members freely absented themselves from debates on 'their' (i.e. the Scots') educational system. And these habits of the imperial period have made it exceptionally difficult for outsiders who take London to be typical of British life, and who accept English assumptions and prejudices on such issues, to understand what the present fuss is all about. What references there are to Scottish, Welsh or Irish differences continue to be accompanied by a ritual, sheepish grin which clearly implies that to respect such differences or even to take them seriously is to indulge in a pedantry that can only be made tolerable by being placed within a humorous framework. This grin can be good-humoured. It can just as easily be the grin of an imperial master race irritatingly indulging the harmless fantasies of 'natives'.

It would be over-crude, however, to think of English attitudes towards the Scottish differences in particular in quite such simplistic terms. In the first place, generalisation is obviously impossible. Theories based on stereotypes always teeter on the edge of spuriousness. There is no one English attitude to Scotland. But in the second place, English attitudes have always been ambiguous. Indeed, so far as Scottish education is concerned, the problem has often been not to demonstrate Scotland's separateness to an English audience but to tone down their exaggerated and inaccurate notions of alleged Scottish superiority. Yet even those who praise the virtues of the Scottish system are just as likely to generalise about British education as the next man and to regard too great an emphasis on its separateness within a general context as an inexcusable pedantry. Moreover, even when lauding the cultural and intellectual success of Scottish schools, the English are likely to discern in them the absence of that virtue which secretly they value more highly in a school than those cultural or intellectual developments which they praise—the virtue of social grace.

In the meritocratic atmosphere of a postwar England which has come to prize intellectual achievement, it has too easily been forgotten that the most despised figure in the prewar English school was the 'swot' or 'mark-grubber' who ranked intellectual activity or a talent in the arts above skill at games or other 'gentlemanly' pursuits. And such a prejudice was just as common in the universities where dedicated scholars and even libraries were in constant danger not just of neglect but of physical attack. The English anti-intellectual often despised the Scots for an intellectual devotion that was usually accompanied by little social grace, while the English intellectual despised the Scots for their lack of formality and grace in their institutional arrangements and demanded of Scottish MAs, on arrival at Oxford or Cambridge, that they should become undergraduates again in order to submit themselves to the socialisation process of true scholars. One turns to the opening chapters of the mid-nineteenth century autobiographical novel *Lavengro* by George Borrow. Borrow was an exceptionally humane writer noted especially for his defence in middle-class circles of the usually despised English gypsies. He is also one who speaks well of Scottish schooling on a quite exaggerated scale. Yet he puts into the mouths of his characters sentiments about Edinburgh, the Scots and their social shortcomings that could have done service just as easily in contemporary 'tolerant' accounts of learned India. He speaks of the life of his family, an English military family in Edinburgh.

> My brother who, for some years past, had been receiving his education in a certain celebrated school in England, was now with us, and it came to pass, that one day my father, as he sat at table, looked steadfastly on my brother and myself, and then addressed my mother:— 'During my journey down hither I have lost no opportunity of making enquiries about these people, the Scotch amongst whom we now are, and since I have been here I have observed them attentively. From what I have heard and seen, I should say that upon the whole they are a very decent set of people; they seem acute and intelligent, and I am told that their system of education is so excellent, that every person is learned—more or less acquainted with Greek and Latin. There is, one thing, however, connected with them which is a great drawback—the horrid jargon which they speak. However learned they may be in Greek and Latin, their English is execrable; and yet I'm told it is not as bad as it was. I was in company with an Englishman who has resided here many years. We were talking about the country and its people. "I should like them both very much," said I, "were it not for the language. I wish sincerely our Parliament, which is passing so many foolish acts every year, would pass one to force these Scotch to speak English." "I wish so, too," said he. "The language is a disgrace to the British Government ..." "... Were it not for the language, which, if the boys were to pick it up, might ruin their prospects in life ... I should very much like to send them to a school there is in this place ... the High School, I think they call it. 'Tis said to be the best school in the whole island, but the idea of one's children speaking Scotch—broad Scotch!"[5]

The dangerous barbarities against which the British parliament was called upon by Englishmen to legislate were perpetrated in an Edinburgh renowned at that time throughout the Western world for its intellectual, artistic and scientific achievements. The uncouthness of Scottish speech was being despised by a nation that was still to develop a modern university and secondary school system, and at a time when Scottish (and, indeed, Irish) schools and universities were already far wider and more influential in their curriculum and far more socially comprehensive in their intake than either the well-spoken and socially exalted ancient English universities or the celebrated public schools whose curriculum remained cramped and whose pedagogy was still largely medieval.

Nor indeed at the beginning of the nineteenth century could the English even claim that superiority that comes from sheer numbers. In 1800 as many inhabitants of the British Isles lived outside England as inside it and it was only as a result of the massive emigration from Scotland and Ireland during the early years of the nineteenth century—during the famines and the deliberate 'clearance' of people from the

Scottish Highlands in favour of sheep and deer—that the population of England began far to outnumber that of her neighbours. At that time English domination was still based far more on straight economic, military and political power than on numerical superiority or cultural development. As the English population began to grow and the population elsewhere in the islands to decline, only then did her dominance and her sense of superiority achieve the dubious legitimacy bestowed by numbers and the presence of lately developed cultural institutions.

Yet, ironically, as England's size and power increased during the nineteenth century so were sown also the seeds of that complementary defensive self-assertion which now characterises the other countries of the British Isles. The nineteenth century saw not merely a decline in the Irish population, unparalleled elsewhere in Europe, it also saw that massive increase in Irish nationalist feeling which was eventually to produce crucial cracks in the structure of the British empire itself. This nationalism was in part a reaction to the economic depression that helped to cause the demographic changes but it owed something also to quite separate cultural developments including far-reaching changes in the nature of Irish religion among both Catholics and Protestants. And although Scotland on the whole accepted for a much longer period her membership of a centralised United Kingdom than did Ireland, there was, nevertheless, a growth of nationalist feeling there also. The closing years of the nineteenth century, the period of the greatest agitation for Irish home rule, also saw a revival of government interest in Scottish political institutions, the first appointment of a powerful political Secretary of State for Scotland and the establishment of a separate Scottish Education Department unknown before.

As we now know, the period between and following the two wars was to see an even more significant growth of national self-assertion in Scotland and indeed in all parts of the British Isles outside England. And all this took place, ironically, at a time when English financial control and English dominance of cultural agencies such as television, radio and newspapers within the British Isles were becoming stronger and more influential than at any time in previous history.

We think it is of some importance, therefore, to notice how, during the last ten years, when most of the world and indeed most of the population of the United Kingdom have expected a growing homogeneity of culture and educational arrangements within the British Isles, there has in fact been a greater tendency towards heterogeneity. Even before devolution, the Secretary of State for Education and Science in the British Cabinet oversees a far smaller area of the national educational systems than he did in 1966 and the responsibilities of his Scottish, Welsh and Northern Irish colleagues have all become appreciably greater. In view of the plans for devolution it looks now as if his power and influence will decline even further while the heterogeneity of administrative arrangements will increase. It is important, therefore, that not only British comparativists but comparativists throughout the world should recognise clearly the increasingly fragmented nature of educational structures within the British Isles and the scholarly and political dangers of generalising about 'British' educational phenomena at any time.

Primary and secondary education in the United Kingdom[6] are, in 1976, the responsibility not of one ministry but of four—the Department of Education and Science (for England), the Scottish Office, the Welsh Office and the Northern Ireland Office. Thus the interests of primary and secondary schooling are represented in the Cabinet by four separate secretaries of state, none of whom need take instruction from any of the others. The Scottish Office is, in addition, responsible for the administration of all post-secondary education (with the exception of that carried on in universities) while the Northern Ireland Office, as a relic of the days of earlier parliamentary independence, controls the whole of higher education.

Superficially, of course, the system resembles a federal one in which each province enjoys separate educational government and structures. In fact, however, it is a perhaps unique development of centralised government whereby each province's education is run by a separate department of central government.

It is, of course, possible to exaggerate the differences between, and indeed the degree of autonomy exercised by, each of these British and Irish systems. There are throughout the British Isles great social, climatic and economic similarities and indeed many common linguistic and cultural characteristics. All the islands have shared a host of common historical and cultural experiences both before and during the imperial period. Moreover, four of the systems (those within the United Kingdom) have been subject to legislation by the same Parliament and are at the mercy of the common ideologies of the same national political parties which (within the island of Great Britain at any rate) operate across national boundaries. Like their neighbours in other parts of Western Europe and indeed like countries throughout the world, they have to respond to similar modern problems and naturally they often respond in similar ways, while all of them are subject to the same international influences emanating from the universities of North America and from other parts of what is now the increasingly internationalised educational world of the English-speaking countries. They are all now subject to more and more pressure and suggestions from world agencies such as UNESCO as well as from agencies such as OECD or the European Economic Community which can offer both financial incentives for suggested educational developments[7] and plans for general economic development which will have educational consequences. In addition, the two Irish systems, like those of Scotland and Wales, have always had to bear in mind the fact that large numbers of their products would be emigrating to England or to countries where English qualifications were recognised.

Migration has also caused educational problems for the Isle of Man and the Channel Islands though there, so to speak, in reverse. In recent years they have had to cope with large numbers of English immigrants and thus had to take account not only of the previous educational experience of pupils arriving from England but also of the expectations of mainly middle-class, English-educated parents. Amidst such pressures, autonomy must perforce be limited.

In addition, of course, all ten educational systems tend for economic reasons to be dominated by the products of the English publishing industry and of broadcasting media whose career structures centre upon London, while the cultures within which they operate tend to be more and more dominated by the norms of English journalism. In recent years also English scholars in the field of educational studies and the highly prestigious schools of pedagogy in England, such as the London Institute, have tended to be the principal mediators of educational thinking within all the British Isles.

But such common influences are not always necessarily English. Very many educational posts in England are occupied by Welsh or Scottish men and women (for reasons we shall discuss later), while an international tone has also been imparted to the systems by the fact that everywhere there are Roman Catholic schools drawing on a common stock of teachers from religious orders that are mainly Irish in their intake.

This internationalisation of the academic profession poses a particular threat to national differences and it is accentuated by the recent English domination of the higher education sector throughout the islands.[8] This domination results in part from the fact that university education within the United Kingdom is overseen by a single University Grants Committee supervised in turn by the English Department of Education and Science. In the name of egalitarianism the UGC has imposed a new homogeneity and uniformity on what were once far more varied structures—a homogeneity and uniformity too often reflecting the style of the (English) majority.

The Isle of Man and the Channel islands are, of course, too small to support their own higher education system so that they are even more subject to the influence of the (usually English) universities and colleges within the United Kingdom, where not only their schools' products but also their teachers seek their training.

Paradoxically, however, such centralising influences have, as we have said, developed alongside a growing tendency towards devolution of administrative structures, not merely to the constituent countries of the United Kingdom, but also, within England, Scotland, Wales and Northern Ireland, to local education authorities which enjoy a degree of autonomy not enjoyed by many apparently autonomous provinces under ostensibly federal constitutions. And even within the Republic of Ireland, whose educational system has remained more centralised than those of her neighbours, a new cry has recently gone up for the establishment of just such local education authorities on the lines of Northern Ireland or of England.

There has, then, for long been a complex situation within the British Isles whereby a growing homogeneity of career structures and curriculum has been accompanied by a growing heterogeneity of administrative structures and cultural priorities. Certainly it is a more complex situation than one might discern in the bland documents of those international organisations which too often treat British and Irish education as a simple unitary phenomenon. Thus, whether you put your money on the eventual triumph of homogeneity or of heterogeneity, growing complexity is a sure winner in the short term—especially as the devolution legislation promises no standard governmental structure for the four countries of the United Kingdom.

We have already said that the legal independence of the ten educational systems in the British Isles can disguise the existence of many shared characteristics, but there are still many differences, distinctive problems and activities which are the result of differing local conditions and distinctive educational histories.

Some of these differences, for example, are the results of differentials in social and economic conditions.

Irish concern in particular has had to be demonstrated within a context of resources far more restricted than those available in Britain itself. And these resources have not just been restricted as a result of Irish independence. Even when both parts of Ireland were under the control of the Westminster Parliament, in the period between 1801 and 1920, the payment of Irish teachers usually fell far short of that of teachers in Scotland or in England for there was in Ireland far greater competition for the few posts available within a failing economy.

Free, compulsory education came to an Ireland even under British rule some thirty years after it had already become the norm elsewhere in the United Kingdom. An emigration-dominated economy with little industrial development and few fashionable natural resources required less educational efficiency than did a Britain which, in contrast, found itself a promising contender in a fierce competitive world which also contained the educationally advanced United States and Germany.

But dominating both Irish and British provision alike—in

different ways and to varying degrees—were the needs of the Empire, which often ascribed differing roles to the inhabitants of the different 'home' countries. Thus, the Scots tended to be in demand not merely as professionals (medical and administrative professionals in particular) but also as engineers and as middle management in the public services and industry. This tended to encourage the further development of an educational system traditionally drawing as efficiently as possible on a national pool of ability deemed to embrace all social classes. The particular imperial role of the English, on the other hand, seemed to lie almost exclusively in the field of leadership. Until the 1930s her proletariat could not even satisfy the manpower demands of home industry and although there was obviously considerable emigration by the English working class to all parts of the Empire, English education did little to prepare it for specifically imperial functions. Instead, general educational developments in England were concerned with industrial needs at home while the imperial needs of the army officer and middle-rank administration were catered for in the characteristically English and socially elitist public and grammar schools.

The imperial role of Ireland was a far more complex one. The Irish educational system, like that of Scotland, produced professionals. These were often the children of small farmers or of comparatively poor doctors and solicitors, but it also produced (very cheaply and often from the poorest classes) hosts of religious 'leaders' (many of them indispensable doctors and teachers) whose highly influential imperial role has been largely neglected by historians. Much of Australian and African education was developed by such people who (free from overtly imperialist ideology) were able to continue their work in Third World countries once the British had gone. But most of the Irish Empire-builders, alas, were enforced emigrants, cast in the role of, at best, common soldiers, or, at worst, of coolies. For them little educational provision needed to be made and, because of their fate, the quality of Irish education at its best has often been judged unfairly by the outside world.[9]

More recent political change has of course also produced obvious differences in the educational provision on the two sides of the Irish border and presumably devolution of government to Scotland and Wales is likely to produce a similar growth in differentials. Moreover the nature of such change can often reflect directly a political ideology. In the Irish Republic and in Wales, for example, the prevalence of a strongly nationalist ideology based on perceived cultural differences has at various times in history produced an overwhelming emphasis on the promotion of the native language; on the other hand the absence in Scotland of any prevailing ideology featuring the Gaelic language has meant that the promotion of Scottish Gaelic (unlike that of Irish Gaelic and Welsh) has never become such a potent political and educational issue.

But perhaps the crucial difference that has marked off English education from that elsewhere in the British Isles is not so easily explained in purely political or economic terms—its apparently irrational failure to exploit its native talent, to draw on its true pool of ability. In Ireland, Scotland and Wales there has been an emphasis for many centuries on maximising the opportunities for the able child whatever his home background. There has been a feeling within such countries, beset by great natural difficulties, that the national pool of ability should be thoroughly tapped and that no social barrier or prejudice should allow such a process, important for the community as well as for the individual, to be impeded. As a result, as we have already said, the Irish and Scottish universities of the eighteenth and nineteenth centuries contained a far greater proportion of boys from humble backgrounds than was the case in England, where the universities were never until recently seen primarily as places for developing the individual's or the state's economic, let alone intellectual, capability. Oxford and Cambridge for most of their history have been concerned, on the one hand with organising and supplying the ecclesiastical career structure, and on the other, with the functions of a social finishing school. Professional men and scientists were never expected in England until recently to develop their skills within educational institutions, and any technical advantages derived from their presence there were largely accidental. Their schooling—and even their university career (if they bothered to have one) were meant to 'gentle' rather than to train them. They were expected to develop professional skills either on the job, in specialist institutes, in teaching hospitals, at the Inns of Court, or, if necessary, in Scotland! Even as late as the second half of the nineteenth century, it was difficult to get Oxford and Cambridge to reaccept medicine as a legitimate and socially acceptable subject of university study and in the case of engineering, this process took considerably longer.

Thus, until recently, English university education tended to be linked in the public mind almost entirely with the social distancing process, with the study of 'useless' subjects seen as the true mark of a 'gentleman' who was not particularly interested in the acquisition of vocational skills. Even now, one of the major differences between English educational thinking and that in the remainder of the British Isles lies in this over-valuing of education for its power to confer social status and to develop 'character', accompanied by an undervaluing of education as a means of economic advancement or as a means of securing a place in a truly vocational structure. At first, such an idea sprang from a leisured class that professed to despise 'trade' and an overconcern with filthy lucre. In more recent years, it has been just as readily embraced by ostensibly egalitarian educationalists who wish learning to be 'pure' and free from mercenary objectives. This transfer of an aristocratic concept to an egalitarian context has had an economically disastrous effect on the English curriculum.

The concept may have withered somewhat in recent years and particularly among parents, but it is nevertheless still a dominant one in much educational rhetoric and organisation and it still underlies many English assumptions. The English educational system is still far more dominated than is usually realised by the old assumptions of a Victorian upper class. It has certainly encouraged far too many English parents, unlike most of their Scottish and Irish contemporaries, to seek places for their children in a grammar school or in a university, not so much for vocational reasons, as for purposes of social labelling and to ensure a position in society, rather than to ensure a genuinely useful training for a chosen occupation. Until recently the low social status accorded to technical studies in England was in marked contrast to the higher status which they enjoyed in Scotland. Significantly those Scottish and Irish schools founded with the intention of conferring social status in the style of English public and grammar schools have often been regarded locally as 'English' schools which usually find it more convenient to follow English curriculum patterns, to despise technical instruction and even to take English examinations and to follow English holiday patterns, to the discomfort of families with some members in 'native' institutions.

Wales on the other hand has continually emphasised the advantages of education to the poorer members of society and indeed her first university college at Aberystwyth was built by the contributions, not of government departments or of rich patrons, but of working people at a time when working-class students in England very rarely had ambitions for a university education. Here, as in Presbyterian Scotland and in Catholic Ireland, education was given considerable priority by the churches and it was church-sponsored efforts in mid-eighteenth-century Wales that gave birth to modern British adult education as we know it.

In strongly Protestant areas of the British Isles literacy and high scholarship were actually seen as enhancing the chances of personal salvation through their encouragement of a more fervent study of the Bible, just as education in Catholic areas was seen as enhancing the chances of producing an intellectually enriched priesthood made up of native candidates drawn from the same social classes as the faithful. In England, the Anglican compromise seems to have produced neither a great fervour for literacy nor a great fervour for the promotion of working-class candidates for the priesthood. Thus even in the nineteenth-century church schools for the poor, though some attention was paid to religious and aesthetic education, the main emphasis was always on the utilitarian aspects of literacy and numeracy, designed to fit working-class children for their current station in life; except in rare cases, individual development was given little encouragement. Certainly it was never seen as a national necessity as in sixteenth-century Scotland or nineteenth-century Wales.

The English elitist insitutions, the boarding schools and the Oxford and Cambridge colleges with their emphasis on programmes of total social training, have probably most usefully exported, as models, their systems of pastoral care which have been adapted for use even in the least socially prestigious sectors throughout the islands—especially in the new comprehensive secondary schools. But in Scotland, until the beginning of this century, the institutional boarding of students had usually been regarded as an affront to a national tradition and institutions had refused to accept the role 'in loco parentis'.[10] Traditionally, Scottish students at college and university remained within the local community, often living at or even below the same economic level as their parents, and the university disclaimed all responsibility not only for their welfare but also for their behaviour.

On the other hand the actual pedagogical process was more early discussed, developed, formalised and professionalised in Scotland than in England where the public and grammar school teacher was essentially an amateur, ostentatiously proud of the fact that he was untrained. Often he was primarily a clergyman rather than a schoolmaster, and saw the training place of the elementary teacher less as the nursery of a professional than as that of an artisan.

Nevertheless, this Scottish emphasis on the professionalism of the teacher did sometimes produce a rigidity and harshness against which other celebrated Scottish figures have reacted, notably the extreme anti-authoritarian A. S. Neill who, in his work, was reacting to what he saw as the unsympathetic methods and classroom atmosphere common in the Scotland of his boyhood. Moreover, as a relic of those sterner days, physical punishment even now continues to be autonomously administered within the Scottish classroom by the class teacher with few of the restrictions on its use now enforced by the English and Welsh authorities—and this is true in classes for every age group (and for both sexes) from 5 to 18.

Even the establishment of an elaborate guidance system with its own distinctive career structure within the Scottish secondary school has not materially altered the situation. All too often the guidance teacher, meant to be a personal counsellor figure, has found himself settled with a special responsibility for this infliction of physical punishment.

On the other hand, as a result of the high value placed on pedagogical skills in Scotland and Ireland and the development of a strong professionalism, the teaching profession there, even in the elementary sector, has for long enjoyed a higher social status than that enjoyed by English non-elitist teachers. Certainly this is especially true in rural areas where the class system (despite the apparent feudalism of certain Highland areas) still lacks the extremes of that in England. Even in Victorian times, the master of the parochial (elementary) school in rural Scotland would probably have had some experience of university life, putting him on a social level with the doctor or the minister, while even in the 1970s the teacher in an Irish village school is still often addressed in the village street as 'Master' on the analogy of 'Doctor' or 'Your Reverence' ...

In Scotland and Ireland, teaching is still a profession of some dignity and in Scotland, at any rate, that dignity is still thought sufficiently worth preserving for some local authorities to be even now extremely unwilling to allow much relaxation in the mode of dress. In certain parts of Scotland young teachers are still expected to wear dark suits in the classroom (or even academic gowns) at a time when many of their English contemporaries relax in their jeans and sweaters.

But, needless to say, not all Scots teachers mercilessly wield the 'tawse' and not all the Irish and Welsh share the classless value systems which we have outlined; nor, of course, were all English teachers in the nineteenth century Anglican elitist clergymen acting as housemasters in public (boarding) schools. Indeed, since the Reformation, there have been thousands of English non-Anglican and, indeed, Anglican working people who have shared the educational views and practices of their Scottish and Welsh neighbours rather than those of their own country's leaders. By the beginning of the nineteenth century Protestant non-conformist churches in England had, for example, developed their own 'academies' as rivals to Oxford and Cambridge and although these failed to establish themselves as places of higher education, they did in many ways provide the prototype of the modern, widely-based, academically ambitious secondary school as well as a training ground for many famous scientists.

In the pages which follow, we shall have to talk of 'national' characteristics and in somewhat broad general sweeps we shall talk of 'national' events, but we accept the proviso that there *were* Scottish middle-class Anglicans or English working-class Methodists or Quaker Irish teachers who stood aside from the main national tendencies. The proviso is a legitimate one and we hope that, as you indulge our generalisations (as we hope you will), you too will bear it in mind.

We emphasised earlier that the nature of the domination which English exercises over the British Isles has changed somewhat during the past two centuries. At first this domination was based on military, political and economic strength—in particular, on the presence of the sovereign and his court in London. During the eighteenth century the fashions and social graces of London also began to make their mark among the purse-proud elsewhere and English forms of social training began to appeal to the middle classes of Edinburgh and Dublin in particular. But it was only during the nineteenth century that the English actually began to outnumber the rest of the islanders and only late in that century that England became for the first time the chief centre of intellectual and high cultural activity. This appeared to spell the end for the Celtic-speaking cultures. Yet, paradoxically again, such an apparent triumph for English was met by a literary revival and a resurgent interest in those Celtic cultures that were so firmly based and politically influential that they are with us still.

Originally, the British Isles had been peopled entirely by people speaking just such Celtic languages. Broadly speaking, the Christian era began with one group (the so-called P-Celts) occupying Great Britain and its satellite islands while another major group (the Q-Celts) occupied Ireland and Man (see Chapter 5 below). Linguistic barriers prevented a close cultural integration of the two major islands and the division was made even greater by the centuries of Roman occupation. For, while most of Britain was firmly brought within the empire or, at least, extensively explored by Roman armies, Ireland was virtually untouched by Roman invasions. Both during and after this Roman occupation there was naturally some intercourse between the islands, and in the post-Roman centuries this increased considerably. Nevertheless, until the major settlements of Irish-speaking Gaels in the west of Scotland (to be discussed later), Britain was mainly a 'Brittonic' (i.e. a P-Celt) island, speaking a language much akin to modern Welsh. Thus parts of Britain no longer in 'Wales' are still covered with Welsh place names (Aberdeen, Aberford, Carlisle, Penrith, Penicuik) while the Welsh-speaking Arthur not only has left folklore relics all over England but has also given his name to the mountain, Arthur's Seat, which dominates the Scottish capital.

Edinburgh was in fact for long a centre of Brittonic culture. Indeed, Kenneth Jackson gave his recent edition of the great Welsh epic, the *Gododdin*, the subtitle *The Oldest Scottish Poem*,[11] as it was almost certainly composed somewhere in the Edinburgh area by the local poet, Aneirin.

Only with the gradual infiltration of invaders from Ireland, Scandinavia and Germany did this 'Welsh' hegemony in Britain come to an end. The northern British and the southern British were finally divided by a great battle near Arthuret in Cumbria (the land of the Welsh-Cymri!) and although pockets of P-Celt culture remained (in the Forest of Elmet in Yorkshire, for example) the main body of 'Welsh' speakers were gradually forced back into the two peninsulas they now occupy, into Cornwall and, (first as settlers and then as refugees) into the first 'British' colony, Britanny—Petit Bretagne.

Despite the fact that these four 'Welsh' peninsulas were united by the sea (a far more efficient communications link until the eighteenth century than any route by land), their cultures and even their languages eventually fell apart, with only the two northern peninsulas developing that common modern language and, to some extent, that social structure that we now recognise as Welsh.

In the remainder of the island, the situation became more and more confused. Various Germanic tribes spread over what are now England and southern Scotland but they settled alongside Scandinavian peoples who sometimes fought and sometimes intermarried with them, while in what is now Scotland, the situation was further complicated during the sixth century by the arrival in the west of the Irish (in Latin, Scoti) who gave the eventual country of Scotland both its name and its central monarchy. Thus the three nations of Britain developed. The P-Celts survived in their twin peninsulas and became the modern Welsh, the Irish invaders of Argyll and those P-Celts, Germanic and Scandinavian peoples whom they could conquer became the Scots, while the remainder—and racially the least pure of all (i.e. all those occupying the remainder of Great Britain) became the English.

Certainly none of these three British groupings is as racially 'pure' as the Scandinavians, and even the Irish, isolated though they were, had mingled sufficiently with invaders to be far from purely 'Celtic' by the year 1000. In any case, the word 'Celtic' has never been more than a linguistic term. Within the veins of the English flows probably just as much of the blood of old aboriginal P-Celtic speakers as of the Vikings or the Angles; in a similar way, the most culturally 'Irish' of the modern Irish, the Aran islanders off the west coast of Galway, seem to have descended in part from English Cromwellian soldiers who were shipwrecked and chose to settle there. The western islands of Europe were always on the main trading and marauding routes and their peoples—despite all the physical stereotyping and the spurious racial claims made by nineteenth-century historians—are not divided by their cultures and their national historical experience rather than by race. The Victorians, Matthew Arnold in particular, did a great disservice to the understanding of the separate British cultures by emphasising racial origins, linking the 'English' to the Germans and emphasising their superiority to the more institutionally 'primitive' Celts.[12] Such Victorian attitudes have been perpetuated by irresponsible journalists' references to a 'Celtic fringe'.

In fact, the parts of Scotland, Ireland and Wales occupied by the majority of the population have never been purely 'Celtic' since the time when England itself was Celtic in its speech and culture. The culture of the populous Scottish central belt in particular became a Germanic culture at much the same time as that of York or London.

In some parts of Europe, racial differences *have* dominated political events—in the Balkans, for example, or in Finland—but rarely in the British Isles. Those who see the difficulties of Northern Ireland, let alone those of Scotland and Wales, as racial problems are deceiving themselves.

At the same time those who suggest that racial similarities between the English and Scots (or the possession of a common mongrel culture based on common ingredients) make nonsense of the idea of Scottish separation from England are also deceiving themselves. There is little to choose racially between Norway and Sweden but between the two countries had grown up such historical and cultural differences that political separation was essential even in the twentieth century, a century when those who scorn the idea of independence for Scotland and Wales assume that such 'old-fashioned' separatist concepts must be unthinkable for Europeans.

By the year 1000, then, the population of the British Isles was a thorough racial mixture and the modern 'countries' of Britain had still to take their final shape. What has been crucial since then has not been abiding racial characteristics but cultural survivals (such as Scots law or the Welsh language) and the political and institutional arrangements that have developed over the ensuing 900 years.

It is probably possible still to find examples of the old 'pure' Scandinavian or 'pure' Celtic-speaking stock in certain remote areas of Britain such as Cumbria or Galloway but it is difficult to prove that your tall blond or short swarthy native is a true descendant of primeval stock rather than a Mendelian throwback to some fecund Norwegian sailor shipwrecked in the sixteenth century or to some Napoleonic prisoner-of-war who fathered many local children. Historians from earliest times until the nineteenth century destroyed their credibility by following just such racial will-o'-the-wisps. The Scots and the Welsh are different from the English not because of their race but because of their traditions, not because of their origins but because of their institutions and because of the separateness that their political history has imposed upon them.

In the first centuries following the year 1000 the boundaries between the three countries of Great Britain were far less well-defined than they have later become. The Norman conquest of England gave a new solidity to its centralised government and William II in particular attempted to stabilise the Scottish frontier. It was he who made the 'land of Carlisle' English for the first time, although both that city and Berwick-on-Tweed still became intermittently Scottish for many years afterwards. David I later ruled Scotland from Carlisle while Berwick was for long the major

Scottish port. It was the English Edward I, however, the 'Hammer of the Scots', who most consciously tried to establish English sovereignty over the remainder of the island, making his son Prince of Wales and eventually provoking that specifically Scottish struggle for independence from English influences that culminated in the victory of Bannockburn in 1314 and the Scottish Declaration of Independence at Arbroath in 1320. It is an interesting demonstration of the non-racial aspect of such events that the Scottish leader Bruce and most of the signatories of this Declaration of Independence were clearly Norman in origin, fighting (like the later American colonists) to establish their independence from political masters who were demonstrably racially identical with themselves.

Until the sixteenth century, English influence in Ireland extended only intermittently beyond the so-called Pale surrounding Dublin, and the Norman rulers to whom the English kings had committed provincial government became largely assimilated by the Celtic/Viking civilisation in which they found themselves. We say 'Celtic/Viking', because not only had Scandinavian settlers supplied Celtic Ireland with its first taste of urban life in towns such as Wicklow and Dublin, but these Vikings had themselves become assimilated by one of the intellectually and artistically most sophisticated backwaters of Europe, where much of classical learning had been preserved in the 'universities' of the early Irish church, whence it was to spread eventually to the intellectually devastated remainder of post-Roman Europe. As elsewhere, the Anglo-Norman kings had little to offer Ireland but stronger centralised rule and a set of colonial governors who needed to be civilised by their own vassals.[13]

Wales was never able to establish the centralised monarchy that saved Scotland or to offer the military challenge (in terms of both armies and geography) that saved Ireland from falling under England's control completely. By 1485 when a Welsh family, the Tudors, succeeded to the English throne, Wales's institutions such as the law and the church were already assimilated with those of England and unable to develop independently within a modern context. Thus, of all parts of the islands, Wales has been the one most completely and continuously dominated administratively by England and it is difficult to see how her identity could have been preserved had it not been for her language and her general rejection of the established 'English' church.

Yet even Ireland, more of which did finally shed English political control completely, also went the way of Wales in one respect. Although it maintained a separate legal system, that system operated according to the law of England, the law of the official government in Dublin, and this law eventually prevailed over native customs even if at first its jurisdiction was severely limited by circumstances. Gradually, as English power widened, the old native Brehon laws ceased to operate and much of the distinctively Gaelic culture and administration disappeared with them. And after the Reformation, when the church in England and Wales became Anglican, so, in step, the official church in Ireland became Anglican also, even though (as in Wales) its tenets were never embraced by the majority of the population.

None of this was true of Scotland with its separate, central monarchy, whose laws were never those of England and indeed were based on continental Roman-Dutch principles often quite unlike those of the English. Moreover, although the Scottish church became Protestant and although on a number of occasions it temporarily embraced an episcopalian form of government identical with that of Anglicanism, it was never automatically in step with England; when, after the union of crowns, Charles I attempted to make it so, he met with a fatal resistance which finally ensured that Presbyterianism rather than Episcopalianism would not only remain the most popular form of Protestant Christianity but would be accepted as the officially established form of church government in Scotland.

Given the existence of such a tradition of legal and ecclesiastical as well as of political independence, the union of the English and Scottish crowns in 1603 did not therefore produce the United Kingdom that many people had expected. Instead, there was a dual monarchy like that of Austria and Hungary or of Sweden and Finland but there was far less of an attempt on the part of the dual monarch to integrate his kingdoms. James VI and I, having already been king of Scotland for many years before moving to London, was very much aware of Scottish differences and sensitivities and did nothing to integrate either the legal or the ecclesiastical structures. Thus he set a pattern (that has endured) of non-standardised government under a British crown that can now tolerate in its ostensibly United Kingdom two legal systems operating on sometimes quite different principles and has in one part of that kingdom an Anglican established church (in England), in another a Presbyterian established church (in Scotland), and in two other components no state church at all (in Wales and Northern Ireland). Such constitutional untidiness was further compounded by James's maintenance in his three kingdoms of three independent parliaments—in Westminster, in Edinburgh and in Dublin. The complexity of twentieth-century constitutional patternings was thus ensured.

In practice, of course, the independence of the Scottish parliament which, before 1603, had been maintained for so long by force of arms and a lively foreign policy, was severely damaged by the new arrangements. The continual presence of the king in England and his growing dependence on the City of London meant that he naturally put his interests as king of England before his interests as king of Scotland. The resultant tension between London and Edinburgh reached a climax with the virtual destruction by William III (under English influence) of the so-called Darien scheme, an attempt supported by the Scottish parliament to establish a rival Scottish colonial empire in the Caribbean. Into this scheme the leading financiers of Scotland, as well as its bourgeoisie, had disastrously poured much of their wealth, and national disaster unavoidably ensued. The reality of parliamentary independence became less and less and despite severe misgivings on the part of possibly the majority of the population, a Scottish parliament, dominated by commercial interests, joined itself to that of England in 1707 under the so-called Acts of Union, Acts guaranteeing among other things the maintenance of existing legal and ecclesiastical organisations in Scotland and, *inter alia*, those institutions of Scottish education that depended in turn on the legal and ecclesiastical structures.

Ironically, as a result, Scotland, which had maintained its independence for over a century even under an English-based king, was now less independent than the hitherto more subservient and anglicised Ireland. Scotland had never had to adopt English laws and state religion or to accept an English viceroy imposed upon it as a military governor, as Ireland had. Nevertheless Ireland entered the eighteenth century, unlike Scotland, with its own separate parliament and was still no part of the new United Kingdom. Despite English restrictions on her trade, the eighteenth century was in fact one of Ireland's most prosperous periods with the only major example of her habitual violence occurring at the very end of the century. During the 1700s Dublin became a major cultural centre, not just of Europe but of the whole North Atlantic, influencing the American colonies and their revolution quite considerably. By 1800, London may have been the largest city in the world but Dublin had become the seventh largest and certainly showed far more of the outer signs of a political capital than Edinburgh which, though it had considerable intellectual and architectural attractions, still lacked the atmosphere that political power gives.

On the other hand, Ireland's success was in many ways deceptive and held in it the seeds of its own destruction. For just as Jefferson and the American founding fathers talked of liberty but ignored slavery, so the Dublin parliament talked of patriotism and democracy but remained doggedly an Anglican (as opposed to an English) parliament and although it did much to improve the lot of the Catholics and Presbyterians who formed the majority of the population it consistently resisted their claims to political emancipation. Symbolically, therefore, it was they who joined in the Great Rebellion of 1798 and precipitated a crisis which enabled the Anglo/Scottish parliament to force Ireland into their United Kingdom. Within this larger unit, not only the interests of

Irish Catholics and Presbyterians but even those of Irish Anglicans were formally subordinated to those of England and Scotland and many would say that the disastrous results of this enforced Act of Union are with us still. The nineteenth century, despite subsequent Catholic emancipation and the opening of civil offices to non-Anglicans, proved to be one of the most turbulent in Irish history, and was to be followed by a twentieth century of even greater turbulence during which sectarian antagonisms reached a peak that they had never known even during the Anglican-dominated semi-independence of the eighteenth century.

The Union of 1707 (unlike that of 1801) had not, however, spelt such disaster for Scotland. Much of her social and commercial independence remained. Indeed, the departure of many of those most keen on aping English ways to the court in London did in some degree restore to provincial Scotland its self-confidence. Edinburgh and Glasgow, newly prosperous from the growth of the West Indies trade and the greater stability which followed the suppression of the Highlanders in 1746, had their fair share of English dancing masters and English-style finishing schools for the genteel, but life in Ayr or Brechin went on as it had done for centuries. There was considerable decay in Scottish politics, with Lord Dundas spreading across Scotland a network of patronage that emasculated much of Scotland's independence on the British political scene, but the country's new commercial prosperity was reflected also in a revival of intellectual and artistic life using as its base a set of universities that were far freer to improvise in their curriculum than were their English counterparts. Indeed, these institutions did not always think of themselves as universities in the restricted modern sense at all. At a time when professors' salaries depended on the number of students they could attract, they became academic entrepreneurs in open competition with the schools, the medical colleges and the other commercial establishments which sprang up to meet educational needs of all kinds. Some pupils attended classes in school and university concurrently, while Edinburgh's 'college' (a term still favoured over 'university' even in the nineteenth century) was successfully overseen not by an independent body of scholars but by a subcommittee of the corrupt town council, whose Lord Provost was also, *ex officio*, Lord Rector of the University.[14]

This was a period of untidy organisational arrangements but a period of great creativity particularly in Glasgow and Edinburgh where the late eighteenth century and early nineteenth centuries saw the development not just of a peculiarly Scottish school of architecture and painting but also of many pedagogical experiments, such as those in the education of the deaf and of the modern medical student and political scientist.

That Scotland's Gaelic culture was concurrently being destroyed in the wake of the 1745 rebellion was noticed by few and welcomed by most of those who did notice, as the once proud and independent Highlanders flooded into the cities and embraced the delights of 'civilisation'.

Wales had nothing to equal the eighteenth-century glories of Dublin and Edinburgh. Until the twentieth century she contained no major city (in 1800 Cardiff's population was still 1,018), no university and very few grammar schools of national stature. Her (minority) state church and her legal system were part of England's and her native Welsh-speaking aristocracy, such as it had been, had virtually disappeared. But such a situation did have eventual advantages. Her language was less threatened than those of the Q-Celts in western Scotland and the populous counties of the eastern Irish seaboard and an unexpected interest in its welfare suddenly came to life as a result of the Gothic and other Romantic enthusiasms of the late eighteenth century.

The ancient Eisteddfodau were revived (eventually with suitable, synthetic ritual dating from the 'druids') and they acted as a rallying point for national feeling at a time when the Welsh began to feel less shame in taking their language and customs seriously. Thus an ancient oral bardic tradition, which was still extant in rural areas of Scotland and Ireland as well as in Wales, began to be saved from extinction. Moreover this revival of Welsh culture went hand in hand with a religious and educational revival movement that valued self-cultivation for both spiritual and moral reasons so that a new cultural consciousness spread among the ordinary people of Wales of a type that one rarely found in the newly industrial areas of Scotland and England.

As the eighteenth century ended, there was thus a definite, if different, buoyancy in each of the non-English countries of the British Isles. Scotland had had a commercial and intellectual revival based chiefly in her cities, Ireland had had an equally brilliant development of urban life depending on a lively parliament whose revolutionary ideas had scared London and inspired Americans, while Wales's native culture had come back into its own along with a new dedication to modern learning. However, only some of this buoyancy was able to survive the rigours of the following century. Ireland lost her independence immediately and had to spend another two centuries facing up to her internal contradictions. Scotland was overwhelmed by the problems of urban expansion as well as a new and deliberate attempt by certain landowners to clear whole rural counties of people in favour of sheep and game, while Wales, too, faced a new phase of vast urban expansion based on her coalfields that brought, in the south at least, a wave of alien immigrants and a new challenge to her always embattled culture and sense of independence.

In all three countries, English cultural influence, linked as it was to industrial development, was considerably extended. This would probably have happened in any case as London's prestige as an international cultural centre grew and as the new urban middle class attempted to adopt London's ways in the style of the eighteenth-century genteel; but it became inevitable as the coming of the railways and of the steamship made communications within the British Isles so much easier and cheaper. London newspapers circulated to every island before the month's end and journeys that had once taken days or even weeks could now be accomplished in a few hours or two days at most. And this new geographical mobility exaggerated and encouraged a characteristic that had always been present in the non-English British since Renaissance times, a desire to have the best of both worlds—to be both a separate and a patriotic Scot/Irishman/Welshman and yet to feel accepted and at home in London/Oxford/Cambridge—the centres of international, 'non-parochial' prestige.

Nowhere is it clearer than in the character of James Boswell, who thought more than most about questions of patriotism and national identity. Thus, Boswell, describing in his journal his departure for London from Edinburgh on 15 November 1762.[15]

> I made the chaise stop at the foot of the Canongate ... walked to the Abbey of Holyroodhouse [the Royal Palace of the Kings of Scotland] bowed thrice: once to the Palace itself, once to the Crown of Scotland above the gate in front and once to the venerable old Chapel ...

Patriotism indeed! But by 1 December his enthusiasm for things English has already once more a grip on him.

> This afternoon I was surprised with the arrival of Lady Betty Macfarlane, Lady Anne Erskine, Captain Erskine, and Miss Dempster, who were come to the Red Lion at Charing Cross ... To tell the plain truth, I was vexed at their coming. For to see just the plain *hamely* Fife family hurt my grand ideas of London. Besides, I was now upon a plan of studying polite reserved behaviour, which is the only way to keep up dignity of character.

And later ...

> The great art of being easy and happy in society is to study proper behaviour ... As I was therefore pursuing this laudable plan, I was vexed at the arrival of the Kellie family, with whom when in Scotland I had been in the greatest familiarity. Had they not come for a twelve-month, I should have been somewhat established in my address, but as I had been but a fortnight from them, I could not without the appear-

ance of strong affectation appear much different from what they had seen me.

Wednesday 8th December ... At night I went to Covent Garden and saw 'Love in a Village' ... Just before the overture began to be played, two Highland officers came in. The mob in the upper gallery roared out, 'No Scots! No Scots! Out with them!,' hissed and pelted them with apples. My heart warmed to my countrymen, my Scotch blood boiled with indignation. I jumped on the benches, roared out, 'Damn you, you rascals!,' hissed and was in the greatest rate. I am very sure at that time I should have been the most distinguished of heroes. I hated the English, I wished from my soul that the union was broke and that we might give them another battle of Bannockburn.

So Boswell makes a clear distinction between patriotism on the one hand and 'Scotch manners' on the other. 'National culture' is clearly less of an integrated concept for him than for us.

The attraction of London manners to an excessively patriotic Scot could therefore be very great and it is such a tension that underlies much so-called anglicisation—the tension which results from attempting to reconcile patriotism or ideology with desirable but foreign models. Boswell's eighteenth-century tensions and contradictions are not entirely different from those of the twentieth-century European Marxist intellectual, inescapably attracted by the blue-jeans, coke-drinking, joint-smoking and essentially capitalist life-style of modern America.

This tension between loyalty to the idea of Scotland and the fear of being thought parochial is found in very many other famous Scots, not least in Walter Scott who not only rehabilitated the kilt for royal use and first articulated many of Scotland's national myths in respectable literary form, but also helped to found the most self-consciously anglicising of all Scottish schools, the Edinburgh Academy, as a competitor to his own 'traditional' old school, the Royal High School, and even embraced the Anglican religion of the English, which he found more congenial than the Presbyterian form—though this is perhaps less surprising in view of the Scottish Anglicans' traditional espousal of Jacobitism.

Even Robert Burns, though firmly fixed in his rural Scots environment, felt the need occasionally to put himself through what he found the 'gravelling' discipline of writing in standard (or at least Augustan) English in order to satisfy his patrons and indeed to place himself in the mainstream of current literary fashion. For the serious Scottish artist must always live in fear of being patronised by the English, or being placed by them in a special peripheral category of the 'quaint' or 'couthy'. When Scots entertain them, the English have always expected them to be either grotesques like Harry Lauder or Billy Connolly, sugarly sentimental like Annie S. Swann and James Barrie, or fiercely romantic like Scott and Stevenson. No wonder the serious Scottish artist often tries to be 'normally' English as well, like Shaw, Wilde and Sheridan, who always reserved their Irishness for special occasions, and always made sure they maintained a secure London base, from which they wrote of English matters in a standard English.

If such Scottish deference was shown so often to the English in the literary field and in the field of social manners, it is not surprising that deference was for long shown also in the field of politics.

The fight first for Catholic emancipation and then for land reform and home rule meant that Irish politics, unlike Scottish politics, remained distinctively Irish and firmly in Irish hands, but by 1900 Scottish seats were often regularly allocated by the major parties to essentially London-based rather than to Scottish figures. The aristocratic fashion encouraged by Queen Victoria of using Scotland as a holidaying place began to give rural Scotland the air of a Bath or a Scarborough—an extension of fashionable London once the season was over. Trollope summed up the situation in *The Eustace Diamonds*:

> A great many people go to Scotland in the autumn. When you have your autumn holiday in hand to dispose of, there is nothing more aristocratic that you can do than go to Scotland. Dukes are more plentiful there than in Pall Mall, and you will meet an earl or at least a lord on every mountain.[16]

In an era of political hostesses and the disposal of seats by a central caucus, it was not surprising therefore that Scotland should also become politically fashionable and that there should be a takeover of Scottish politics by those with primarily English interests in mind. By the time the Liberal Government took power in 1906, such a takeover was pretty extensive and posed a clear parliamentary threat to the proper defence of Scottish interests. The English Asquith recalls how he (himself MP for East Fife) had climbed a hill at Raith above Kirkcaldy with some Liberal colleagues and Birrell had gloried in the fact that every constituency in sight (i.e. the whole of Fife and much of the Lothians) was represented at Westminster by a London barrister.[17] Moreover, the situation in many parts of Wales was little different. It is not surprising therefore that there was a predisposition even among Scottish and Welsh MPs not to take national traditions too seriously—especially in education. Most Tory and Liberal MPs, even when they were Scots or Welsh by birth, sent their own children to English boarding schools or to local schools run on English lines, though in Ireland such a following of English models was far less dominant and affected far fewer politicians.

On the other hand, despite the strength of such tendencies in Scotland and Wales their effects must not be exaggerated. The involvement of so many English MPs in Scottish affairs did at least provide a link between English and Scottish politics of a kind that has not always been present in the more recent era of the exclusively Scottish MP. Moreover the lump was always considerably leavened. Alongside the expatriate Englishmen and anglicised natives representing Scots and Welsh interests at Westminster, there were always radicals who tended to represent, sometimes in small numbers but virulently, a growing national consciousness which developed in the late nineteenth century and which expressed itself in straight political terms.

The supreme example was, of course, Lloyd George, who combined the role of world statesman and British war leader with that of Welsh national hero—pushing through parliament such distinctively Welsh measures (highly unpopular with the English majority) as the disestablishment of the Anglican church in Wales and persuading George V to 'revive' the elaborate rituals of installing the Prince of Wales in the castle of Caernarfon. Moreover, Lloyd George was a great patron both of the Welsh language and of the national religion as embodied in the nonconformist chapels. Many of the Welsh have mistrusted him but more of them with hindsight than at the time of his successes. He, more than any man, was responsible for the growing realisation among the Scottish and Welsh middle class that loyalty to the Empire or to the United Kingdom need not involve the embracing of Englishness or even of English social manners. During the war he demonstrated that the Empire was not necessarily unsafe in the hands of a Welsh-speaking elementary schoolboy with a regional accent and a radical outlook, and the success of Lloyd George formed part of that immense ideological breakthrough reflected in the rhetoric of the 1918 Education Acts which for the first time in Britain reflected a genuinely egalitarian (if somewhat paternalistic) set of educational guidelines.

In Scotland a new national consciousness, after the setbacks of the eighteenth and early nineteenth centuries, had been encouraged also by the growth of newly potent, if sometimes tawdry symbols. After the flamboyant and shallow display by a kilted George IV (stage-managed by Walter Scott) of his devotion to the traditions of Scotland, his niece Victoria did a more solid job of reviving kilt, tartan and Highland Games in a synthetic but far more socially attractive way, in a way now too easily dismissed by the purists with the scornful name of Balmorality. For whatever the artificiality of the world of sword dance, caber-tossing and 'The Stag at Bay', Victoria's tartanry certainly entered the Scottish consciousness and imposed itself as a unifying set of national symbols even on the Lowlander to whom kilts and tartan had hitherto been at worst a threat, or at best unknown. Royal favour meant that a kilt had become a distinctively Scottish and universally acceptable middle-class dress by 1900, even in areas where it had struck terror in the period before the 1745 rebellion; and this whole panoply of highlandism as conceived by the mid-nineteenth-century aristocracy was quickly communicated to the working class not only via the biscuit tins and ribbons of the new manufacturers and the fancies of the music halls but even more fundamentally by the new army of the kilted regiments which by 1918 had loyal representatives in about every street and family in Scotland. One can laugh at the tartan on the shortbread tin or the plaid-collared terriers on the calendar, but they did and do symbolise a feeling of national separateness common for the first time to both Highlanders and Lowlanders and now underpinned with more respectable certainties. They were only some of many phenomena (the cult of Burns was another) that gave Scots a new feeling of common separateness and new confidence in their national institutions and customs. At last they became proud of their accents, their haggis and their oatmeal without any longer fearing social derision at the hands of the English. They remained loyal to the Union, but as equals, not inferiors. Boswellian tensions were subsiding.

Opposition to the disbanding of the Argyll and Sutherland Highlanders in the 1960s represented far more than the nostalgia of a few militarists or right-wing fanatics. Many saw it, probably foolishly, as a threat to a whole century of growing national confidence.

This growing Scottish consciousness of separate nationality in the late nineteenth century was not just a manifestation of fashionable romanticism as, to some extent, the cult of the Eisteddfod had been. It was underpinned also by more tangible social realities: there was the realisation by the Scottish learned professions, for example (the law, the church and the professors in particular), that a great deal was to be gained by rehabilitating the glories of Scotland's separateness if only in their own interests. Thus the ceremonial surrounding the Scottish courts and the meetings of the church's General Assembly became far more formalised and elaborate than they had ever been before. High kirks were again referred to as cathedrals (sometimes on the basis of very short-lived histories as the seats of temporary Reformation bishops). The universities of Edinburgh and St Andrews in particular played up the picturesque nature of their settings in the style of Oxford and Cambridge. In a sense it was still anglicisation but with a difference. Instead of deriding national institutions in favour of English ones, their claims to acceptance even by an English touchstone were asserted instead. Students who had never bothered to go through the mumbo-jumbo of graduation ceremonies or the wearing of academic dress (irrelevant as they probably considered both) began to do so in order to prove they were as good as the Oxford patronisers who, at this time, were widely claiming that Scottish universities were only a form of grammar school.[18]

Even some members of a Scottish aristocracy who had for many decades played down Scottish differences, who had bought houses in Leicestershire and assumed that progress was always to be sought on English lines, began to look back again, to wear the kilt, to stir their porridge and resume their kirk-going. Indeed, the continued loyalty of some aristocrats to Presbyterianism had in itself often given them a continuing feeling of separatism from English Episcopalian friends, and the growing religious fervour which accompanied the 'Disruption' of the kirk in 1843 had in some cases accentuated this feeling (see page 62 below). It was appropriate therefore that in the late 1860s a Commission presided over by a Scottish aristocrat, the Duke of Argyll, should assert the rights of Scottish children to proceed from village school to university in the traditional Scottish manner, a manner highly unsatisfactory to British Cabinet ministers and to the English-minded professors and civil servants who were to plan Scottish secondary education during the next fifty years.

The strength of this feeling of separateness was, however, such that it seemed quite natural for the 1872 (Scottish) Education Act to be followed by the setting up of a separate Scotch Education Department to replace the section of the Privy Council Office that had previously dealt with grants to Scottish schools. The following decades saw even more important developments, in particular the creation of the crucial post of Secretary of State for Scotland who was to oversee that growing body of affairs that were once more seen to be peculiarly Scottish. At first, the Secretary of State was seen, particularly by the English, as a largely ceremonial figure meant to ape the Lord Lieutenant of Ireland, not in his military and political power, but in his power to open bazaars and to appoint academics to Regius chairs; but, gradually, as the feeling of Scottish separateness grew and began to be allied more and more with radical politics and as social legislation expanded, so grew the powers of the Scottish Office at Dover House in Whitehall and so grew both the powers of the Secretary of State and his influence in the Cabinet, to which he was admitted during the 1920s.

This growth was to continue in fits and starts but incrementally. Every new upsurge of national feeling or political agitation brought new progress until government concern over the rise of the separatist Scottish National Party and other popular agitation on so-called Red Clydeside and elsewhere produced a major governmental change, the removal in 1939 of most Scottish Office staff from London to Edinburgh—to the new St Andrew's House perched symbolically on a hill overlooking the Palace of Holyroodhouse, the seat of royal power in the years before the Union.

Following 1945, separatism temporarily became less obviously important as an element in Scottish politics. The Scottish section of the

Labour Party had played a major part in the British success of the Labour movement as a whole. A new primary concern with economic planning on the part of politicians gradually persuaded Labour leaders, if not the party's rank and file in Scotland, that a centralised Britain rather than a separate Scotland was likely to produce more favourable results for all parts of the United Kingdom, especially as the continuance of a Labour Government in London seemed dependent on success in Scotland. Nevertheless an earlier nationalism had made its mark. A new and more Scottish political world had been created which, as Kellas has rightly emphasised,[19] now became responsible for much of the decision making on Scottish affairs. Instead of always imposing solutions on Scotland from without, London began more and more to rely on the advice of civil servants based in Edinburgh, interacting with politicians who were also essentially based north of the border.

The introduction of air travel accelerated this process. Scottish MPs were less inclined to live permanently in London during the parliamentary session. Instead, they usually flew down to Westminster on a Monday or a Tuesday morning and returned on Thursday evening and this kept them far more in the centre of local as well as national affairs. They worked in both countries at once, instead of being ambassadors to an imperial court. As a result it became increasingly rare for English career politicians to seek or to be acceptable in Scottish seats. Indeed by 1960 all but a handful of Scottish MPs of all parties were Scots themselves or had strong Scottish connections. By 1974, the exceptions could be counted on the fingers of one hand.

In such a comparatively closed political world a new call to separatism based on economic arguments was likely to appeal, and when the Scottish National Party became revitalised during the 1960s, it made its chief appeal, not to the romantic, Gaelic-speaking fringe areas like the Highlands—the sort of areas where Welsh nationalism was having its success—but to the hard industrial areas of Dumbartonshire, Clackmannan and West Lothian where economic recession was taking its toll. In this new situation of hard-headed separatist agitation, in a more than ever separate world of Scottish politics, entered a further crucial factor that gave a new reality to a hitherto shadowy tartan world—the end of the Empire that had for so long occupied the attention of Scotland's talents.

As Christopher Harvie has put it,[20]

> [The Scots] provided the Empire with its Bibles and opium, its steamers and railway engines, its non-commissioned officers: engineers, bankers, clerks and missionaries. This success was largely due to Scots distinctiveness, to the relative excellence and accessibility of secondary and higher education; in the 1860s one Scot in every

1,000 went to university, one Englishman in every 5,800. Yet by depriving the country of the resident intelligentsia which, in 19th century Europe, acted as the focus of nationalism, the expatriate Scots yielded place to the antiquarian tartanry of (resident) Scotland, the pseudo-patriotism of a non-nation.

Harvie believes that the reinvolvement of Scotland's intellectual leaders in the fate of their own country was bound to produce considerable change.

During the interwar depression the birth of political nationalism was essentially 'the revolt of the MAs'. It produced a poet and ideologist of genius (though scarcely a political leader) in Hugh MacDiarmid ...

The final withdrawal from Empire and the greater competition for jobs outside Scotland from the products of a modernised English educational system had now finally forced the MAs into total concern with their own country's future.

As a result of this Scotland seems to have been trying to pack into the last decade and a half the cultural evolution of a comparable small European state over the last two centuries ... The complacent conservatism which characterised middle-class Scottish culture seems almost completely to have disappeared. The old Scottish institutions are admitted to be in dissolution; the hold of the churches has been broken; law is seen more and more as a restrictive practice; education is badly in need of reform ...

If [the returned intellectuals] maintain their traditional loyalty to the Union they will end up being exploited by an alien elite—oilmen, Whitehall and Brussels bureaucrats ... If they maintain their traditional elitism they must emerge as leaders of nationalism. In present circumstances there's little doubt about which course will be taken ...

To some extent a similar series of events took place in Wales. It had fewer separate institutions to build on but the post-1945 world saw a further revival of interest in a language that had been rehabilitated in official eyes by Lloyd George and which was given a considerable boost by the growth of broadcasting. Throughout the war the entire United Kingdom, sharing a single network, had heard the news in Welsh each evening at five o'clock preliminary to the highly popular *Children's Hour*. They were certainly no longer ignorant of its existence and the self-respect of ordinary Welsh speakers was considerably strengthened by the ever-growing national respect shown to it by the BBC. Other official recognition was slow in coming, scandalously slow for many nationalists, but there was no doubt about which way the tide was flowing.

Most important of all, a stimulating literary revival was in full flower, led by a major Welsh-speaking figure, Saunders Lewis, whose encouragement of Welsh met with far more success than the efforts of Hugh McDiarmid in Scotland whose attempts to revive 'Lallans', the ancient Lowland Scots dialect, were largely ineffectual outside his own popular writings.

The poet Dylan Thomas and the charismatic politician Bevan became symbols in the non-Welsh British consciousness of a true Welsh significance and, encouraged by Irish and Scottish examples, Welsh politicians of all parties pressed for a greater recognition of Welsh needs. This was in a part a manifestation of the common postwar agitation by individual British regions for greater economic help, but, to the surprise of most people, election rhetoric during the 1960s carried Wales a little further than Birmingham or Tyneside for she was also (unexpectedly) given a Secretary of State, and if his powers were considerably less than those of his Scottish counterpart, this was largely because there were fewer separate national institutions for him to oversee. However, once the ball was set rolling, 'giving power to Wales' (i.e. to the Secretary of State) became a popular electioneering ploy and in 1970 the Welsh Conservatives, never hitherto significant supporters of Welsh separation, promised him control of primary and secondary education, much to the annoyance, it is reported, of the subsequent Conservative Secretary of State for Education and Science, Margaret Thatcher. She had to preside over a shedding of her own Welsh powers that was not only reluctant but is even at the time of writing, under her successors, far from complete. The development of the Welsh Office provides perhaps the most startling example of the haphazard and unco-ordinated way in which British constitutional change has taken place during the past century.

Like the SNP in Scotland, the Welsh nationalist group, Plaid Cymru, was considerably strengthened rather than weakened by the ease with which such concessions were gained. Plaid also began to profit, like the SNP, from the anti-metropolitan ideology which began to grip provincial Britain generally in the post-imperial years. Moreover, far more than the SNP, Plaid was able to appeal to a youth protest movement, based on the defence of a separate language, that fitted neatly into the international scene of 1968, had its own appealing world of folk music and could provide opportunities for the pop star as much as for the professor of economics. Superficially at any rate, its early development has been far less bourgeois and far less middle-aged, far more radical and far more adventurous than that of the SNP, whose stock political ploy has been the cavalcade of saloon cars rather than the sit-in at the court-room.

Least bourgeois of all, however, has been the tiny nationalist movement in the Isle of Man, Mech Vannin, putting up a forlorn rearguard action against the influence of an English tax-evading middle class. They have little but the memory of a dead Manx language and an increasingly eroded folklore to give colour to a political platform based on the simple defence of the small man against the rich who have chosen to buy him out and to leave him without housing and without a job. The cause of the Manx nationalist is very much the cause of the central London working class or of the Welsh farm labourers, all of whom are equally at the mercy of a gentrification that is wiping out their traditional ways of life by leaving them with nowhere to live. It is in a real sense not a nationalist cause at all, though in an independent island it can easily function as one, especially in an island with a long tradition of independent parliamentary government.

The development of national consciousness in Ireland had taken a very different course, for no part of that island has ever really been accepted by the inhabitants of the larger island (especially by the English) to be 'British' in the full sense at all. This is a sentiment, of course, which shocks the Ulster Unionist and his political supporters at Westminster, yet the mere fact that for many years (even before the present troubles) the Unionist headquarters in Belfast, at the entrance to the main railway station and air terminal, had to be draped with a large slogan saying 'Ulster is British' implies that a large number of visitors as well as some locals still needed to be convinced. By 'British' the Unionists do, of course, mean 'part of the United Kingdom', but the official description of that kingdom has always been 'Great Britain and Ireland' or (later) 'Great Britain and Northern Ireland'—never 'Britain' alone.

Interestingly, many Irish emigrants to London have clung to their own areas, Camden Town, Kilburn and Cricklewood, as if they found more difficulty in integrating with the general population than do the London Scots and Welsh who are dispersed throughout the capital.

In fact, Irish history has always marked the Irish out as separate—their experience overlapping with Britain's at many points perhaps, but still essentially different.

Such separation dates back, of course, to Roman times, but even within the period of maximum British influence following the spread of British settlements beyond the Pale in the sixteenth and seventeenth centuries, the native Irish themselves remained distinct—marked off by their Catholicism, certainly, and to some extent by their language and customs, while even the English-speaking Protestant settlers, like the Vikings and the Normans before them, eventually developed a life-style at least as distinct from that of England and Scotland as that of the American colonists whom they so often resembled and, indeed, supported during their War of Independence. In fact, this separateness has continued to give all Ireland a curiously American air, reinforced and developed by the comings and goings of many generations of both

Protestant and Catholic emigrants. The 'Yank', the returned emigrant, is a familiar figure in the Irish village and even remote Irish farms can have an atmosphere of cosmopolitan experience rarely found in English villages—with a son back from Seattle, a nun daughter on holiday from Lagos, a father back from Nottingham and a mother hot-foot from a pilgrimage to Lourdes or Rome. The entrepreneurial style of Irish small town shopkeepers, the dress of the priest, the atmosphere of the village dancehall (often a nissen hut with a Las Vegas frontage) or of the Protestant gospel mission tent, all of those often remind one more of Illinois or Ontario than of Lancashire and Ayrshire and the feeling is reinforced, in the North at least, by the omnipresence of guns, whose ownership is now widespread, but was even twenty years ago (uniquely in the British Isles) a feature of policemen's uniforms.

At the same time, while noting such Americanisms, it would be ridiculous to suggest that Irish interaction with Britain and the rest of Europe, both culturally and politically, has not been of crucial importance to both parties. It was, after all, invaders from Britain and Scandinavia who began the destruction of Ireland's distinctive Celtic culture.

In fact, this early Irish culture had been rich not merely in ecclesiastical learning, in architecture and the visual arts generally; it excelled also in literature. Old Irish works, first of an oral tradition and then written down as a monastic sideline, have not only survived in greater quantities but outshine in variety and versatility the entire surviving corpus of Old Welsh and Old English works. The ancient Irish were, after all, greatly in demand as literary figures. Not only did Irish monks establish much of Western Europe's medieval scholarship, they also spread many of the legends (of Tristan and Isolde, for example) that have since been carelessly labelled Teutonic or Wagnerian while the Irish provided also many of the key myths of Anglo-French Arthurian writings. Irishmen were specifically imported as story-tellers by bored Icelanders, many of whose sagas are laced with Irish legends—just as in a later period, the Irish Congreve, Sheridan, Goldsmith, Shaw and Wilde dominated the London theatre even when writing in a non-Irish style and idiom.

But whatever the durability of Ireland's literary and religious influence, there is little trace now of her former legal customs and of her other early institutions. Irish law courts—for example—are far more like their English models than are the law courts of Scotland.

Unlike Scotland (but like Wales) she was conquered by the English and, as in Wales, English government demanded standardisation. Thus, sudden death is investigated even in the Irish Republic by a coroner's court as in England and Wales. In Scotland there are no such coroners. An Irish 'barrister' trains at an Inn of Court as in England; a Scottish 'advocate' knows no such 'Inns'. Until 1870, the Irish established church was Anglican and united to the Church of England (and Wales).

Even so, it is important to remember that despite the similarity of treatment accorded to Ireland and Wales by England, Ireland was always accorded far more cautious treatment. The Welsh were too weak and divided to resist such innovations. The Irish were in every century extremely resistant. It is true that this resistance often came only from a minority but, as Pearse reminded the world before the 1916 rebellion, even a minority can keep a sense of nationhood alive.

Pearse's sense of nationhood was not, of course, shared by all his fellow Irishmen, especially in Ulster, but the mere existence of nationalist opposition to a London government has always had a potent effect on the cultural and political attitudes even of the Protestant Unionists, if only because it has led them to exaggerate those 'British' qualities and loyalties in themselves that the inhabitants of Great Britain take for granted. No Scottish party has (as yet!) had to print posters saying 'Scotland is British' (though, significantly, by the end of 1976 a small inter-party group of anti-devolutionists had begun to do so). Moreover, Wales was prepared to accept an English constitution in the sixteenth century because she was not divided from England by religion in Reformation terms.

But Ireland's problem is the problem of the two minorities—the large minority of Protestants in Ireland as a whole and the large minority of Catholics in the North challenging Ulster Unionist dreams of a cosy homogeneity. These tensions existed even before the country was politically divided in 1921—indeed that very division was caused by them and their effects on educational provision in particular have always been enormous.

This tension has been continually increased because at no time has government managed to stand aside from the religious struggle. Before the Union of 1801 the 'free' Irish parliament, liberal as it was in many ways, was nevertheless not just a Protestant but an exclusively Anglican parliament—for a nation predominantly Catholic and Presbyterian; while after 1921, when both parts of Ireland came once more under the 'native' rule of two separated parliaments, far too many decisions of both the Dublin and the Belfast governments appeared to be mercilessly dominated by an intolerant local majority opinion. In fact, both governments could argue that, in the educational sphere in particular, they showed remarkable magnanimity to their minority populations. But too often it *was* magnanimity rather than the administration of a truly impartial system believed by all sides to be fair. Had governments been trusted, fewer schools and parents would perhaps have opted out of the state education systems in a country where the social status attractions of private schooling have always been less than in Britain.

Even when attempts were made (as in the 1831 scheme of national education) to establish a non-denominational education system, the forces of denomination proved too strong. In Dublin, for example, attempts to establish a non-denominational University College alongside the Protestant Trinity College were technically successful in the sense that such a non-denominational college was established and was forbidden to teach theology or religion, but social divisions were such that Protestants largely refused to patronise it, preferring their own college. Thus UCD was and is widely seen as a 'Catholic' college by default, though through one of those unexpected quirks of Irish life that happily foil the stereotypers many Catholics defied an episcopal ban on attendance at Trinity College and regularly joined their Protestant fellow citizens in a college with a longer tradition and certainly a higher social status.

The concentration of so much modern (English-style) high culture in Irish Protestant hands might have cost the Irish majority more dearly, had the Catholic church itself not maintained links with France, Italy and the rest of Catholic Europe as well as with the often fashionable, cultural world of English Catholicism during its Victorian 'Second Spring'. Indeed the essentially Oxonian Newman himself was invited to establish a Catholic university in Dublin to be run on Oxford lines. This project failed, largely because many of Newman's ideas (embodied in his Dublin lectures, 'The Idea of a University') proved too liberal for a newly ultramontane hierarchy. He did however succeed in encouraging a movement for the establishment of Catholic secondary schools which international orders such as the Jesuits and Vincentians were keen to satisfy, while that peculiarly Irish order of teachers, the Christian Brothers, were to revolutionise Catholic secondary education not just in Ireland but throughout the British empire.

Rome, the Empire, America, the salons of London and Paris, all of these provided scope for the socially ambitious Irish during the nineteenth century. On the other hand, Ireland itself (compared with Scotland) had little trade with the world outside and there was not the same scope for fortune making as existed in nineteenth-century Edinburgh or Glasgow. Belfast, it is true, was built up virtually from nothing on the shipbuilding and linen trades but it never developed the entrepreneurial empires of the Scottish cities, and Irish ambitions (particularly Catholic ambitions) tended to run on administrative or religious rather than on commercial lines. In this it resembled other Catholic communities such as that of Quebec, also existing in the shadow of commercially dominant Protestant centres and, as in Quebec, there were those who expressed their financial and career frustrations in politically rebellious terms. For alongside the international ambitions that have for long been the true mark of the aspiring Irish existed, of course, the equally typical nationalism that was to be a prototype not only of such movements throughout the British empire (in India, in particular) but also specifically within the British Isles. The Irish De Valera has been regarded as an elder statesman not just by Nehru and the Indian Congress but equally by Plaid Cymru and the early leaders of the SNP.

Nor was this nationalism, until recently, seen as a primarily Catholic preserve. The Anglican Irish parliament before the Union of 1801 horrified London by its separatist sentiments while the rebellion of 1798 (itself the result of collusion between Catholics and Presbyterians) and the rising of 1916 both had significant Protestants among their leaders. Two of the five presidents of Ireland since the adoption of the 1937 Constitution have themselves been Anglicans.

At the same time, it must be admitted that since the latter part of the nineteenth century the division between nationalists on the one hand and those advocating union with Britain on the other has tended to reflect the old Catholic/Protestant divide as embodied in the Ulster Unionist battle-cry, 'Home Rule is Rome Rule'.

Before the First World War when the only home rule envisaged was devolution to an Irish parliament within the United Kingdom, it was still possible to be, as Irish Liberals were, 'moderate' nationalists and unionists at the same time. But 1916 and the guerilla wars which followed changed all that. The settlement of 1921 meant that the Catholic/Protestant divide became for the first time an official South/North divide which often ignored the interests of the minorities left stranded on either side of a largely artificial dividing-line. For nothing has been more exaggerated than the clear-cut cultural divisions implied by the modern rhetorical treatment of the Irish border. This arbitrary line simply does not divide two races or two cultural entitles. It is indeed straddled by parishes and villages but even more by overlapping traditions and loyalties that the outsider, seeking neat dichotomies, finds it difficult to comprehend.

If one listens to the Northern Ireland Unionist rhetorician (*on* the platform as opposed to *off* it) one would assume that the people of Northern Ireland (and especially the Protestants) were and always have been a race apart from the remainder of the inhabitants of Ireland. In fact, as we have seen, this is racial nonsense. The modern Irish are just as much mongrels as the remainder of their fellow islanders, while both parts of Ireland, though they do have certain separate historical experiences (just as the Highlands and Lowlands of Scotland do), equally have a common history and to a remarkable extent still share common institutions. All the major churches, for example, are still organised on an all-Ireland basis as are the trades unions and many major sports. Very many Northern students (virulently Protestant Unionists as well as Catholics) attend schools and universities in the dreaded and 'backward'

Republic (their description not ours), while Southern actors and other entertainers regularly tour in the North among people as culturally loyal to them as the people of Kilkenny or Cork.

The truth is that, whatever their political rhetoric, most Irishmen, both North and South, do in their everyday lives treat Ireland as a single country with their cultural loyalties far more affected by social class and geographical background than by political ideology. It may be that the recent troubles have differentiated the whole Northern experience (for Catholic and Protestant alike) more fundamentally than was the case before, but it remains to be seen whether any new sense of difference survives the warfare.

In the meantime it is still possible to discern a number of cultural groupings on both sides of the border that form more meaningful, rational divisions that those created by the crude political fiat of 1921. The long experiences of Empire, of rural life, of London's social domination still have a greater influence on personal decisions—especially in the educational field—than the rhetoric of fifty years of political separation.

If one extends an examination of the old dichotomies to the whole of Ireland, the complexity is easily demonstrated. In Appendix 2 we reproduce an attempt to analyse what correspondence there was in, say, 1970 between the holding of Unionist/Nationalist views and the practice of Protestantism/Catholicism.

The major difference that marks off Northern Ireland from the remainder of the United Kingdom has, of course, been its failure to become integrated into the general British political system. There the writs of the Conservative, Labour and Liberal parties just do not run in terms of deciding the general lines of political debate. Until the recent acquisition of strength by the Scottish National Party, they certainly ran in Scotland and once an ideological commitment had been made in London (on comprehensive schooling, for example) then its consequences were felt in all parts of Britain; but even a Labour Government practising direct rule has been unable to force comprehensive schools on Northern Ireland where a decision must be made, if it is to be acceptable, within its own closed political system. It is still one of the characteristics that mark the Northern Irish off as an abnormal part of the United Kingdom and force upon them the need to cry 'Ulster *is* British!' more and more.

It is, of course, true that the Protestant Ulsterman does have a lot in common with his Protestant contemporaries over the sea—in particular, his very non-Catholicism—but to attribute this to his Scottish or English ancestry can get us nowhere. Many Scottish immigrants to Northern Ireland—from Kintyre and the Highlands (or from Glasgow!) were Catholic and have remained so, while many Scottish 'Protestants' (often now agnostics at most) have Irish Catholic forbears that in no way influence their current cultural attitudes. At the same time many fervently republican, Catholic families in Dublin watch the same television programmes—from London, use the same washing powder, eat the same chocolate, have a whole domestic culture in common with the Protestants of modern Scotland but this has far less to tell us about their *political* attitudes or their image of themselves and their national identity than we might think.

Amazing as it may seem to many English and Scottish observers, people who never speak Irish really do sometimes want it to be taught compulsorily in schools just as Catholic Irishmen (traditionally mercenaries) really can still join the British army without becoming unionists or anti-patriots. The Irish, like Canadians and Belgians, have developed the art of sharing a neighbouring culture without being completely swallowed by it.

In the 1920s what is now the Republic was willing to risk its prosperity in order to guarantee its cultural independence. There can be no doubt that in material terms its educational system suffered for it, especially in contrast with that of Northern Ireland. To some this seemed mere foolishness, but others would argue that the somewhat rootless aping of London that ensued in the North was educationally harmful and just as damaging to the creation of an indigenous and constructive culture in the long run. With the growing prosperity of the 1960s, the Republic could again begin to expand. For a time it seemed like a tortoise overtaking a Northern hare still stuck in the attitudes and styles of *its* 'Reform' period—the 1940s and 1950s.

Moreover the changes in the Republic were backed and strengthened by her close links with a wider international world. These were not just the result of emigration and Catholicism, but were strengthened, as in Scotland, by the return of imperial exiles, by the arrival of British tax-evaders and by the impact of that independent diplomatic world of which she was now a full and even celebrated, independent member. Dublin became buoyant and self-confident once more after a century and three-quarters of obscurity. The world of Belfast on the other hand, like that of early eighteenth-century Edinburgh, was that of a purely provincial capital and of a province no longer of great importance either to London or to Dublin. Its cultural influence, unlike Edinburgh's, was almost non-existent, its industries and commerce were declining. By a tragic irony it has been the troubles of more recent years that have renewed Belfast's importance and made it a centre of international interest. It remains to be seen whether it will hold world attention when it eventually rebuilds its shattered culture and whether something new and exciting will emerge, whether the old Northern hare will streak ahead of the tortoise once again. Certainly some of the community enterprises it has thrown up during its adversity suggest that this may well be so and that its institutions will be firmly and locally based instead of being mere artificial transplants from the world outside.

Compared with Ireland, or even Scotland, the Channel Islands have had a remarkably passive history during the past hundred years. Even the terrible interlude of being the only British Isles in enemy occupation during the Second World War seems to have left their institutions and their sense of nationality largely unimpaired. The assertion of Britishness in the face of their gigantic neighbour France has, isometrically, appeared to create a British cultural homogeneity and a unanimous loyalty to the London crown that is rarely equalled elsewhere in the Commonwealth. But it was not always so. The nineteenth century in particular saw many cultural strains as the old Norman French culture was gradually ousted by metropolitan standardisation. And the insult was even greater for, far from being militarily conquered by the English, like the Irish and Welsh, or economically subdued, like the Scots, the original Channel Islanders, the Normans, had actually conquered the English themselves and started them on their path to international success and, indeed, to hegemony within the British Isles. Their Norman/French language had for long been the language of the London court and was (indeed, still is) used for giving the royal assent to Bills at Westminster.

By the beginning of the nineteenth century this French culture was still sufficiently alive in Guernsey for a new church, the 'English' church, to be needed in St Peter Port to cater for English soldiers and officials.[21] But erosion finally became inevitable first with the development of the tourist and horticultural trade (almost totally dependent on England) and then with the increasing influx of English residents seeking first a pleasant climate and then a tax haven in the renewed independence of the postwar years.

There are none of the signs of a backlash—of a revival of French or even a nationalist retort to English bourgeois domination in the style of the Isle of Man or rural Wales. But central Wales seemed equally dead politically for most of the nineteenth century and until very recently the Isle of Man seemed as politically somnolent as Jersey or Sark. It would be an incautious man who forecast no revival of Channel Island self-assertion in an economic and cultural future that remains unknown.

NOTES AND REFERENCES

1 For a detailed description of both the major and minor systems see the opening chapters of *Education in Great Britain and Ireland*, ed. R. Bell, G. Fowler and K. Little (London, Routledge & Kegan Paul, 1973).

2 Ingeniously, Churchill suggested that, if Scots would accept this, then the English would accept Scottish numbering next time there was a King David or a King Robert.
3 See for example the football column of *The Times* for 23 October 1975.
4 'Unionist' throughout this work refers to those wishing to maintain the unity of the United Kingdom.
5 George Borrow, *Lavengro: The Scholar, The Gypsy, The Priest* (World Classics Edition, 1904), p. 53.
6 The Isle of Man and the various Channel Islands are not part of the United Kingdom, do not send members to its parliament and are not subject to Westminster legislation on education.
7 The introduction of free secondary schooling to the Irish Republic was a direct reaction by the government to an OECD report.
8 A domination demonstrated in an *Irish Times* headline of 1971, 'Irishwoman appointed to New Limerick Lectureship'.
9 Trollope, after eighteen years' experience of the country, believed the Irish working class to be 'very much more intelligent than those of England'. (A. Trollope, *An Autobiography*, Berkeley, University of California, 1947, p. 54.) As a Post Office surveyor, he probably got to know all the British Isles better than any other Victorian writer.
10 See, for example, M. Cruickshank, *History of the Training of Teachers in Scotland* (University of London Press, 1970), pp. 102-3.
11 Edinburgh University Press, 1969.
12 Particularly in his *Celtic Literature* (Popular Edition, London, Smith Elder, 1891).
13 Like earlier invaders, they became 'Hibernicis ipsis Hiberniores' (more Irish than the Irish themselves). See Maire and Conor Cruise O'Brien, *Concise History of Ireland* (London, Thames & Hudson, 1972), p. 47.
14 The best account of the educational scene in eighteenth-century Edinburgh is to be found in A. Law, *Education in Edinburgh in the Eighteenth Century* (University of London Press, 1965).
15 J. Boswell, *London Journal 1762-63* (London, Heinemann, 1950), pp. 40-72 *passim*.
16 A Trollope, *The Eustace Diamonds* (Oxford Trollope, Oxford University Press, 1950, p. 292.)
17 Lord Oxford and Asquith, *Memories and Reflections 1852-1927*, Vol. 1 (London, Cassell, 1928), p. 105.
18 See, for example, an article in *Mind*, vol. 2, p. 74, 'Philosophy in the Scottish universities'.
19 J.G. Kellas, *The Scottish Political System* (Cambridge University Press, 1973), pp. 1-19.
20 In 'The devolution of the intellectuals', *New Statesman*, 28 November 1975, pp. 665-6.
21 See A. Rowan, 'Slow progress at St Peter Port', *Country Life*, 29 March 1973, pp. 848-50.

Chapter 2

The Development of the Systems

Even before the time of the Reformation there had been notorious regional cleavages within the British Isles so far as religion was concerned. The directly Roman church established by St Augustine of Canterbury and his followers had its chief base in the southern and eastern parts of England and often found itself in conflict with the more old-established Celtic churches in the northern and western parts of the Islands. Although the doctrinal and administrative divisions between the two groups were largely set aside following the Synod of Whitby in 664, there is no doubt that this initial separation continued to influence not only clerical habits and doctrinal attitudes but also educational arrangements for many centuries. However, Rome, working through the more highly centralised churches of the Norman period, undoubtedly did manage to impose a greater unity on the church's education systems in England, Ireland and Lowland Scotland so that by the time of the Reformation, educational provision within the British Isles had probably reached the highest level of uniformity that it has reached at any time in written history. Moreover, at the time of the Reformation itself, the educational arrangements made by Protestant monarchs for education within the three kingdoms were in many ways broadly identical. In those areas which persisted in their Catholicism (such as Ireland, the Western Isles and Lancashire) the establishment of Protestant Schools was seen as a major device for bringing dissent to an end. At the same time, those centrally placed grammar schools which already existed, particularly in the cathedral cities, were overhauled both in curriculum and pedagogy and in accordance with renaissance ideals as a way of improving the educational standards of the new Protestant clergy.

We speak of 'cathedral' cities, although, of course, it was for a time by no means certain whether the new Protestant churches would be episcopalian or Presbyterian in their organisation and in Scotland the Reformers wavered over this question for a century or more. In any case, the educational significance of such differences was at first limited. The Scottish Presbyterians in their *First Book of Discipline* of 1560 drew the outlines of an educational system very similar to those being promulgated by Luther and Episcopalian governments elsewhere in Europe and indeed very similar to those supported by the English crown not only in England but in Ireland. In the latter country of course, such

Protestant arrangements were seen by the persistently Catholic native population largely as a means of proselytising and this was not an unfair interpretation. Following the settlement of Ulster by Englishmen and Scots mainly from the wild, uncultured Scottish border country at the beginning of the seventeenth century, King James VI and I set up throughout the Ulster counties a system of royal (grammar) schools similar to the cathedral schools in England which were meant to impose a system of English-speaking Protestant education on what he saw potentially as a vital buffer zone between two major groups of religious and political enemies—that is, between the Gaelic-speaking Catholics of western Scotland and the Gaelic-speaking Catholics elsewhere in Ireland. However, neither in the case of the royal schools nor in the case of the other Irish Protestant schools envisaged for each country parish was any adequate, permanent provision made for their financing, and although many Irish schools still claim a history stretching back to this period, very few of them can claim that that history was a period of unbroken prosperity, at least before Victorian times, and few of them have been able to function satisfactorily on the endowments made at the time of the Ulster plantation.

Similarly in England, although the cathedral schools were reformed and refurbished and although the Tudor monarchs covered the land with all those grammar schools that so often in more modern times have rejoiced in the names of 'Queen Elizabeth' or 'King Edward', they too usually had a pretty inadequate permanent provision made either for their maintenance or for their inspection; while there was a similar lack of adequate endowment and supervision of the parochial elementary schools also envisaged in the Reformation legislation. In any case, even where schools *were* adequately endowed, they were unevenly spread over the whole country and their presence often depended less on evidence of need in the locality, than on the fortuitous piety of some local grandee endowing schools partly for pious and partly for tax-evasion purposes. Thus a village producing two lord mayors of London might for centuries enjoy far better educational provision than a much larger town which had not had the good fortune to produce any such distinguished progeny.[1]

Some of the grammar schools (particularly those that dated back from before the Reformation, such as Eton and Winchester) were superbly endowed and were able not only to survive but to cater continuously for the highest levels of society. But many of the Reformation grammar schools, especially those detached from the cathedrals and thus from clergy training, soon degenerated into elementary schools or worse, and many village elementary schools themselves disappeared altogether for want of adequate staffing and financing. Certainly, until the nineteenth century, there was no assumption in England either that every town should have a grammar school, or that every village should have an elementary school. Indeed it was never assumed, even among the middle class, that every child should attend any educational institution whatsoever at any time in his life. Among many of the very poor, full-time schooling was seen as an economic liability, as a distraction from earning a living while among the more genteel members of the middle class, schools (especially the great public boarding schools) were seen as at worst dens of iniquity and at best a threat to the unity of families.

On the other hand the civil and religious advantages of at least basic literacy were of course obvious; and while, for a minority of middle-class and upper-class families, adequate education was usually provided within the family circle, literacy had to be bought elsewhere by the majority of the population. Thus, by the beginning of the nineteenth century, a vast number of private teachers and establishments had sprung up among all social classes, and although many of these establishments would not be schools in the modern sense, (i.e. demanding total commitment for the whole of each day) they did at least spread basic literacy and numeracy among a far greater number of the population than has usually been supposed.[2] It was their unsatisfactory nature rather than their absence that caused such a public outcry in the 1830s when the first state subsidies for elementary education began to be paid. By that time the churches and other charitable organisations had already done a great deal to help spread elementary education (and indeed some elements of a wider curriculum) across the face of England, while a new interest in the reform of secondary education had begun to develop, partly under the influence of the nonconformist academies, partly in imitation of the French, Germans and Americans. The influence of the latter in particular has been greatly under-rated, for many of their educationalists acted as interpreters of the continental scene to British audiences.

Many of the old-established and often derelict grammar schools now began to be refurbished by enterprising headmasters, often in the style of Winchester and Eton, and despite what were sometimes legal prohibitions, they began to despise and drop their local connections in favour of attracting a clientele from all over the country. This process was considerably assisted by the development of the railway system near whose junctions many of the more successfully developed 'ancient' grammar schools were situated.[3]

In Scotland things had developed rather differently. Although the reformers' plans were very similar to those elsewhere in Western Europe, the still independent Scottish parliament and privy council had taken several further steps during the seventeenth century to encourage and consolidate a system whose construction the church had begun in the previous century. In various Acts passed between 1666 and the end of the century, Scottish government had arranged a far more adequate provision for the maintenance of elementary schools than had been the case in England or Ireland. By 1600 many (possibly most) parishes in the more prosperous parts of rural Scotland had already established reasonable parish schools; and these in turn were meant to play their part in a proposed network by which able pupils were to be directed from them to the district grammar schools in the larger towns and, if appropriate, subsequently to the provincial universities.

Such a system of course largely remained an ideal. Certainly it never functioned in quite such a simple and convenient way. Nevertheless some of its components were already in existence. No less than five institutions claiming to be universities were already functioning by 1600 (two of them in Aberdeen) and many of the high-level grammar schools were already either competing with those 'universities' for a similar type of pupil or were concentrating on the task of supplying them with students. However, in the poorer parts of the country and in those parts of the country where parishes covered extensive areas (some in the Highlands covered 100 square miles or more) the reformers' intentions were far less near being realised. The seventeenth-century legislation demanded therefore that the local property-owners (or 'heritors') should be legally responsible for providing and maintaining a school in every parish of Scotland. The legislation also fixed the minimum and maximum payments to be made to schoolmasters and arranged for a system of inspection supervised by the General Assembly of the Church of Scotland and carried out by its lower assemblies. Such arrangements mark a clear advance on any arrangements made in England and although some parts of Scotland, such as the western Highlands and the Borders, were still too wild by the beginning of the eighteenth century for the rules to have ever begun to be applied satisfactorily and although in other parts of a still ill-governed country the heritors could prove either too defiant or too poor to do all their duties, a remarkably comprehensive system of parochial elementary schools was already established within most of the Lowlands and even in many Highland and Island areas by 1700. Where the system creaked, it was often helped out by church and other charity organisations similar to those operating in England.

On the other hand it must be emphasised that although this Scottish system was compulsorily financed, attendance for the pupils was never compulsory nor was it usually free, and (most important of all) it did not operate within the cities where provision was often the same hit-and-miss affair as in major English and Irish centres of population. Moreover by 1830 the considerable migration of population from the Scottish countryside to the city suburbs, particularly in the central belt, meant that the parochial school provision in such areas was soon hopelessly overstretched and village schools previously catering for a population of

6,000 or 7,000 could now, in some extreme cases, find themselves 'catering' for a population of 100,000 or more. By 1830 therefore the most populous parts of Scotland were in no better and no worse an educational state than similar areas in England and Ireland and there can be little doubt that the standard of many of the private enterprise establishments then operating and, indeed, the standard of many of the parochial schools themselves had produced a considerable educational deterioriation so far as many sections of the urban population were concerned. Ironically, the improvement in agricultural methods had also brought an educational decline even in prosperous country areas, for with the greater complexity of operations on the farm, parents were more reluctant to allow their children to 'waste' their time in school, particularly on purely cultural pursuits, and no longer saw schooling as the only way of salvation, either economic or spiritual. An earlier peasant society had been more favourably disposed to general cultural training and had placed a greater stress on the religious benefits of Bible reading. To the modern farmer, even literacy seemed less important than the availability of manpower.

By 1830, then, no part of the British Isles could be said to have an adequate system even of part-time state education of a type that had already been established in most of industrial Western Europe and in the more settled parts of North America. Levels of illiteracy may well have been exaggerated by some subsequent historians and our view of the period may also have been coloured by the contemporary reports of empire-building civil servants anxious to make a case for the development of an adequate state system to be controlled by themselves.[4] Nevertheless what schooling there was was clearly inadequate to cope with the greater complexities of modern industrial and commercial living. Moreover by modern standards it was often only schooling in a very limited sense. Many of the children attended only for certain hours on certain days and there was never any question of that total commitment to a single institution which has characterised schooling in more recent years. Parents and children regularly 'shopped around' educationally and pupils could often be attending a number of institutions or establishments concurrently, learning, perhaps Latin here, and dancing there.[5] Moreover even the greatest defenders of the private enterprise system of elementary schooling in this period make no attempt to defend the inadequacies of the English and Irish secondary schools which, where they did exist, were all too often tied to a narrow and outdated curriculum, of a type that the Irish and Scottish universities, unlike some of their feeder establishments, had long since thrown overboard.

In Scotland the absence of an adequate system of secondary schooling covering the whole country was in many ways far less important a problem than it was in Ireland or England, for the university background of many village schoolmasters meant they could themselves prepare candidates directly for university studies, much to the surprise and distaste of English politicians. The latter, with the usual English class-based assumptions concerning education, saw it as both pointless and dangerous to encourage the study of higher mathematics and classics among lower-class village schoolboys. Some members of Victorian Cabinets felt that at worst this encouraged a dangerous restlessness and at best gave such village boys scholarly tastes which they could not hope to satisfy on later incomes.

In England such secondary education as did exist was largely restricted to the middle and the upper classes and although some poor boys, particularly aspirants for the church, were able to slip through the class net and were on occasion sponsored by leading churchmen or rich benefactors, the grammar schools and the public schools provided a totally inadequate tap for the national pool of academic ability. Even in the 'dissenting' academies where academic aspirations were highest, the standard of studies for the vast majority of students was probably low by modern standards as indeed was the bulk of the work undertaken by Victorian university undergraduates, very few of whom attempted honours and very few of whom saw their studies as essential for the following of subsequent vocations.

Although the ending of patronage during the nineteenth century saw the introduction of more exacting entrance examinations for both the universities and the professions, the business of guiding candidates through such examinations was seen by most parents to be a matter not so much for the schools (whose main concern was with social training and labelling) as for specialist 'cramming' establishments, perhaps the least adequately studied of all Victorian educational structures. Boys were even in the habit of leaving Eton and other comparatively efficient public schools for such 'crammers' in order to gain entrance to the army, or to Oxford and Cambridge and the institutions thought fit for such purposes could include the new, socially inferior 'university' establishments in London such as University College and King's College.[6]

With a growing sense of international rivalry in commercial and industrial life, it was felt more and more generally that other countries solved their educational problems more satisfactorily and the attractiveness of foreign models of schooling, particularly those of the United States and Germany became considerable. From the 1830s onwards, the British government was very much involved in the adoption of such models for new state-subsidised schooling throughout the British Isles. In England and Scotland this initially took the simple form of subsidising and augmenting worthy charitable enterprises, particularly the schools already established by the churches. But in the Channel Islands and in the

Isle of Man the reign of William IV in particular saw a much more far-reaching reorganisation by government of general educational provision, including that at secondary level. Most significantly his reign also saw in Ireland the establishment, some forty years before the establishment of a similar system in England, Scotland and Wales, of an actual system of national elementary education under the supervision of a government board.[7]

This pioneering effort in Ireland is rarely discussed in English and Scottish books of educational history. But it must have provided not just the authorities in Dublin, but British government in general with invaluable preliminary experience, later to be of relevance elsewhere in the United Kingdom. In particular, it must have prepared London for the sectarian squabbles which made the development of English state education so difficult; for the Irish scheme was, from the beginning, plagued by the most violent sectarian disagreements among those who were meant to work the system. However, the lessons were not all depressing. It also demonstrated to the bureaucrats the possible financial advantages of state accountability; while the textbooks and copy-books produced by the state printers in Dublin were imposed not just on Irish schools but also on many of the English and Scottish schools in receipt of government assistance, thus providing Whitehall not only with a way of recouping losses at a time when government subsidies were under great suspicion but also with a semi-covert method for imposing a standardised and politically satisfactory curriculum.[8]

It is often assumed that the Irish system of 1831 was largely established in order to cope with Ireland's habitual social and political turbulence for which a better educational system appeared to offer one possible solution. For just such reasons, the British government also undertook the maintenance of the main Catholic seminary for the training of priests at Maynooth in an attempt to purchase the political assistance and loyalty of a native and potentially revolutionary priesthood. But there is some evidence that the national system of 1831 was just as much the logical outcome of genuinely ideological commitment to educational egalitarianism on the part of the Irish parliament in the period before the Act of Union in 1800,[9] and certainly there had been for some thirty years a growing number of initiatives on the part of both Protestant and Catholic leaders to establish a non-denominational system of elementary schools throughout the country, led notably by the Kildare Place Society which included both Catholic and Anglican bishops among its keenest supporters. Such aspirations towards non-denominational schooling did not, however, long survive the establishment of the national scheme, for both the Presbyterians of the Ulster Synod and some of the increasingly ultra-montane Catholic hierarchy soon set aside the comparative liberality of earlier decades and insisted on having their own national schools, restricted to 'their own' people.

It must be said, however, that all too often they had cause to mistrust the motives of some influential Protestant bishops for whom, as in England, 'national' schools meant 'Anglican' schools.

Thus the distinctively denominational system of national elementary schools, now such a typical feature of education in the Irish Republic, was already well established by the middle of the century and was not the later creation of fifty years of rule by native Catholics.

These events have left a legacy in Northern Ireland also, where the ostensibly non-denominational 'county' primary schools have been so exclusively Protestant in most areas that parents have even objected to Catholic student teachers doing teaching practice in them, while some Belfast Catholics attending such 'undenominational' institutions have been punished by their bishop with the withdrawal of confirmation, such has been the assumption on both sides that the 'right' place for Catholic children and teachers was in the Catholic voluntary schools of their own ghettos or townlands. One suspects that, in Northern Ireland, opposition to mixed schools at least at secondary level has been motivated more by a fear of mixed marriages (with the demographic threat that they pose to the communities) than by a desire to protect pupils doctrinally. Certainly it has been wasteful for some small towns have had to support four grammar schools (two for boys, two for girls) when one would have sufficed elsewhere. Even now, there seems less prospect of desegregation in the North (where non-denominational education already officially exists) than in the Dublin area where many middle-class parents are positively demanding non-sectarian schooling. Indeed, the question of 'secularising' schools is now perhaps the major point of controversy in the Republic's education system.[10]

Many of the current troubles of Ireland are, of course, attributed by politicians and journalists to just such a system of educational 'apartheid', of separate and equal development (which incidentally has never affected technical or vocational schools in which Catholics and Protestants of all ages have always mixed together, nor the Northern universities where such a mix is equally surprisingly acceptable, given the even greater chance of its providing marriages); but it is far too easily forgotten that there is often little to choose organisationally between the Irish system of denominational schooling and that which operates in England and Wales where large numbers of both primary and secondary schools are still supervised on much the same lines as in Northern Ireland, both by the Roman Catholic church and by the established Church of England. The English and Welsh churches are also, as in Northern Ireland, 'voluntarily' paying a certain proportion of the costs of such schools in order to maintain a say in their government. The whole question of whether such church schools should continue in existence after the establishment of a national system of education in England and Wales in 1870 was a matter of intense political controversy which continued into this century. Non-Anglican Protestants in particular objected to the paying of rates for the partial upkeep of far from impartial establishments. Nevertheless, although Roman Catholic primary schools have on the whole maintained their distinctive nature, the Church of England schools in many villages and towns are by now quite indistinguishable in terms of their intake from the surrounding schools run entirely by local authorities; and many parents (even those not nominally Anglican) often remain largely unaware that the primary school attended by their children is in fact a denominational one run by the Church of England.

Nevertheless even in Anglican schools the churches do maintain certain powers over the curriculum and staffing while, particularly in strongly Catholic areas, the existence of this 'duality' in the national school system can be a matter of great, if sometimes latent, political significance. It is certainly a matter which most politicians treat with great caution and if it has appeared recently to be a non-issue, this is often because attention has deliberately been steered away from it in most educational discussions at election times.

In Scotland, the issue of denominational schools began by being more complicated but has now become much simpler than elsewhere. As we have already seen, a great network of parochial schools was originally established and supervised by the established (Presbyterian) Church of Scotland. However in 1843 a great division occurred within that church, ostensibly over matters of lay patronage but embracing greater issues. This splitting of the kirk became known as the 'Disruption' and involved the departure of a major group of ministers and laymen. Their newly established Free Church of Scotland insisted that it, rather than the establishment, was now the true national church and that it should embark upon the collection of funds in order to establish its own national system, not merely of parochial churches, but also of parochial schools.

Thus at a time of crucial need in industrialised Scotland, these newly raised funds were sometimes unnecessarily squandered in duplicating the provision of schools in sparsely populated rural areas, although of course in certain more congested areas the new Free Church school provided yet another agency for the relieving of pressures. In any case there was certainly continuing tension between the 'old' church and the 'new' and as preparations were made for setting up a national system of state education for Scotland in 1872, the problems of reconciling the interests of the Free and the established churches were a major theme of the debate. In the end, as the vast majority of Scots were Presbyterians of one persuasion or another, all national schools were to be run by the new school boards on non-sectarian, though broadly Presbyterian lines, while only the Roman Catholics and the small group of Anglicans in Scotland retained their distinctively denominational schooling. However, in 1918, by an arrangement unique to Scotland within the United Kingdom, it was agreed that denominational schools should be maintained completely by the local authorities, even though the church concerned was to retain central control over the religious teaching and, hopefully, over the staffing.

In the Republic of Ireland there were (and are) no such local authorities and there clergy-control over what are invariably denominational elementary schools has been virtually unlimited, though recently schemes have been devised for giving parents and teachers a greater say in school government. In the United Kingdom, on the other hand, the influence of LEA advisers and inspectors on church schools has been considerable and thus their differences from surrounding 'secular' schools have been greatly diminished. Moreover, throughout Britain, it has sometimes become increasingly difficult (especially as methods of teaching religion in church schools have become more and more similar) to provide adequate staffing for denominational schools from the ranks of the church concerned and one story of a Catholic school in Edinburgh (by no means apocryphal) tells of its acquiring a Pakistani communist as its principal teacher in that most doctrinally sensitive of disciplines, history; though it is true this might not have happened so easily in an English or Irish Catholic secondary school which is slightly less directly dependent on the secular authority than is the case in Scotland.

But it is not only the denominational arrangements that have distinguished the development of Scottish secondary schooling from that elsewhere. As we said earlier, the Scottish parochial schools, as well as some of the schools which were later set up in competition with them, were in the habit of sending boys directly to the university and while sometimes the training they provided had to be topped up by 'preliminary' classes, provided by the professors themselves (never loath before this century to supplement unstable incomes) there was an atmosphere of high scholarship among the best pupils of some village schools, particularly in more prosperous country areas.

At Dalkeith in Midlothian, the parochial school actually developed, under the patronage of the Duke of Buccleuch, into a fully fledged English-style grammar school, teaching the classics to a high standard and acting as a rival to the high schools of Edinburgh and the other large towns that dated from the Middle Ages or had been established as a result of the Reformation plan.[11] Thus, although by the mid-nineteenth century Scotland was not well supplied with secondary schools in any modern sense, especially in comparison with France or Germany, she did nevertheless have a widespread system of secondary tuition and many parish schoolmasters, like their colleagues in the high schools, had a continental rather than an English view of the curriculum. Up to 1914, Scottish universities enjoyed far greater links with continental universities than did Oxford and Cambridge, and George Davie has suggested in his *The Democratic Intellect*[12] that this link had far-reaching effects on Scottish pedagogy. Certainly the curriculum was more generalist and experimental (in continental style) than the more narrow, tradition-bound curriculum of the most socially prestigious English establishments and although Davie has probably exaggerated the extent to which teachers allowed genuine, mutually critical dialogue at school and university, certainly methods of teaching the classics and mathematics could differ enormously from those operating in English public and grammar schools.

The latter tended for example to emphasise the minutiae of grammar and the skills of Latin and Greek versifying at the expense of any discussion of the content and ideas of the classical authors they were reading. Political and philosophical discussion was, they believed, beyond the minds and experiences of those of tender years. Not so the best of Scots teachers, who attempted to broaden their pupils' view of the world as well as their linguistic ability. The Scottish high school boy or undergraduate had usually a smattering of philosophy and in some cases a knowledge of the physical sciences even if his knowledge of prosody and the exact use of the Latin subjective left something to be desired.

But however desirable all this might have been educationally, it eventually began to tell against him in strictly practical terms for such a diet prepared him badly for the new English-based examinations that began to dominate nineteenth-century career structures following the end of patronage in the civil service and the army.[13] In these examinations English drilling as opposed to Scottish mind-broadening paid off handsomely. As Davie laments, the Scots learnt the lesson quickly. The adoption of English models was accelerated.

Even as early as the 1820s, before the examinations had even begun, some leading Scotsmen had hastened this process. During that decade a group, (paradoxically anglophile and yet nationalist in the style of Boswell, including Cockburn and Sir Walter Scott), had actually founded in Edinburgh an English-style grammar school for the education of the 'better classes'—Edinburgh Academy. It is true that it was not typically English. It had a wide curriculum in that Scottish style increasingly revered by frustrated reformers south of the border, but it had an English, Anglican headmaster whose ideas of pedagogy were characteristically English and were based on a meticulous attention to detail hitherto largely unknown in Edinburgh.

The founding of Edinburgh Academy was to have a far-reaching effect on the development of secondary education in the Scottish cities. For it not only introduced an English pedagogy, it also introduced to Scotland the notion of the prestigious school as the major device of social labelling. Symptomatically it was established in the 'New' Town of Edinburgh, in that area of classical elegance which the Edinburgh middle class had built in order to distance themselves from the squalor of the 'Old' Town (situated on both sides of what is now the Royal Mile) where, for centuries, they had lived promiscuously with their social inferiors and even shared some of their schooling. Edinburgh Academy was a symbol of an end to all this. It marked the first major formal step towards the establishment of a school system based, like that of England, on the class distinctions of society. Symptomatically, it was the first Scottish school to encourage the playing of organised team games, and these were organised initially by its 'Former Pupils', the first group of Scottish 'old boys' to rejoice in that most overt form of social labelling later symbolised throughout the British Isles by the 'old school tie'.

Even the academically prestigious high school, still in the Old Town, found competition from the Academy too strong and had, itself, to move on to the edge of the New Town, perching regretfully in handsome new classical buildings looking down on its old premises amid the squalor of the High Street.

From this point onwards, Edinburgh's secondary education in particular came to be dominated by English models and by English social divisiveness. In the 1860s and 1870s the first professor of education in the University of Edinburgh, S. S. Laurie, saw as one of his main tasks the establishment of academically and socially high-level English-style secondary schools in Scotland, and in the later part of the century Scottish developments were considerably influenced by developments south of the border. Initially, the biggest influence was the Taunton Commissioners' Report on the English endowed schools,[14] the most significant of which were the grammar schools. Taunton suggested a new system of secondary education with three tiers of schools each catering for a different division of society—the richest class who were able to keep their children at school till the age of 18, those who were prosperous enough to keep them there till 16 and those who felt it necessary to withdraw them at 14 or earlier. This notion of a secondary system catering in turn for each branch of the middle and upper classes affected Scottish as well as English decision making. Eventually charitable institutions such as George Heriot's Hospital (previously designed to cater for the impoverished) were refurbished and reorganised to cater for the more prosperous. Most grotesquely of all, perhaps, an orphans' fund under the Fettes Trust was diverted to the provision of a new boarding school for the Scottish upper class, the group deemed to be least well provided for in Scotland according to Taunton criteria! Hence, the fashionable Fettes College, like Wellington College in England, was created from funds originally earmarked for the service of the destitute.

The Taunton Commission had been preceded by an earlier Commission (the Clarendon) that reported in 1864. It had been concerned entirely with the nine most distinguished public schools and although its Report included an extensive discussion of curriculum (especially the poor treatment of science in English schools), the consequent legislation was concerned only with finance and methods of school government. Taunton's effects were more far-reaching, for its work eventually resulted in the appointment of *ad hoc* Commissions for the reorganisation of individual schools and trust funds. Some of the latter had been legally restricted for use in the education of boys. The post-Taunton Commissions released money to establish girls' grammar schools or more rarely, coeducational schools—the existence of which in rural areas of Scotland had so impressed the Taunton Commission's own correspondent. The Taunton legislation and its aftermath also finally released many schools from earlier restrictions that limited them to the subjects of the Renaissance canon.

As a result of the Taunton reforms and the ending of patronage, there was a new, if gradual, upsurge in academic standards to cope with the new demands of a public examination system. The English universities came to place greater trust in the secondary schools and success there began to give exemption from sections of the undergraduate course.

Many rich families still chose to educate their children privately at home, but by 1900, it was almost universal for children of all middle- and upper-class families to attend some secondary school or another, and by 1900 it was felt to be more and more appropriate that the brightest children being thrown up by the new state elementary system should also be given a place on the ladder that led via the grammar school to the universities and professional life in general.

As a result of the 1902 Education Act, the new local education authorities then established in England and Wales to replace the old (and generally smaller) school boards were enabled to develop grammar schools of their own. Sometimes they started from scratch. In other cases, they adapted old-established schools or purchased private enterprises. Thus the whole network of popular English and Welsh grammar schools such as we have known in this century was eventually born and in order to assist the poor boy to climb the ladder on which his foot was now (theoretically) placed, a system of 'merit' scholarships was established for promoting able pupils from the elementary schools.

This 'merit' system was followed in Scotland also and it was from such beginnings that the system of secondary selection called in England and Wales the 11 plus was developed. In Scotland, of course, the transfer usually occurred a year later (see Appendix 1) though the principle was similar. By the 1940s, the provision of such grammar school places was virtually universal, though only a small minority of children were awarded them and not every place was taken up. Some families felt themselves too poor to provide the necessary books and uniform or to forgo the children's earning power. Thus they did not always pose too great a threat to the grammar school's middle-class flavour, especially as in England and Wales until the forties, and in Scotland until the seventies, it was possible for aspiring parents to 'buy' a way for their children into such local authority schools at comparatively low rates, even if they failed the 'merit' exam. Poorer children who only just 'failed' were often accommodated in 'central' schools providing a high level of commercial and technical education and after 1944, these central schools were often turned into grammar schools themselves, sometimes taking the second string of 11-plus successes, although they were rarely accepted as socially equivalent to 'real' grammar schools given the strong and continuing social bias in favour of schools with an academic, non-utilitarian purpose.

The prewar county grammar schools in England and Wales had managed to capture much of the atmosphere and prestige of the elitist Victorian English public school and did everything to identify themselves with the public school sector by way of dress, sport and curriculum.[15] Moreover, this model was embraced also by the new senior secondary schools (the selective grammar schools) of Scotland and by all those schools in the British Isles outside England which aspired to equivalent social status.

The 'merit' children, like those who later passed the 11 or 12-plus, were by their very attendance in such schools destined, whatever their home background, to become part of the middle class and often themselves became enthusiastic followers of public school models. Despite their own entire dependence on academic success, they even began to share the common public school tendency to venerate the games field and 'character' at the expense of classroom 'swotting' or 'mark-grubbing'.

In the century following 1870 then, England, and to some extent Scotland, had developed a socially stratified secondary school system and it was stratified even for those who were being given a grammar school education; for among the grammar schools themselves there was a distinct pecking order. The old-established tended to take social precedence over the newly established, while among the old-established themselves, there was a clear social distinction between the most distinguished of the public schools (especially those with boarders such as Eton, Winchester and Harrow), and the older local grammar schools, some of which were being entirely administered by local authorities (in itself a matter of some social disgrace). In theory, the grammar school, at whatever level, opened up the same set of opportunities for all, but even by 1976 the proportion of pupils from the more socially elitist public schools and grammar schools is still greater on entry to the ancient universities, to the professions and to the most prestigious sections of the public service than might have been expected from the spread of an egalitarian ideology and the situation has not been dissimilar in the major cities of Scotland. Indeed, it has become almost unthinkable for professional families in Edinburgh to send their children to anything but a fee-paying school of some kind and the middle classes of the four Scottish cities have actually opted out of free local authority education on a scale unknown even in south-east England.

In rural Scotland on the other hand, and in Wales, where the system was technically the same, the social pressures were not so enormous. The Welsh grammar schools in particular were never either as highly selective as they were in England and Scotland, or as socially divisive, and by the time national moves were made during the 1960s to end the 11-plus examination, some Welsh counties were already allowing as large a proportion as 60 or 70 per cent of the age-group into the grammar school. In other words, the Welsh non-grammar schools in some counties had become, in effect, remedial establishments for a minority rather than the socially damning destination that they were for the majority of English and Scottish pupils. Thus, when comprehensive secondary education began to spread during the 1960s, the process was much quicker in Wales for the majority of the school population was already either attending comprehensives or was not as aware of secondary selection as a crucial, social selection process. In rural Scotland also there was already a core of schools, particularly in small country towns, where those following a grammar school curriculum and the rest of their age-group were already accommodated under the same roof. (Indeed, in some cases, the school also included the only local primary school.) Such 'multilateral' schools (with only internal selection) provided one of the models for the new comprehensives elsewhere in Britain, although such a model was of course in the end largely rejected even in Scotland in favour of more thorough-going change.

The social divisiveness of secondary selection in England and urban Scotland eventually meant that the move to comprehensive education did not just consist of a crusade for educational change, based on dissatisfaction with the selection procedures and the need to tap more efficiently the pool of ability from which eventual leaders and skilled operators were chosen; it sprang also from a general feeling that the superficial labelling involved in secondary school selection was dividing the nation socially, as well as educationally, a feeling never felt as acutely in Wales and rural Scotland.

In Ireland there had never been such a feeling either. There the effects of Taunton had been considerably restricted by finance and the influence of the public school was minimal. Some potential candidates for gentrification, the royal schools for example, even wanted to develop their day-boy entry at the expense of boarding.[16] Thus the class basis of secondary selection never became so highly developed and although Northern Ireland, following its usual pattern of moving 'step by step with England', had introduced a provincial 11-plus system in the 1940s, the great majority of Northern Ireland's grammar schools, both Protestant and Catholic, continued to be either independent or semi-independent of government without anyone feeling that this posed a major social problem. Fee paying in local authority grammar schools had remained both common and acceptable even among the poorer classes of Northern Ireland society in a way that was never true in England and Scotland, while in the Republic of Ireland, the differences from the British situation were even more marked. There the vast majority of Catholic secondary schools providing an academic education were run by the religious orders or by diocesan secular priests who were able to devote at least some proportion of their salaries and general endowments to the provision of scholarships for poor children on a scale that was quite impossible for any financially viable school in Great Britain or indeed for any other type of Irish school. As a result virtually every Catholic child in the Republic who wanted a grammar school education, was able to get it at very low cost or even no cost at all to his family, particularly if he was a candidate for the priesthood or had some other religious vocation. Thus when, in order to bring the Republic into line with the rest of Western Europe, the Dublin government introduced in the 1960s a system of free secondary education for all, those instituting it actually found it a very cheap operation indeed. The demand for academic education was already being satisfied so fully that the providing of extra secondary places for those excluded hitherto by poverty actually cost far less than a concurrent move to introduce free transport schemes for rural pupils.[17]

In Northern Ireland where almost half the school population (unlike the adult population) is Roman Catholic, it was even easier for the religious orders to satisfy Catholic demand because of the higher salaries they commanded and the greater state subsidies available to the grammar schools. Whether pupils with poorer qualifications benefited once they had arrived in grammar schools is quite a different issue—but arrive they did in far greater numbers than their 11-plus success would warrant, such is the value placed on academic education by the emigration-minded Irish population.

Social success in Ireland is guaranteed far more by grammar school success than by grammar school attendance. Thus when pressure began in the remainder of the United Kingdom for the ending of secondary selection on educational and social grounds, the demand for such a change was minimal in Northern Ireland. Both the status consequences of 'failure' and the chances of actual exclusion from a grammar school were considerably less. Eleven-plus success guaranteed a place, 11-plus failure did not rule it out. The first formidable opposition to the 11-plus in England had come not from convinced ideologues but from the parents of 'failures' and any parent who, for a modest fee, purchased a place for his child in the junior department of a Northern Ireland grammar school could almost certainly count on that child being eventually transferred to the senior school regardless of an 11-plus 'failure'. Moreover once that child had been promoted, he was entitled to financial relief in respect of the place at a 'free' school which he had not taken up. It is not surprising, therefore, that there was little pressure to end selection (as in England and Scotland) from the more articulate parents of 'failures'.

In the Republic, there was never until recently any real development (except in the most affluent parts of Dublin) of rigorous selection by secondary schools and grammar or vocational secondary education is now generally available to all who require it. Thus, having avoided the tensions caused by an 11-plus, the Republic has found the introduction of comprehensive schooling a comparatively painless process—in political if not in economic terms. Opposition in the cities has been minimal. Indeed, the enlarged facilities that comprehensive and community schools[18] provide have been generally welcomed. Only in the country towns has there been concern—not so much over the loss of grammar schools as such as over the loss of the 'atmosphere' created by the dominance of a particular religious order, over the loss of a school to which there are strong family loyalties, over proposed methods of government deemed (in the absence of a local authority) to be undemocratic, or over the mere lack of local consultation in the planning stages. The question of a school's social or historical 'traditions', so important in England and Scotland, has arisen hardly at all.

In the 1970s, the grammar schools of England have of course been defended mainly as centres of intellectual excellence, but it is interesting to recall that when the passing of the 11-plus became, in the 1940s, the sole method of entry to the state-maintained grammar schools, both teachers and parents at such schools objected to the imposition of such a rigorously intellectual *rite de passage*. They deplored the ignoring in such a selection process of 'character' and sporting qualities and indeed defended academic heterogeneity as a virtue in itself, thus revealing the extent to which they saw their schools, not as the intellectual hot-houses they were proudly to become, but as the natural nurseries for the whole of certain classes in society. Parents in rural Scotland, in Wales and in Ireland on the other hand, although they also desired the social advancement of their children, seemed to be more interested in solid training that would lead to job success (guaranteeing social success) rather than the mere social badging of the old school tie. Certainly their devotion to the grammar school has been less fanatical and their defence of it less of a major political issue than it has been in England and in the largest cities of Scotland.

Because of the major invasion of the Isle of Man and the Channel Islands by English middle-class immigrants following the Second World War, England's problems on this issue have tended to be their problems, and even before then, it became clear that the English model of secondary education was the strongest for them to follow. It will be interesting in the next decade to see whether this continues to be so, and whether the new English model of the comprehensive school will prove satisfactory in islands now dominated by middle-aged populations whose educational ideology was established in the England of more than a decade ago.

Some readers, of course, will deplore our concentration on the grammar school. After all, they could rightly point out, the grammar school has always been the school of a small minority. The 1944 Education Act in England and Wales and its successors in Scotland and Northern Ireland all declared that they were concerned with providing secondary education for all and the grammar school has been only one of the vehicles by which such secondary education has been provided. However, undeceived by such rhetoric, most people in the British Isles have clung to an earlier belief that only the grammar school has been a 'real' secondary school and that the secondary modern school in England or the junior secondary school in Scotland have only been the old elementary school writ large.

We have concentrated on the grammar school, because in a sense it has been the most positive element in British and Irish educational development during the last century. For even though the majority of the population do not attend such schools, the form of their education has tended to be dominated by the presence of schools from which their teachers are drawn and by which they feel they have been rejected. All too often, particularly in the United Kingdom outside Wales, they have in the past been fobbed off with scraps from the grammar school table—literally, on occasions, for education authorities have all too often allocated their abandoned textbooks and classrooms for the use of 'non-academic' pupils; and while it is true that in the thirty years following 1944, the more enlightened and the better endowed secondary modern or junior secondary schools often adopted a more positive attitude towards their intake and tried to develop a separate pedagogy and pastoral system, to do so was to accept the claim of the 11 or 12-plus at its face value—that it really had sorted out children into distinct groups for which separate and different provision should be made. In fact, of course, such a claim was highly debatable. Not only were the instruments it used fallible but its cut-off point varied enormously from district to district, depending not on objective 'academic' standards but on the number of grammar school desks available. Thus in Gateshead less than 10 per cent of a yearly intake were at one time deemed 'worthy' of grammar school treatment. In Merioneth, 50 per cent or more could make the grade.[19]

The more realistic of the non-grammar secondary schools accepted that they were the potential losers in what was essentially a grammar school dominated game and attempted to play the game by the grammar school rules—entering the maximum number of pupils for external (academic) examinations and even, on occasions, organising prestigious A level programmes and sixth forms. Only by moving in that direction could they hope for social acceptance by parents and employers.

The school system of the Republic of Ireland has been more honest. Those who do not make their way to grammar schools (which they can of course do on a free voluntary basis with no national entrance requirements[20] either leave school with nothing but an elementary school experience that nobody pretends is an aspect of 'secondary education for all', or, more commonly, turn to the vocational school, which provides them with a technical and commercial training and the possibility of later transfer to a higher-level regional centre. In some places the vocational school has joined the grammar schools in new 'community' establishments which, like the schools they replace, are judged far more by the qualifications and the training they provide than by the social prestige which they confer.

The domination of the secondary sector by the public/grammar school model is echoed in the higher education sector by the domination of the universities. Whereas in France, Germany and the United States, institutions devoted entirely to technical or vocational education were able to equal or exceed the more generalist universities in terms of social or even academic prestige, this was never so in the British Isles. Here the older type of institution, and especially Oxford and Cambridge, managed to maintain a social supremacy and appeal even after the realisation that new forms of higher education were required in an industrial or post-industrial world. Instead of giving way to or sharing pride of place with institutes of technology, universities attempted to incorporate many of their characteristics into their own structures. Thus engineering and management began to be taught alongside Latin and anthropology. Yet, at the same time, British employers, the public sector in particular, continued to value 'liberal' studies above all others and pooh-poohed the notion that potential civil servants, for example, should acquire a particular technical training rather than the general intellectual experience encouraged by the 'traditional' universities.

In fact, most of the British universities' pedagogical traditions did not stretch back much beyond the late nineteenth century, but the medieval atmosphere of Oxford and Cambridge or St Andrews and Aberdeen gave them an air or authority which seemed to depend on many more centuries of experience.[21]

As a result, even the new universities founded in the late twentieth century, despite minor innovations and experiments, have felt it safer to adopt the prestigious general patterns of their predecessors and have joined a club which, through the University Grants Committee and the system of external examining, attempts to impose more and more uniformity of standards and practice upon its members. Oxford and Cambridge in particular, because of their high social prestige, continue to act either as a nursery or as a coveted destination of many university teachers within England and to a remarkable extent elsewhere in the British Isles.

The Irish and Scottish universities had begun the nineteenth century with their doors far more open and their courses far more cheaply bought than those of their English counterparts. Only a minority of Scottish undergraduates proceeded ceremonially to degrees or even completed degree programmes. They took what they needed and departed. Even as late as 1912 hardly any of the students in the Glasgow law faculty bothered to graduate. By 1880 Glasgow was already admitting more male students than it did in 1960, during the age of so-called unprecedented expansion. Yet of the many thousands then matriculated, only some half dozen per year were taking honours degrees. Clearly the conception of university education which it then embodied was very different not only from that of contemporary England but from that of modern Glasgow.

However, in the ensuing century not just Glasgow but all the Scottish and Irish unversities were to move appreciably closer to the Oxford/Cambridge or American elitist model, as did those English universities such as London and Manchester which had begun with mainly Scottish models in mind. Durham had been the first provincial university in England to realise the commercial attractions of offering a Taunton-like spread of university fare to cater for all pockets, offering colleges at different social levels. By the end of the century, a clear pecking order had been fixed equivalent to that of the public school/grammar school spectrum, while other institutions of post-school education were accorded the low status accorded to the central and the elementary schools. This social extrapolation from the secondary to the tertiary sector embraced even Scotland where university numbers dropped in the name of 'standards', and unions, clubs and halls of residence grew up in Oxford and Cambridge style, making the old plebeian student and those from the village school feel less welcome and less wanted.[22]

London, which had begun simply as an examination board acting as external examiner for courses done in cheap institutions throughout the United Kingdom, gradually began to concentrate more and more on its internal degree programme requiring full-time attendance at increasingly middle-class institutions in a more and more expensive metropolis. Until the Second World War, university entrance requirements in Britain, though higher than in the nineteenth century, were still on the whole quite unexacting; but with the introduction of more widespread university grants during the 1950s, competition for the few places available demanded higher and higher intellectual standards in entrants, thus introducing into British universities for the first time an air of intellectual as well as social elitism. Before 1939 there had been distinguished scholars in large numbers at such institutions but they had rarely if ever formed a majority even on the teaching staffs who were often selected for their pedagogical or pastoral qualities as much as for their scholarship. Certainly the majority of English undergraduates had made no claim to intellectual distinction, though this was probably less true of Wales where the notion of upward mobility by education was more readily accepted by the working class.

It is in the field of higher education that the distinction between Scottish and Irish education on the one hand and English on the other is now at its weakest. It is true that courses in both countries have retained distinctive characteristics. Irish and Scottish institutions still have far more 'general' candidates doing 'Ordinary' degrees than is the case in England where the vast majority of students attempt Honours. It is true also that the governmental and degree structures of the Scottish universities still contains distinctive elements such as the rector, a figure who in five of the eight universities is elected by the students to chair the supreme financial body of the institution, the university court. In the same five universities, also, the first degree in Arts is usually not the BA as in England but the MA.

But symptomatically, recent changes have been English-style changes. The Ordinary degree is losing favour. In the Arts Faculty at Edinburgh, for example, it now merits only an English-style BA rather than an MA (despite the fact that Oxford and Cambridge both award the MA on the basis of a first degree examination—after a delay of some years). At Edinburgh also (and English influence is strongest there) it is proposed to strip the rector of his chairman's powers, while the newer universities, particularly the 'technological' Heriot-Watt and Strathclyde, have largely ignored the Scottish pattern altogether in favour of a more 'normal' (i.e. English) structure, though even they have had to incorporate generalist elements into their curriculum if only out of deference to the schools that prepare their students and to the career structures which they serve—both of which are still geared to the older Scottish patterns.

As so often, of course, England itself has been changing at the very time that Scottish and Irish imitation has been strongest. The coming together of the grammar and elementary traditions in the comprehensive school has been reflected in a blurring of the edges between the university system on the one hand and the remainder of higher education on the other. Until the 1960s it seemed natural in an English context (though not a Scottish one) to see university teaching as a quite different activity from teaching of a technical or vocational kind such as was carried on in teacher training colleges, technical colleges, art colleges, and so on. This ascribing of lower status to technical education seemed a natural part of educational life, despite the fact that it did not happen in Germany and France and despite the fact that purely 'technical' training for prestigious professions such as medicine and law was happily, even 'traditionally', accommodated in the university sector. Economic need, international example and social change all conspired during the 1960s to alter this situation. New technological universities were created, the Royal College of Art became a university and, above all, a new Council for National Academic Awards (CNAA) was empowered to validate 'genuine' degrees to be awarded in non-university institutions. In an attempt to rationalise the situation, civil servants developed the concept of the 'binary system' (a subject returned to in Chapter 3)—dividing control of the 'independent' universities from control of the rest, as much to protect and encourage the non-universities as to formalise and to defend a class structure. But it smacked too much of the old discredited 11-plus dichotomy and soon the flood began to sweep away the distinctive marks of the university sector.

The flood was further increased by the founding of the Open University operating on an all United Kingdom basis and granting properly validated degrees not merely to those who had never been near a grammar school but also to those who offered, as part of their qualifications for the degree, certificates obtained in lesser colleges and technical institutions. The new polytechnics offering CNAA degrees became as fashionable as universities among the anti-elitist young while the Open University, by 1975, had already in Scotland alone more undergraduates than four of the existing Scottish universities (including two of the oldest).

With the development of a system for transferring credits between institutions (already being pioneered in an arrangement between the Open and Lancaster universities) there seems no foreseeable end to the revolution in English higher education. It remains to be seen whether the Scots, always traditionally more tolerant of technical education, will follow suit. A more likely repository of older English attitudes is, however, the higher education system of the Irish Republic where plans for an English-style post-binary revolution are already being set aside in favour of a less far-reaching proposal. There the power to confer degrees is likely to remain largely in the hands of universities at whose feet lesser institutions such as colleges of education and colleges of technology will sue for approval.

It would be ironic if an all-powerful English university model of the imperial period survived within the British Isles only in the anti-imperialist cloisters of the Irish Republic. On the other hand, the concentration of degree-granting powers in the hands of a single type of institution may lead in a quite different and less elitist direction. Ireland, through her insistence on 'traditional' forms, may find herself accidentally with some of the first comprehensive universities in Europe (see Chapter 3).

We have so far dealt in the main with the state system of education and those institutions such as universities which are now generally recognised as being an integral part of such a state system. In a sense, of course, this term 'state system' is misleading in a United Kingdom context for, as we emphasised earlier, the administering authority is usually the local education authority rather than a government department as such, but in practice, such is the level of state as opposed to local expenditure on the education service, that the phrase is not as misleading as much of the rhetoric tries to suggest. On the other hand, it would be misleading to think of any of the British and Irish education systems as being purely state systems, for in all ten of them there are two factors that prevent total state control from becoming a reality. One is the continued educational involvement of the churches; the other is the existence of an extremely lively and influential group of independent and semi-independent schools.

Despite the egalitarian ideology which has dominated political discussion of education for most of this century, there has, ironically, been a continual strengthening of the independent sector, particularly at the secondary stage. The immediate postwar period, indeed, saw various attempts to expand the public schools in particular by opening more of their places to scholarship children from state primary schools, though, significantly, the Fleming Report (which embodied such proposals) opposed their expansion in Wales where, it was felt, they posed a threat to the national culture![23] Totally independent schools have been comparatively rare, and far rarer in Scotland and Wales than elsewhere, but a major group of semi-independent schools in receipt of some state grants have become an ever more important sector particularly in certain large cities of England and Scotland. By following the educational patterns of the most socially exalted independent institutions, they have helped to increase the prestige and appeal of those independent schools in the public mind. In England these semi-independent secondary schools have been in receipt of what has been called the 'direct grant', and in exchange for certain financial support from central government, they have undertaken to apportion a certain number of free places to children passing the local authorities' secondary selection examination. Because of their selectivity they have usually remained grammar schools and provided a major stumbling block to the establishment of fully comprehensive secondary schemes in many areas, particularly larger towns.

In Scotland a similar group of schools has existed, particularly strong in Edinburgh and Glasgow, called 'grant-aided' schools. These schools, although they receive a direct grant like their colleagues in England, have not, however, been under any obligation to accept local authority selected children, and although they have in many cases offered scholarships on their own initiative to children from all social classes, their clientele has tended to be mainly middle class in origin.

Their position was strengthened in Scotland by the fact that, by a curious administrative anomaly, certain local authority secondary schools were able to admit fee-paying pupils who had failed to pass the local selection exam, pupils who had been excluded from English local authority grammar schools since 1945. Naturally, because of the social prestige resulting from the presence of so many able and socially exalted pupils, parents were anxious to enter their children at such fee-paying grammar schools and in Edinburgh in particular fee-paying secondary schools, whether independent, semi-independent or local authority, began to dominate the whole secondary system so far as academic activity was concerned. Indeed by 1970 some 70 per cent of all students attempting Highers in Edinburgh secondary schools were attending such fee-paying schools.[24]

The 1970s have seen a transformation of this situation. The English direct grant and Scottish grant aid have both been wound up and fee paying has been forbidden in Scottish local authority secondary establishments. But throughout the British Isles the power of the independent and semi-independent sector as a model will probably survive for some considerable time, for attendance at such schools was and is seen to bring academic and occupational as well as social promotion. The majority of places at the most prestigious universities and a far higher proportion of the highest posts in the public service than their numbers would suggest are still going to candidates from just such schools. And this situation has in some curious way been reinforced rather than eroded. In particular, they provide an escape route, for richer parents, from a comprehensive system providing no social badging.

In neither part of Ireland, nor in the Channel Islands and the Isle of Man, has there as yet been any intention of changing the position of such schools, while even in Great Britain the future of the totally independent school has been threatened by no major party. The independent sector still provides the ultimate joker in the pack so far as the national organisation of British and Irish education is concerned—not least in Northern Ireland. But then to many who oppose standardisation as such, that joker spells salvation—particularly in the case of those independent schools such as Neill's Summerhill or Kilquhanity House in Galloway which are more concerned with educational experiment than with the badging of a social class.

One sector of education we have hardly touched upon at all—that of part-time and short-term adult education. We have mentioned the Open University but it shines out as the sole major initiative in this sector taken by British government since the war and significantly it is concerned with the most elitist form of education. However, both the Russell Report[25] on adult education in England and Wales and the Alexander Report[26] on adult education in Scotland draw a sombre picture of how, in this century, Britain has fallen behind the Scandinavian and other continental countries. Nor is the situation in Ireland very different.

This conceals a long history of enterprise, particularly in Wales, enterprise that has now lost some of its steam and failed to produce modern parallels to the folk high school and the study circle in countries such as Ireland, Scotland and Wales where they would be particularly appropriate. The trade unions have produced courses for their own purposes but there have been few of those colleges for adults who have missed out at school that one finds elsewhere in Europe. There are exceptions, Coleg Harlech in Wales, for example, or Newbattle Abbey in Scotland, but they are totally inadequate to deal with a much wider need.

This is the great black disaster area of British and Irish education.

There are many who talk of 'lifelong education'; there are few authorities who will finance it.

NOTES AND REFERENCES

1 For a discussion of this poor distribution, see S. J. Curtis, *History of Education in Great Britain* (6th edn) (London, University Tutorial Press, 1965), pp. 155 *ff*.

2 See E. G. West, *Education and the Industrial Revolution* (London, Batsford, 1975).

3 In particular, Rugby and Marlborough (near Swindon). See T. W. Bamford, *Rise of the Public Schools* (London, Nelson, 1967), p. 26.

4 This is the argument of West, op. cit.

5 See Law, op. cit.

6 See F. J. C. Hearnshaw, *The Centenary History of King's College, London* (London, Harrap, 1929).

7 A full account of the origins and decline of this system is given in D. H. Akenson, *The Irish Education Experiment* (London, Routledge & Kegan Paul, 1970)

8 This is discussed, *passim*, in J.M. Goldstrom, *The Social Content of Education 1808-70* (Irish University Press, 1972).
9 Akenson, op. cit. pp. 17-59.
10 See article in the *Irish Times* of 14 July 1976 by Christina Murphy.
11 For an account of Dalkeith see A. K. Mackay's unpublished M.Ed thesis at Edinburgh, summarised in *Scottish Educational Studies*, vol. 2, no. 1, May 1970.
12 G. Davie, *The Democratic Intellect: Scotland and her Universities in the Nineteenth Century* (Edinburgh University Press, 1961).
13 ibid.
14 Schools Inquiry Commission (Endowed Schools), 1868.
15 See R. Bell and N. Grant, *A Mythology of British Education* (London, Panther, 1974), *passim.*
16 See article in Portora Royal School Magazine (Old Portorans edn), vol. 1, no. 18, 1975, by N. A. Dodds and B. S. Arnold.
17 Though, of course, the scheme did not give any assistance to families unable to forgo the child's earning power, nor did it provide adequate supplies of books and other equipment. Even so 75 per cent of the secondary school population were now attending grammar schools (*Irish Times*, 4 July 1972.)
18 This is a special type of comprehensive school providing general community facilities as well as academic and vocational schooling.
19 See P. E. Vernon, *Secondary School Selection* (London, Methuen, 1957).
20 In the Irish Republic, there is no pretence of providing secondary education for all. It is *available* for all, but no one is obliged to take it. At the end of 1974, there were still 400 pupils over 14 at national (elementary) schools (*Irish Times*, 4 December 1975).
21 See Bell and Grant, op. cit., *passim.*
22 See A. McPherson, 'Selections and survivals' in R. K. Brown (ed.), *Knowledge, Education and Cultural Change* (London, Tavistock, 1973).
23 *The Public Schools and the General Educational System* (HMSO, 1944), ch. 9, 'Wales'.
24 The Public Schools Commission 2nd Report, Vol. III (HMSO, 1970) suggests that about one third of all Edinburgh pupils were then at fee-paying schools, but a local authority breakdown suggested that this proportion increased as children grew older. In the fifth year of secondary school it was 60 per cent and in the sixth year, it was 75 per cent.
25 *Adult Education: A Plan for Development* (DES, 1973).
26 *Adult Education: The Challenge of Change* (SED, 1975).

Chapter 3

The Systems in Action

Despite common generalisations to the contrary, the United Kingdom is not a highly centralised state like France where all major decisions remain under the control of one centralised ministry of education; nor is it a federal state like the Federal German Republic or the United States, where educational decision making is left to the constituent provinces. The United Kingdom is probably unique, in that while control is retained over all the educational systems by a central parliament and government, the latter chooses to exercise the control of schooling through four separate central ministries.

One of the reasons, of course, why such a complicated situation has arisen has been the absence of a written constitution. Indeed, not only British politicians, but British constitutional lawyers have prided themselves on the absence of such a rigid framework. They claim that while the situation produces apparent anomalies such as the continuation of a second chamber recruiting its members partly on the basis of heredity, the absence of written rules has made the whole thing far more 'flexible' and 'human'. Until the beginning of the Northern Ireland tragedy, less attention was paid to the fact that the absence of such a constitution denied the ordinary citizen the right of appeal to a Supreme Court such as exists to set aside constitutional disadvantages in most other Western democracies. It may well be that the establishment of such a court will be made necessary either by the eventual settlement in Northern Ireland, where the permanent defence of civil rights has been a central issue, or by the need to curb the powers of any subsidiary parliaments or assemblies established elsewhere within the United Kingdom following the devolution of power to Scotland and Wales. Certainly during the heyday of unionism, the absence of a specific constitution worked to the advantage of England rather than her smaller neighbours in that the cards were all left in London's hands to be played in a magnanimous or tyrannical way as was seen best in England's interests.

The London government could afford to be magnanimous for example (in order to avoid local difficulties) over continuing the Presbyterian established church in Scotland when the Anglican church was being disestablished in Ireland and Wales. The anomaly of the sovereign having to subscribe to different forms of ecclesiastical government on crossing the border appeared to pose problems for none but pedants and doctrinal purists. Moreover the Quebec separatist, René Levesque, has drawn attention to the subtle way in which, by apparently insignificant gestures, London has quieted Scottish national aspirations during the past century—by allowing the continued circulation of Scottish banknotes originally authorised by a pre-Union Scottish parliament, by establishing a fine-sounding but largely hollow Scottish Grand Committee in the Westminster Parliament and by scattering throughout the country London-controlled national enterprises with the word 'Scottish' somewhere in their title.[1]

This loose-knit, unformed constitutional situation has always enabled London politicians to respond easily to Scottish pressures without giving too much away and the same has to some extent been true of the policy pursued by London government in the education of the Welsh, whose language in recent times has been the subject of far greater magnanimity and encouragement by London than many English-speaking Welsh people or English immigrants would like. This undefined situation has meant that actual decision making has tended to be shaped by circumstances and by individual personalities rather than by rigid constitutional formulae. At one stage, for example, an actual formula was developed for regulating government expenditure in Scotland, the so-called Goschen formula, which estimated the actual proportion of the British national income to which Scotland was entitled. But Goschen has, fortunately for Scotland, been ignored as often as it has been applied, just as Scottish differences from England are not always taken into account when block grants are made. In the educational field for example, little or no account appears to be taken of the theoretically shorter length of the Scottish secondary school course or the greater length of the Scottish university course in assessing the needs of secondary and tertiary educational establishments.

Nor does any actual machinery exist for co-ordinating actual educational policy throughout the kingdom. The extent to which the four ministries responsible for schooling work together seems to depend largely on the personalities of the ministers involved. There is some evidence for example, that when Bruce Millan was the Under-Secretary of State responsible for Education at the Scottish Office his relationships with his English colleagues were far from close. Indeed, in a radio interview, he suggested that he had visited the English Department of Education and Science less than half a dozen times during his reasonably long period of office. A Conservative successor, however—Neil Munro— claimed in the same programme to have been in constant touch with his English colleagues and to have joined them regularly in formulating policy.

Nor do Scottish ministers appear always to give in readily when pressurised by English colleagues. While the situation was not one of constant struggle, Bruce Millan suggested that there were crucial points at which Scottish ministers would not budge. He claimed, for example, that the decision to enforce the attendance of 15-year-olds in secondary schools as opposed to further education colleges when the school-leaving age was raised to 16 was a decision which the Scottish Education Department forced upon their English colleagues even against the will of the English secretary of state at that time. On the other hand, when general national enthusiasm in the governing party is great enough (as, for example, over the comprehensivisation of secondary schools or the ending of the direct grant to grammar schools) national boundaries have meant little (in Britain if not in Northern Ireland) as the ruling party put into operation those measures for which it believed it had a mandate.

Moreover, the London government sometimes acts from time to time without taking too much notice of Scottish or Welsh views, even when the consequences for Scottish or Welsh education may be considerable. For example, London appears to have established such major United Kingdom institutions as the Council for National Academic Awards (CNAA) and the Open University without any major consultation with Edinburgh or Cardiff on their desirability, as opposed to their subsequent operation. It was presumably assumed that the presence of the Scottish and Welsh Secretaries in the Cabinet was enough to signify their approval.

More usually, what uniformity there is has been brought about by a programme of concurrent legislation for all the four component countries of the United Kingdom. Thus, between 1944 and 1947, a series of broadly similar Education Acts were passed for England and Wales, for Scotland and for Northern Ireland.

In the end broad uniformity *is* usually achieved in many areas but this does not mean that all four countries are always or even necessarily in step. Indeed sometimes individual parts of the Kingdom have been out of step with their partners for years or even decades. Even now, within the parameters laid down for school attendance, the Scottish office chooses to end primary schooling at the age of 12 rather than 11 and to exercise its right to separate decision making on such issues as teacher training, child guidance, and so on. Often there is a tortoise and hare situation where each of the partners in the Kingdom may take its turn to be the pioneer within a particular field, and although it may be followed subsequently by the others, this may only happen many years later. The establishment of national elementary education in Ireland, for example, was not followed in England and Wales until thirty-nine years later and in Scotland until forty-one years later and although on occasions (as in 1918 for example) major Education Acts for the different parts of the United Kingdom have coincided, their contents have not always done so.

Scotland, for example, did not immediately follow the English example of 1902 in handing over control of education from the school boards to the general county authorities; instead she maintained until 1920 a system of separately elected *ad hoc* authorities existing to run education only[2] (a system to which Northern Ireland has now returned in the 1970s after a long period when the English pattern was followed there), while Northern Ireland has also maintained a centrally controlled 11-plus system for secondary school selection despite its dismantling by local authorities elsewhere in the United Kingdom.

It must be emphasised, of course, that, in all of this, Scotland, with her own ecclesiastical and legal establishment, has been most often the partner with the strongest degree of educational independence. It is perfectly natural that the second largest partner in such a union, with an articulate if sometimes purely rhetorical defence of its educational independence always at the ready, should regularly assert her remaining autonomy. In any case, the Scottish Education Department, unlike that of Wales or of Northern Ireland, has had a separate existence for over a century, and has produced some extremely powerful civil servants who have given Scottish decision making a continuity and independence that one does not readily find in Cardiff or Belfast. In comparison with them, the efforts of some politicians seem extremely feeble. The occupants of the political under-secretaryship carrying responsibility for education are continually changing; only a few individual ministers at the Scottish office have made their mark in the educational field, while major changes in Scottish arrangements have been determined by strong permanent under-secretaries and a particularly strong inspectorate.

Independent decision making for Wales is by comparison a relatively feeble affair. Most people in the United Kingdom, including senior civil servants who ought to know better, all too often still think of England-and-Wales as a single educational unit. Welsh education, though strong in terms of its separate language and culture, is weak in terms of its administrative autonomy and has no legal or ecclesiastical establishment to defend it. Moreover, it has inherited from the English connection a set of local authorities far more fiercely independent of central control than many of their Scottish counterparts.

Significantly, the only 'traditional' home of Welsh higher education is at Jesus College in English Oxford; and while one must not underestimate the considerable significance of the Welsh University and particularly the University College in Aberystwyth as a creation of Welsh working people themselves, it would be wrong to suggest that in its basic organisation it is anything but a modern institution based largely on Anglo-American models. It may have become the great guardian of Welsh culture, but it is not the guardian of a distinctly separate educational tradition. Indeed, if it is that to some degree it is so not so much by its internal operations but by the encouragement it gives extramurally to the adult education movement which is far stronger and more ambitious in Wales than in England.

Northern Ireland's independence of decision making was quite clear-cut for fifty years; not only did it have its own ministers and civil servants dealing exclusively with education but they were responsible to a subsidiary parliament which tolerated (officially at any rate) no interference by London in its day-to-day decisions. London might control Belfast financially but appeared to have no detailed say in how money was actually spent on education. Certainly, the London parliament was forbidden by the so-called 'Speaker's rules' ever to discuss it—before the holocaust of the 1960s. On the other hand, the Ulster Unionist ideology demanded a policy of moving 'step by step with England and Wales' so that in fact differences in the decisions made in Belfast and those made in London became less and less obvious. Strictly speaking the Belfast ministry (unlike the Scottish Department) maintained its control even over the university sector using the University Grants Committee merely as a consultant and did show its independence in this sector, for example during the 1960s by refusing to raise the fees charged for overseas students, when this was in effect made mandatory by the University Grants Committee in the remainder of the United Kingdom. Nevertheless, the whole examination structure as well as the local education authority structure of Northern Ireland came to be more and more modelled on those of England, generally regarded in Belfast as the guardian of the most advanced educational thinking. During the 1960s in particular, the Northern Ireland system was 'brought up to date' (as was generally believed) by the substitution of the English-style GCE for the native Irish exams with their Scottish flavour, while teacher training was reorganised using the models of the English institutes of education established in the postwar period. We have already noticed that Northern Ireland is at present out of step in the matter of the 11-plus examination. Yet even on this issue there is considerable pressure from the department (as the Ministry of Education has been called since the institution of 'direct rule' by the Northern Ireland Office) and from the teachers' organisations to bring Northern Ireland into line with the remainder of the United Kingdom. Local difficulties remain over secondary selection; the proportion of semi-independent schools is too large for their views to be set aside as easily as elsewhere and, of course, the issue of segregated denominational education looms larger and more significantly than in England. But most educationalists in Northern Ireland still assume that in the long term the province's education must, almost by the laws of nature, be brought in line with that of England and this seems remarkably true even of Catholic and Republican opinion.[3]

The recent development in Northern Ireland of a system of

'un-English' *ad hoc* education authorities that no longer links the control of education to general local government was a natural outcome of local administrative and political complexities rather than an assertion of independence in the face of 'anglicisation' (as one might have suspected had it happened in Scotland). In Northern Ireland (as indeed in Ireland as a whole) the question, 'Wha's like us?' expresses the anxiety of the inferiority complex rather than the all too common arrogance of some Scottish educationalists.

It is not, of course, simply the constitutional untidiness of the United Kingdom that causes the untidiness of educational arrangements. More than in most West European countries considerable freedom is accorded to the local education authorities who, for example, between the 1940s and the 1970s could organise secondary education much as they wanted to, while the presence of a strong independent school sector is still a major cause of differentials both between the social classes and between geographical areas, and continues to have an enormous influence on educational practice and thought, particularly in England and Northern Ireland. Moreover, as we have already noted, all four countries continue to have large numbers of schools run by the churches who practise a sometimes uneasy partnership with the local authorities. Wales has the smallest proportion of such schools but in England and Northern Ireland they form a major part of primary school provision.

In addition, all pretence at neatness in arrangements has been abandoned in the post-16 sector throughout the United Kingdom, particularly in the provision of education for those in the age-group 16-19. Some of those in this age-range still attend institutions catering for those of 11 or 12 (which are reluctant to lose their older pupils, partly because the nineteenth-century elitist model of the public and grammar schools demands such a prestigious 'top'); other members of the age-group attend specially designed sixth-form colleges catering for that age-group alone; while even greater numbers attend institutions of further education catering for all post-school age-groups including those following degree courses. Nevertheless, despite the complexity and untidiness of such arrangements, we shall now attempt to examine the various 'systems' in more detail. It is for the reader to decide whether the clear anomalies and confusions seem inefficient and destructive of good government or whether they seem constructively humane, flexible, creative and pragmatic. Both views are widely held and the second is not just held by those with a vested interest in confounding the prying intruder.

The most significant document for the government of education in England and Wales is the 1944 Education Act although one of the most significant things about that Act is that it is almost entirely concerned with primary and secondary schooling as was its Scottish counterpart passed two years later in 1946. So far as the post-secondary sectors are concerned there exists little coherent legislation. What Acts there are tend to deal with individual institutions rather than with the systems as a whole and all too often it has become the practice of ministers to depend not so much on detailed legislative powers carefully discussed in Parliament, as on ministerial fiat and secret negotiation or on the use of circulars and regulations, permitted within a broadly based legislative framework. Such matters may become the subject of parliamentary debates if formal approval is required or if individual members feel strongly enough about them but all too often such debates simply result in views being 'noted' and major educational decisions can still escape virtually all parliamentary scrutiny either in Committee or on the floor of the House. Thus, during the late 1960s, the whole process of setting up what was to be a revolutionary institution of higher education, the Open University, proceeded with only the most cursory and informal parliamentary discussion. The final decision was made without any vote in the House, while the process of closing down many English colleges of education (reducing their student numbers from nearly 120,000 to 40,000 in the space of five years between 1975 and 1980) has also happened with virtually no detailed parliamentary discussion and with no burden on the minister to explain detailed decisions to the world outside. In fact the whole procedure has largely been arranged by civil servants behind closed doors.

The general apathy which Members of Parliament so often show towards educational issues other than the bread-and-butter issues of primary and secondary schooling, is demonstrated in such matters very well. Even where Parliament has acted deliberately, as in passing the 1944 Act, it has usually provided a framework (sufficiently vague) to allow ministers room for incredible manoeuvre, being 'strong on rhetoric and short on controls' as one influential local director of education observed with satisfaction. Thus it talks of the rights of parents and of the facilitating of provision but does little to spell out such rights or the mandatory bases of such provision and the secretary of state cannot easily be challenged in the courts on such basic constitutional issues.

Positively, he is placed in a position to lead public opinion and by the power of the purse he is given considerable control over what happens educationally within the country. But much of the day-to-day power exercised by ministers of education elsewhere in the world is, not only in England and Wales but also in Scotland and Northern Ireland, handed over to local education authorities.

Until the changes in local government during the 1970s these authorities were, in England and Wales, the county councils and the general councils of the county boroughs (that is, the self-governing large towns). In London the outer London boroughs were autonomous education authorities, whereas the central London boroughs with their extremes of richness and poverty were grouped together under a single body, the Inner London Education Authority. However, since the local government changes of 1974, the county boroughs have disappeared from the scene and although the London arrangements have remained as before, over the greater part of the two countries the local education authorities are now the general county councils. The exception is in the so-called metropolitan counties in England, within which, on the model of the outer London boroughs, the local district councils act as the local education authority.

Local education authorities are often seen in England as rivals of the central government. Indeed many students of the English educational system have seen at its base a tripartite rivalry of LEA, DES and the Teachers' Associations, each operating as a constitutional balance to ensure that neither of the other two gains the upper hand in the formation and operation of eductional policies. However, the rhetoric of all three demands that they should be seen, not as rivals, but as partners in a joint quasi-religious enterprise, and some sociologists have recently seen in this threefold 'rivalry' a deceptive coming-together of three parts of the same establishment determined to defend its conventional ideas and overlapping vested interests against social and political criticism.[4] The Schools Council for Curriculum and Examinations in particular, although it is seen by official spokesmen as a place where the local education authorities, the Inspectorate and the teachers can settle their differences, is seen by other writers as a place where they can decide on a joint strategy for defending a common orthodoxy and the whole notion of 'balance' in the system is seen as a smoke screen behind which deals against the public interest can often be made.

Equally deceptive in some respects is the autonomy that is officially accorded by British government to the local education authorities. In fact some 80-90 per cent of their expenditure is a mandatory expenditure on services which they are compelled to provide by statute or on the instructions of the secretary of state. Even in the disposing of the remaining 10-20 per cent, their room for manoeuvre is often limited by regulations or by the availability of finance which has to be found from the general local treasury and not from any specific form of educational rating. Of course, the statutory obligations could not be fulfilled without a considerable subsidy from central government, but this is not just a help but also a further chain that links them to the processes of central decision making; thus, all but the most recalcitrant local authorities were readily brought to heel over the issue of comprehensive secondary education by the merest threat of financial sanctions from the centre, even though the secretary of state had no legal powers to enforce his own ideological viewpoint.[5]

Nevertheless, within such limits, the LEA does have some autonomy both in the way it fulfils its statutory obligations and in the way in which it spends its funds in the non-statutory 'margin'. Some authorities, for example, spend more than others on books and equipment. Others concentrate on the development of pre-school activities such as nursery classes and child-minding facilities. At the time of the amalgamation of the old authorities in the spring of 1974 for example, there was a tremendous range in the provision of facilities for the under-5s among the existing English authorities. Moreover under the terms of the 1944 Act, although local authorities were compelled to provide secondary education for all children within the age-group 11-15, they were left free to decide whether such education should take place in selective or non-selective institutions. Thus Anglesey decided very early to establish comprehensive schools for all the secondary school entry in their county while in 1976, thirty years later, some English local authorities were still operating a 1940s-style secondary school selection system in its entirety. Similarly, patterns of staffing are decided locally and the size of some classes can vary enormously from authority to authority, while, although the actual number of days upon which children have to attend school is laid down by central authority, there is considerable variation, even within the same LEA area, over the length of the school day. (It has been estimated recently for example that in one Scottish county there is a variation of up to three and a half hours in the length of the school week as between different primary schools—almost the equivalent of a whole school day in the primary sector.)

Most important of all, perhaps, the central government has in England and Wales officially delegated to the local authorities general authority for the shape and content of the school curriculum with the exception of religious education which is mandatory everywhere and over which Whitehall still exercises a loose supervision. It is the local authorities who employ the teachers and not the government, and it is they who decide therefore how the time of those employees should be occupied. In practice some of this power has usually been delegated to the governing bodies of individual institutions though, both rhetorically and with realism, most officials now speak of teacher autonomy in such matters. Nevertheless when the curriculum is the subject of local public controversy, certain authorities have readily exerted their right to censor or to forbid certain activities.

The local authorities have (in addition) often taken the initiative in the field of educational research. The National Foundation for Educational Research in England and Wales and the Schools Council for the Curriculum and Examinations are both in many respects the products of local government initiative and although the Schools Council now has a built-in teacher majority on all save its finance committee, the local authorities still have a major and often a financially crucial say in which of its ideas are adopted.

On the other hand, the Secretary of State for Education and Science is responsible in both England and Wales for the final determination of the examination structure which does so much to shape the secondary school curriculum. External examinations and proposals for their reform are matters for discussion by the Schools Council, but over their decisions the secretary of state can still exercise the power of veto and, in theory at any rate, he still acts as a link between the educational system and the general economic and administrative structure of the country. He is the person who is answerable to Parliament for the shape and outcome of the school provision and, while he may leave most of the detail to the local authorities within that structure, he has means of bringing them to heel. Although building programmes are initiated by the local authority, plans costing over £50,000 have to be submitted for the secretary of state's approval before the expenditure is finally authorised. This gives him one power over the curriculum that may not be statutory but is extremely effective. Thus despite their 'autonomy', LEAs continually feel central government looking over their shoulders particularly in formulating their policies for post-secondary education.

If there are limitations to the ostensible powers enjoyed by local authorities, there is even less reality in the legal delegation of authority from the local education authorities to the bodies formed to govern schools in England and Wales. Each primary school usually has a committee of managers appointed by the local council and each secondary school a board of governors originally developed in imitation of the board of governors forced on the public schools during the nineteenth century when it was necessary to put in order what were their sometimes scandalous financial arrangements. Occasionally a group of schools may be governed by a single committee but this is far from usual. The essential purpose of such boards is that of representing the laymen and, in particular, the council who are financing the institution, but in more recent years they have often been reconstituted (as indeed have the education committees of the local authorities) to include representatives of more than merely local authority interests. Some of them now contain parents, teachers and, indeed, pupils. But this widening of their membership happens to have coincided with a period of professional assertion on the part of teacher organisations which has often intimidated governing bodies into not exercising any real control over the actual running of the school; they may, for example, play a part in the appointment of a principal but from then on he is believed to be autonomous and they usually become little more than an advisory group. Most governors are largely unaware of their own legal powers, especially over the curriculum, which they assume to be not only the professional but also the legal province of the head teacher and his assistants, while their moral authority has sometimes declined because of the unscrupulous or careless way in which governors have been appointed, as acts of political patronage, by certain local authorities. Examples of directly elected governing bodies are still rare and the whole operation of such committees is at present being investigated by a special committee.[6]

Strictly speaking, the local education authority in England and Wales is the general council of the County, London Borough or Metropolitan district, but in practice, much of its work is undertaken by an Education Committee which co-opts to its membership representatives not only of local and parental interests but of the teaching profession, the local churches and sometimes the student body. The decisions of such an education committee can be over-ridden by the parent authority, but rarely if ever does this happen except when major political or financial issues are involved. Moreover, it is pretty rare for the decisions of the LEA's officials to be over-ridden by their own committee or authority in an age when education officials are possessors of the most potent professional mystique within the educational world. The awe-inspiring expertise of local education authority officials, like that of the Inspectorate, can usually intimidate lesser mortals and only the most determined 'lay' members of boards of governors, of education committees or of education authorities will dare to question their official pronouncements except in the most exceptional circumstances. The power of such officials has also been considerably increased by the complexity of modern educational and financial arrangements and by political manoeuvres that have encouraged informal decision making at the expense of open discussion in committee (see Chapter 6 below).

In Scotland, local authority schools have usually had no boards of governors and headteachers have been directly responsible to their education authorities. Thus, on occasions, they have appeared sometimes to enjoy an autonomy far greater than their English counterparts. In particular, Scottish headteachers have tended to suffer less gladly than their English counterparts the growth and existence of parent-teacher associations on the American model, whose claims to act not merely as ginger groups but as controlling mechanisms within the system have on the whole been frustrated not just in Scotland but throughout the British Isles. However, the lack of any buffer between the Scottish local authority and its schools has tended to increase the centralising power within those authorities. They have, for example, been far less ready than English authorities to trust headteachers over the appointment of their own staff; and in turn the Scottish Education Department itself has also tended to keep a closer watch than is the case in England over the authorities within its charge.

This maintenance of central control has been made easier by the condition of Scottish local government in recent years. Before the changes instituted in 1975, Scottish local authorities varied enormously in size. As in England, the education authority was usually also the general county council, the only exceptions being the four largest cities, Glasgow, Edinburgh, Dundee and Aberdeen, which in themselves formed 'counties of cities' and whose town councils were the education authorities. This meant that authorities could vary in size from tiny groupings such as Selkirkshire or Peeblesshire with fewer than 20,000 inhabitants to Glasgow with over a million. Needless to say the small authorities were extremely nervous about defying central government, while even the largest authorities were sometimes equally nervous given that within their boundaries were to be found some of the worst and most financially challenging urban problems in Western Europe.

In many respects, therefore, the education authorities in Scotland remain subject to considerable central control in comparison with those in England. They no longer, for example, have the power to distribute grants to university students, nor do they have under their control, as in England, any colleges of education. Until recently they did not even have major colleges of technology, though, through the force of English example, this is no longer true, for many colleges of further education in Scotland have been developed into institutions that compare in their range of subjects and standards with some English polytechnics. In rivalry with them, however, the government itself operates in Scotland a range of what are called central institutions ranging from semi-university establishments, such as Paisley College of Technology, to less ambitious affairs, such as the Queen Margaret College of Domestic Science in Edinburgh, the Galashiels College of Textile Technology and Leith Nautical College, almost all of which would, in England, be under local authority control.

One further fillip to centralisation in recent years has been the suitability of Scotland's size (with the population of just over 5 million) for Scandinavian-type experiments in general national innovation. Curriculum innovation in particular has, in some academic subjects at any rate, been more widely successful in Scotland, if only because the whole process has been kept more firmly in the hands of a central government with considerable influence. There has been established no equivalent to the English and Welsh Schools Council and teacher representatives on curriculum consultative committees have been official appointees, rather than the delegates (or even the selection) of the teachers' organisations themselves.[7] Even the General Teaching Council, controlling entry to the teaching profession (see Chapter 6 below) and containing a majority of members elected directly by teachers, has still been subject to considerable central supervision.[8]

Theoretically, as in England, the secretary of state leaves considerable discretion to his education authorities and indeed to individual schools, but, as in Northern Ireland, the smaller size of the country means that the leading figures at the centre have a far greater personal knowledge of individual Scottish authorities and schools and thus the consequence of even petty defiance can be all the greater.

This quality of smallness as an encourager of centralised authority applies with even greater force to the Channel Islands and the Isle of Man, where not only every headmaster, but possible every teacher is known to the central administration, and where the ostensibly national authority is run more and more like an English LEA.

In 1970 one would have been tempted to say that local authorities in Northern Ireland were a subtle blend of the English and the Scottish, having the characteristics of an English organisation, but being Scottish in their subservience to the central ministry in Belfast, for Northern Ireland is considerably smaller in area than Scotland and has only a quarter of Scotland's population, and with so many of the secondary schools in semi-private hands, the powers of an education authority official there were considerably circumscribed. Moreover, even the all-important 11-plus examination was run from a central point and educational decision making at local level was pretty bland. However, with the recent development of the local education and library boards, the situation has changed perhaps far more than anywhere else within the British Isles. These boards are specifically educational in orientation and are responsible to no other existing authority, save the government itself. They therefore may in the future provide an interesting experiment capable of being copied elsewhere. Indeed, their success may suggest that the old school boards of England and Wales and the local authorities of Scotland which, until 1929, also operated on an *ad hoc* basis might well be revived.

This Northern Ireland innovation is equalled only in its potential importance by the institution in Scotland of a system of school councils (not to be confused with the Schools Council for the Curriculum in England and Wales) which local authorities have been mandated to set up throughout their areas. These councils are meant to act as a link between the schools and the local community and vary enormously from area to area both in their composition and in the number of schools under their control. Under certain local authorities, for example, they are based on each secondary school and include in their jurisdiction all the feeder primary schools. In other areas, they cover a particular geographical division and are meant to take under their wing both Protestant and Catholic schools as an encouragement to integration of educational effort and community development. There is considerable variety also in the powers so far delegated to these councils. It is too soon to see which models will emerge as dominant, but certainly, for the first time since the *ad hoc* authorities disappeared in 1929, the population of Scotland at large is being called on to play a direct part in educational decision making. Whether the reality will match the rhetoric remains to be seen.

Within educational institutions themselves, there has been a general tendency throughout the British Isles to increase consultation with both pupils and staff. In this respect it is difficult to discern any national patterns. Certainly the old-fashioned school staff meeting has been given a new lease of life, while previously revolutionary schemes for consulting pupils have become commonplace, but the growth of such consultative councils and the extent to which they make real decisions has tended to depend upon local conditions and the personal orientations of principal and staff rather than on national policies.

This development is a classic example of how pedagogical and administrative theory has tended in recent years to transcend national boundaries. The growth of student representation on governing bodies, in particular, has been a result of the general agitation throughout the Western world since the year 1968.

And if United Kingdom schools are seen to be more and more similar and to be following more and more similar international curriculum patterns, then the similarity extends also to classrooms within the Irish Republic. Until recently, largely for reasons of finance, Irish pedagogy tended to be more old-fashioned than in most other parts of the English-speaking world, but since the changes instituted in the 1960s, the position has changed somewhat. A whole new modern primary curriculum, housed in more and more modern schools, has been accompanied by major plans for similar expansion in the secondary schools which, during the last decade, have for the first time become open to all. These plans for secondary education are already bearing fruit in new purpose built community comprehensive schools in the suburbs of Cork and Dublin, and, even within the boundaries of many old-fashioned structures, new curriculum fashions are to be discerned within the huts and temporary classrooms which litter the schoolyards and playing-fields of a more ambitious Ireland.

Nevertheless whatever the growing similarity between the British and Irish curriculum, the government of education in the Republic still remains idiosyncratic by British standards. Indeed Garrett Fitzgerald, Ireland's Foreign Minister, has referred to his country's educational administration as 'colonial' in its preoccupation with the detailed supervision of individual institutions.[9] Even minor decisions concerning buildings and expenditure by primary schools in remote villages have to be referred to the central government department in Dublin and are often subject to decision by the actual Cabinet minister responsible. This is strange indeed to those used to the delegated systems found elsewhere in the British Isles, though it is worth remembering that the population of the Republic and certainly its educational turnover is smaller than that of some British local authorities such as Inner London or Strathclyde.

The complexity of administration is often a function of the finance involved and although, for example, the Republic has a higher proportion of the 16-19 age-group at school than is the case in the United Kingdom, its financial investment in them is considerably smaller.

Nevertheless the absence of devolution to the Irish regions still seems strange if we remember the scattered nature of the Irish population, the cultural differences between eastern and western Ireland (whose educational needs at any time vary enormously) and the fact that the Republic's population is considerably greater than that of Northern Ireland, which still sees virtue in delegating power to local authorities. In the Republic, the only existing local authorities in the educational field have the strictly limited role of running the vocational i.e. the non-academic secondary level schools attended by only 25 per cent of pupils and thus although there is a county and regional structure for technical and semi-technical education, the work of the primary and academic secondary schools is still firmly in the hands of Dublin and indeed, to some extent, in the equally centralised and firm hands of the main religious orders who provide the buildings and many of the staff for large numbers of institutions.

Indeed, church influence on Irish education is so all-pervading that it is dangerous to think of the Catholic church in Ireland, or indeed the Protestant churches in the Republic, as forming homogeneous groups with common educational policies as would be largely the case in Britain. There they represent a comparitively minor sector. In Ireland, they cover almost the whole spectrum of practice and opinion. There are for example many different views on curriculum and indeed on administrative issues represented within the ranks of the Irish bishops, and many differences both within the religious orders themselves and between them and the Catholic hierarchy. Indeed, church spokesmen unite less often over saying what schools should do and how they should be organised than over the matter of keeping the state in its proper place, as a supplier of funds, rather than as a dictator of teaching method and content. The conservative clerical managers of some primary schools, for example, have been reluctant to hand over power to the new governing bodies now being proposed in order to produce greater parental and community involvement in the running of the schools, while other more progressive parish priests have welcomed such a change with open arms as being in accordance with the teachings of the Second Vatican Council.

From time to time there is talk of a move towards the establishment of English-style local education authorities or possibly, as a compromise, regional education authorities. Indeed one of the partners in Cosgrave's coalition government (the Irish Labour Party) openly advocates the latter. But it is realistic to remember that, whatever the infrastructure that might be established, real power would first have to be wrested from the hands of the bishops and the religious orders on the one hand and of the minister on the other given that they, between them, supply the funds for what are essentially the schools of a developing country. There has even been a suspicion in recent years that decision making could pass outside Ireland altogether—to the World Bank, for example, one of the main suppliers of funds for the development of the Republic's second-level system.

Nowhere is international interplay seen more readily however than in the field of the British Isles' examination systems. Within Ireland school-leaving certificates are still to some extent an irrelevance, in that employers claim (as English employers once did) to be interested as much in 'character' as in examination results, and a place in a school football team can still count for more at a selection interview than high scores in the leaving certificate. But in the more streamlined of Irish industries paper qualifications do count far more with overburdened personnel managers, while the continual possibility of emigration, traditionally present in the mind of Irish students, has meant that the validity of Irish examinations abroad has always loomed large in Irish educational planning. And there is no doubt that in this context, the English and Welsh examination system has loomed largest both as a rival and as a potential model, not only because the scope for employment in England has been greater but because English-style qualifications are known and acceptable throughout the world while London's assumptions tend to dominate the entrance requirements of international organisations, just as they used to dominate the requirements of the imperial service. Thus while it is true that the Irish government has not yet moved substantially towards the establishment of an English-type GCE examination system, vested interest and bureaucracy are perhaps enough to explain this. There is no doubt in Irish schools and colleges of a great determination on the part of students to obtain either the actual English qualifications or degrees and certificates generally accepted as their equivalents. Moreover, as in many ex-colonial territories, English-style examinations such as the Cambridge School Certificate and the Cambridge GCE have always had a certain social prestige among the Irish middle class.

The finest example of this Irish desire to follow English examination models is to be found in Northern Ireland where the Unionist ideology of step by step with England made its realisation easier. There the socially most prestigious schools led a campaign in the late 1950s which eventually resulted in the total abandonment of the previous distinctively Irish generalist system of group examinations in favour of an English GCE with its single subject entry.

Until that time, all parts of the British Isles had been reasonably content with a situation in which all the systems followed a roughly similar, generalist pattern of leaving certificates for children in academic secondary schools, but the decision of England and Wales to abandon such generalist patterns in the early 1950s threw such interchangeability into question.

In England and Wales, there had developed during the first half of the twentieth century a standardised system of school certificates designed to act as general entrance qualifications, not only for other educational institutions, but also the professions and general employment. These had replaced the host of separate certificates, at one time some 400 or more, issued in the years before the First World War. The School Certificate examination itself was generally taken by the majority of grammar school leavers and success in it provided a satisfactory guarantee of quite high-level grammar school attainment for general employment purposes, as well as a place in the clerical section of the civil service. Admission to the next grade of the civil service, however, required the Higher School Certificate which was taken at the end of the grammar school sixth form course. It too was a generalist examination in the sense that students took a reasonable range of some four or more subjects, but within a more narrowly specialised scientific or arts area than was the case in Scotland or Ireland where a far more genuinely generalist school-leaving test was mandatory. This Higher School Certificate was a relic of what had once been a more generalist undergraduate course in the English universities, from which exemption came to be claimed as a result of taking such examinations in the sixth form of the secondary school. Gradually, as the twentieth century proceeded, the sixth form examination began to copy the more specialised shape of the highly specialised Honours undergraduate course itself which was gradually being narrowed to encompass merely one or at most two subjects in contrast with the courses followed by Scottish and Irish Honours students, who began by studying far more than their eventual Honours subjects.

In view of the continued generalist nature of the Scottish and Irish university courses, the Scottish and Irish secondary schools were constrained to continue a more generalist course even in their upper reaches. Thus the Scottish Highers examination continued to demand English literature even of science students, while for ideological reasons, the Irish Republic continued to demand the Irish language of all candidates.

Scotland and Ireland also provided examinations at a lower level, lower than the English School Certificate, largely as a means of encouraging effort among those who had given up any thought of school careers beyond the minimal school-leaving age but such lower certificates (such as the Junior certificate in Northern Ireland, or the 'inter' certificate in the Republic) had less and less public importance attached to them, and were used more and more for internal selection purposes. However, the possession of such a certificate did at least mean that grammar school drop-outs had something to show for their pains when approaching employers alongside pupils who had never attended such schools.

A further difference between England and Wales on the one hand and Scotland and Ireland on the other was that the English and Welsh School Certificate examinations were run not by government departments but by the universities. Indeed there were in England a number of rival university examination boards running quite separate examinations, and although some attempt was made at standardisation, marking practices could vary quite considerably. This arrangement came about partly because of English fears of state control of the curriculum, but even more as a result of the historical accident of the certificates developing as part of a transfer of university courses into the secondary curriculum. Elsewhere in the British Isles the school-leaving examinations were kept firmly in the hands of national boards.

However, as part of the postwar reconstruction of English and Welsh education, although the university control was retained, it was decided to abandon the notion of package deals and to allow both School Certificate level and Higher School Certificate level subject matter to be studied on a single subject basis. In future the former would be covered by a General Certificate of Education (O level) and the latter by the General Certificate of Education (A or S level). It now became possible for those who treasured such things (a high proportion of the population) to claim that they had 'passed' GCE even though they had simply obtained a pass in one subject, say woodwork, at the Ordinary level.

Holders of Scottish and Irish qualifications began to face more and more difficulties in having their certificates accepted as the equivalent of the new-style English examinations. London University in particular began to doubt the validity of the claim that the old-style generalist school-leaving certificates in Ireland and Scotland were the equivalent of the new highly specialised A level, and this had repercussions not merely on would-be entrants to London University itself, but on entrants to all kinds of other occupations and institutions where the London external degree formed a basic item in the curriculum. For example, the Army College of Science at Shrivenham was closed to Irish candidates at a time when Irish middle-class emigrants were thinking more and more of careers in the British army at a high technical level. Considerable national feeling was also stirred up in Scotland by the growing tendency of English institutions and employers to look sceptically at candidates offering Scottish Highers.

Northern Ireland, with its already greater tendency to follow English and Welsh models, found such a situation insupportable. A group of the most influential grammar schools went to the Ministry and demanded the adoption of a GCE-style examination system. At least one of them even attempted blackmail and entered their best pupils, not for the Northern Ireland Senior Certificate Exam, but for the Cambridge GCE A levels, and warned that they would go over completely to the English examination unless their demands were met. The Ministry did not take long to capitulate in the face of such threats to its prestige and its finances and early in the sixties a new Northern Ireland English-style GCE O and A level system was established, still under a government board, but fully acceptable to employers and institutions in England and Wales. It was a logical step for Northern Ireland, a few years later, to follow the English and Welsh pattern in establishing its own Certificate of Secondary Education (CSE) designed for the academically less ambitious pupils to whom attention had been drawn by the Newsom and other reports. It can of course be argued that Northern Ireland adopted these new examination systems for purely educational reasons and no doubt the argument for adopting them in England and Wales were just as valid in Belfast, but there was considerable evidence at the time of pressures from the occupational structure far outweighing pressures from the school system itself.

In England and Wales as well as Northern Ireland, the establishment of the CSE marked a major new departure, for this secondary school exam was no longer controlled by a purely external body, whether university or national board. It was to be very much teacher-oriented and to be run by teacher-dominated regional committees. Moreover it soon experimented with new ways of evaluating student performance adopting assessment in three 'modes'. Mode 1 was similar to GCE in that the papers were marked by an external group of markers, dealing with papers that had been externally set. Mode 2 used papers set by the teachers actually teaching a specific class, but these were still marked by external examiners. Most revolutionary of all, Mode 3 allowed examinations to be developed in a particular class or school and allowed examinations to be assessed by the class teacher himself under regional supervision. Quite clearly the notion of external examination had moved a long way from the old days of the SC and HSC, while many children who had been previously considered unfit for external examination were now brought into its useful though still educationally uncertain net. With the common prevalence of the English superstition that 'more means worse' CSE has still to achieve the status and credibility of the older examination systems and both employers and institutions still feel uncertain of its value compared with GCE, Mode 3 procedures in particular providing a stumbling-block to the traditionally minded.

Scotland has on the whole proved less anxious than Northern Ireland to follow the GCE and CSE models. This has been partly because of a genuinely widespread and traditional belief in the value of a more generalised course (particularly as a preparation for the generalist university courses still followed there) but there seems little doubt that this reluctance to change was considerably encouraged by the publication of George Davie's book *The Democratic Intellect*[10] which popularised and bolstered a belief in the separateness of the Scottish educational tradition with its loyalty to generalist, continental models rather than to the specialist patterns to be found in English education. In fact this influence was ironic, for Davie's book was meant to describe the decline and death of a tradition rather than its liveliness, and for him the continental links had long since died out under an English influence reinforced by a London-based administration. Moreover some of Davie's followers (though not Davie himself) tended to exaggerate the extent of English specialisation in the days before the comparatively modern development of Honours degrees and the A level exams. In the early nineteenth century, the main difference between English and Scottish examinations lay less in their degree of generalism than in their approach to the subject matter.

The average Scottish student, although he had a larger *à la carte* menu to choose from (ironically in the style of GCE), was probably just as likely as his English counterpart to restrict himself to a very few dishes—particularly as he was rarely interested in completing a whole programme and taking a degree.

Undoubtedly Davie's book played a major part in providing an apparently respectable intellectual basis for the considerable revival of educational nationalism which occurred during the late sixties and early seventies, and this reinforced the view that there should be no attempt in Scotland to follow English patterns where this was avoidable. It provided also a positive philosophical basis for the claim that the Scottish generalist tradition was not only different from, but also superior to, that being followed in England and Wales. Indeed the generalist nature of Scottish education for the older pupil had begun to be specifically praised in England itself—in the Swann and Dainton Reports on scientific manpower for example. Thus when a new Scottish examination was introduced for an age-group similar to that taking the English O level, and was intended as a leaving certificate for the majority of secondary pupils who left at the age of 15 or 16, the Scottish Examination Board was careful to describe it as the O *grade* rather than the O *level* in order to make a clear distinction from its English contemporary; even so, it must be admitted that not only the Scottish public but many Scottish educationists are hard put to it to enunciate the real differences between the Scottish and the English examinations at this level. Certainly it is regarded as an equivalent of O level by most employers outside Scotland, and indeed it is referred to as the O level by many Scottish politicans and journalists as well as by members of the general public. Its major differences from the English O level result less from its own academic qualities than from the place it occupies in the Scottish school structure.

First of all, it has had, most unsatisfactorily, to perform the functions of both GCE and CSE. A far higher proportion of the same age-group takes O grade in Scotland than is the case with O level in England and for many of them such an academically oriented examination is probably unsuitable. Ironically, for the academically able it is of less importance, for many of those intending to go to university take a smaller spread of O grade subjects than their English counterparts. In England O level provides a last chance to take a wide spread of general subjects before proceeding to the narrowly specialist sixth form. However, Scottish secondary schools in general do not have such sixth forms and the still generalist 'Highers' are usually taken (at least for the first time) one year rather than two years after the O grade.

In the more socially elitist schools where the influence of English models has always been strong, the tendency to regard the post-O-grade years as sixth form years has reinforced the demand for A levels of a more specialised kind as a climax to the careers of the most able pupils in the academic sections of the secondary school. So far no such A level (or A grade?) has appeared, but many people believe there has been a covert attempt to introduce it. What *has* appeared is a Certificate of Sixth Year Studies. This was meant to be taken by students who had completed their university or professional entrance requirements, and did not want to follow the earlier, more educationally sterile pattern of simply repeating Highers in order to get better gradings. It was intended that such students should embark on more specialised study within a single subject (perhaps, though not necessarily, the subject they intended to pursue at university). The examination took the form of the presentation of a thesis based on private study supervised by senior staff in the style of university lecturers. In order to forestall the charges that an A level was thus being introduced by stealth, there were constant official assurances that this was not to be a new university entrance requirement and was not intended as such. However, even in Scotland, the universities are autonomous bodies and in the largely hidden process of selection among candidates with similar qualifications there is no doubt that the possession of the Certificate of Sixth Year Studies has been one of the factors used in a battery of selection criteria by more and more university officials. Thus it is now seen by many teachers as an essential guarantee for university entrance in those departments where there is a great demand for places. In fact Sir James Robertson, one of the committee that first introduced the examination, was candid enough to admit in a radio interview at the time that he saw the Certificate of Sixth Year Studies as eventually developing into an enlightened Scottish form of A level and there is no doubt that many people still hope that it will do so. However, as with the A level itself, recent research has suggested that it is a very poor predictor of success in university courses proper, despite the similarity of its procedures to what is supposed to be the more individualised university learning situation.[11]

The absence of any move towards the establishment of a Scottish CSE or any equivalent system to cover the less academically motivated student has caused some schools, in desperation, to link themselves to English CSE boards in order to provide what they consider more appropriate examinations for their pupils, but some regional education authorities have frowned on this and Strathclyde, the largest, has gone as far as to forbid it.

Having the O grade as the sole examination for most secondary pupils has at least avoided the social divisiveness which results from having separate examination structures for the academically able and the rest and it may be that in the end this Scottish tortoise will arrive ahead of the English hare once more if present proposals for integrating GCE and CSE procedures south of the border are accepted.

Because it is taken outside the United Kingdom, the Irish Leaving Certificate has perhaps been regarded as a more exotic qualification by English employers and institutions than was the case with Northern Ireland Senior or Scottish Highers; it has therefore been treated with greater leniency by those in London who decide on equivalences. Nevertheless, just as British television flourishes alongside Irish television down the prosperous east coast, so English-style examinations and qualifications are now tolerated within Irish institutions in a far less surreptitious way than is the case in Scotland. Indeed some professional bodies in Ireland now quote entrance requirements in terms of GCE as readily as in terms of the Irish examinations. This is partly because Dublin's all-Ireland ideology and custom demand an openness of opportunity for candidates from Northern Ireland where the GCE holds sway and ironically this has made it easier for the GCE to be accepted as a 'native' qualification than has been the case in Scotland. Some fifth of the places in Trinity College, Dublin, for example, are reserved for candidates from the North[12] who will be arriving with their English-style O and A levels. These prove as acceptable as their British coins and English banknotes.

There is a certain residual Irish attachment to the idea of a generalist education, but it has never been as strong as in Scotland and a greater pragmatism has tended to dominate the Irish examination structure—the defence of the Irish language always providing an exception.

In the field of higher education, moves towards standardisation have been considerable within the United Kingdom. This has partly been the result of a general surveillance of all institutions either by a London-based University Grants Committee or by the Council for National Academic Awards, but despite the rhetoric of university autonomy, the influence of major professional and employment organisations is also considerable. Few British (or Irish) universities can for long ignore the wishes of the British General Medical Council or indeed of similar bodies in the United States.

Nevertheless, the Irish and Scottish degree systems still retain very distinctive features when compared with those of England and Wales. In particular, less is expected of the candidate when he arrives from school and the Honours course not only includes some generalist elements in the early stages but is also spread over four years. Moreover Irish and Scottish universities are still seen in the main to be responsible for the general education of all secondary and many primary teachers who, in England, would usually seek places in colleges of education or, more recently, in polytechnics. Therefore the presence of Ordinary degree students in the university is far more common than in the average English university where such degrees have often died out.

It was also at one time common for Scottish and Irish students to enter university a year earlier than their English counterparts although the fierce competition for places during the sixties and early seventies has largely removed this age differential.

The dominance of the Irish and Scottish university systems by the needs of future teachers, who form a major group in all arts faculties[13] and a substantial group even in the sciences, has been effected in part by a recent growth in the assertion of teacher professionalism. As a result of the Robbins report in the 1950s, a new degree specifically designed for potential teachers was introduced throughout the United Kingdom called the B.Ed (Bachelor of Education). Arrangements for the award of this degree vary from area to area and university to university, but in general the tendency has been to mount it almost entirely within the colleges of education, which have thus gained added status because they are teaching undergraduate students. Nevertheless the B.Ed examination has still to be supervised either by the local university or by the Council for National Academic Awards and the B.Ed has often tended to be taken only by candidates who could not or would not have attended universities. In Scotland for just such reasons people have been reluctant to accept the notion that the B.Ed is the true teachers' degree, the only worthwhile qualification for a true professional.

It remains to be seen in the next few years whether the professional ambition of teachers succeeds in having the B.Ed accepted as the normal method of entry to the profession, providing as it does an integration of academic study and professional training throughout the pre-service period. However, it may be that students in general will prefer to keep their options open for as long as possible and will register for the more generalised BA, MA and B.Sc courses, thus avoiding that lifelong commitment to teaching that registration for the B.Ed usually entails.

In the Republic of Ireland the situation with regard to teacher graduation is equally far from clear. The colleges of education there had for some years been able to attract a type of highly academic student for whom equally valuable scholarships were not available in the university sector (see Chapter 6). It was natural therefore that such academically viable colleges should demand more autonomy and the right to award their own degrees under the supervision of the Republic's equivalent of the CNAA, the NCEA. But more recently the Minister for Education, clearly influenced by the aspirations common at the time when he was himself a teacher, has suggested instead that the universities should continue to oversee the award of all degrees for teachers, not because the colleges cannot be trusted academically, but because of the suspicion that to award a qualification other than a 'real' university degree was to sell the teacher short as a professional.

This confusion over teacher degrees is simply one symptom of what has been a general confusion over the future of higher education in the Republic. At present the Republic has two universities: Dublin University, (Trinity College, Dublin) is Protestant in origin but now mainly Catholic in terms of its student body. The second university is a federal university, the National University of Ireland, with colleges not only in Dublin but also in Cork, Galway and Maynooth. During the past decade there have been a number of proposals for alterations to this system. It was felt to be foolish, for example, to duplicate facilities in Dublin city and it was suggested that the Dublin branch of the National University should be merged with Trinity College in order to form one major university in the capital. Not only did this raise logistical and political problems of its own; it also left the remainder of the National University scattered and impoverished and lacking many vital faculties and departments. In effect the merger proved politically impossible and while the government has striven to arrange the elimination of unnecessary duplication facilities between the two Dublin institutions (most crudely by the withdrawal of grants to Trinity's veterinary department in early 1976) it seems at present to be opting instead for the existence of two rival institutions, Trinity College in the centre of the city and University College on the southern outskirts. However, the proposed fate of the remainder of the university system had remained far from clear. Cork and Galway had always insisted that they should themselves become independent institutions. The government was initially not prepared to make the extra outlay required for this but in July 1976 it capitulated. In such a situation the fate of the prestigious teacher training colleges, particularly St Patrick's at Drumcondra in Dublin, becomes crucial. For if St Patrick's is drawn into some sort of link with University College, or indeed with Trinity College, then the continued existence of an Irish NCEA is thrown into doubt. Institutes of advanced technology are still in their infancy so far as the Irish Republic is concerned, and any development of a system outside the universities would require a massive investment that cannot be envisaged in the present economic circumstances.

In England and Wales the 1960s gave birth to the new concept in higher education already discussed in the previous chapter, that of the Binary system. As we saw, this is neat in theory, dividing higher education into two sectors, (1) the so-called 'private' or 'independent' university sector (not very independent so far as finance is concerned!) and (2) the so-called 'public' sector including the colleges of education and the newly established polytechnics with their wide spread of students, ranging from Honours degrees candidates to 'day release' students following courses requiring no previous academic qualifications. The institutions on the non-university side of the fence (where they are not run by churches) are usually being run by local authorities who, since the beginning of the century, have been encouraged to develop their own higher education facilities. But we have already hinted at the fact that parts of this so-called binary system are providing courses that could not possibly be described as higher education, while some of the polytechnics and indeed some of the colleges of education are no less autonomous in their academic decision making and no less ambitious in their course provision than are the universities. Indeed, although one of the aims of the proposals was to divide the universities, as the main centres of research, from mainly teaching institutions, it has already become apparent that many polytechnics are pursuing research programmes as ambitious as those being pursued on the other side of the binary fence. The main effect of the enunciation of the binary concept has simply been to confirm the universities in their elitism and their feeling of separateness at a time when it might well have been more advantageous for government to encourage a greater integration of higher education provision in order to avoid unnecessary duplication of courses, in order to consolidate research and above all in order to widen the opportunity for participation in degree courses by a wider section of the community.

That the Department of Education and Science is now wavering in its maintenance of such the system is proved by the fact that in its schemes for the elimination of 'unnecessary' colleges of education during the late 1970s it is equally able to accept schemes for incorporating such colleges into universities or into polytechnics, thus suggesting that in reality, if not in theory, those two groups of institutions have already attained a certain homogeneity in official eyes.

In Scotland the binary system was never officially developed as a concept in quite the same way. This was partly because, until recent years, local authorities did not develop institutions specialising in higher education, nor did any colleges of education exist in the local authority sector. Institutions other than universities were the direct responsibility of the Scottish Education Department, which in recent years granted them a greater degree of autonomy but still continued to exercise financial and general overseeing of their activities. On the other hand, as we have already noticed, the situation was complicated further by the fact that the overseeing of the universities was the responsibility of the English DES rather than of the Scottish SED, and this introduced yet another complexity into the already complex structure of British higher education.

In the midst of this confusion further difficulties have resulted from the massive closure of colleges of education in England and Wales, where students numbers have been reduced from some 114,000 to 40,000 within half a decade. The consequences of this for the universities and polytechnics are incalculable. Ironically it may well mean a restoration within the English university sector of the same Ordinary degree which many of their academic colleagues working in Scotland have been so anxious to eradicate in order to get in line with England.

NOTES AND REFERENCES

1 He was speaking at a conference in Edinburgh on Scottish devolution in 1975.
2 J. Stocks, 'Scotland's ad hoc authorities' in *Studies in the Government and Control of Education since 1860* (London, Methuen, 1970) pp. 69-90.
3 Unlike most Protestant schools, Catholic schools place great importance on the teaching of Irish history and of the Irish language, but they show no keenness for following the lead of Dublin in organisational matters and intercourse between Northern and Southern Catholic colleges of education has been slight.
4 See, for example, M. F. D. Young, 'On the politics of educational knowledge', *Economy and Society*, vol. 1, no. 2, 1972, pp. 194-215.
5 He has since taken these powers by the Education Act of 1976.
6 The so-called Taylor Committee, reporting in 1977.
7 See the article by J. D. Nisbet, 'Curriculum Development in Scotland', *Journal of Curriculum Studies*, vol. 2, no. 1, 1970, pp. 5-10.
8 See the article by R. Bell, 'Lessons of the Scottish GTC' in the *Times Educational Supplement*, 22 January 1971.

9 Speaking in an Open University television programme (E352/6) in 1972.

10 Davie, op. cit.

11 The subject is covered in detail by A. F. McPherson and G. Neave in *The Scottish Sixth* (Slough, NFER, 1976).

12 According to the Provost in a speech at Ballymena (*Irish Times*, 15 June 1971).

13 A. F. McPherson and G. Atherton quote a figure of 71 per cent for female arts students at Aberdeen applying for admission to post-graduate teacher training. 'Graduate teachers in Scotland—a sociological analysis' in *Scottish Educational Studies*, vol. 2, no. 1, 1970, p. 36.

Chapter 4

The Interaction of the Systems

Various though their administrative arrangements are, the educational systems do not operate in a vacuum; they are parts of larger complexes linked together culturally, economically, and in some cases politically as well. Britain could be regarded as a complete legislative unit; the United Kingdom as a political unit; and the British Isles make up a recognisable economic and cultural entity that manages to survive political divisions. It would therefore be astonishing if the educational systems were to function in isolation. Nor do they; there are several powerful mechanisms which lead to continual interaction between them.

The most obvious mechanisms at work are legislative, and are well illustrated by the relations between the Scottish and English systems. As we have seen, Scotland had kept the framework of a distinctive educational system, in spite of political union, in a way that Wales has not. Quite apart from having set up a national school system earlier than any such thing was contemplated in England, Scotland in the Act of Union of 1707 retained the two institutions on which that system was based, the Church of Scotland and Scots law. Not much was said about education, as this was hardly seen in England at that time as a function of the state; but when secular systems did emerge, the survival of the Scottish church and legal system made separate administrative arrangements necessary, as was eventually recognised by the creation of the Scotch Education Department. Even with a single parliament, then, the existence of a distinctive Scottish administrative and legal system has called for separate legislation. Throughout its modern history, Scottish education has been governed by a series of specifically Scottish Acts passed by the Westminster Parliament.

Not that this has necessarily meant separate consideration of policy, however; it has to be emphasised that even specifically Scottish Acts are those of the entire United Kingdom Parliament. Admittedly, that is true equally of those applying only to England and Wales. Scots members can vote on these; but although the composition of the House gives Scotland and Wales more MPs than they would be entitled to on a strict population count, the membership of the Commons is bound to be overwhelmingly English. There is no need to see anything particularly sinister in this—it is a long time since a Speaker could say 'We have catched Scotland, and will hold her fast'[1]—but most members regard the *special* concerns of Scotland and Wales as rather peripheral, time is hard to find in a crowded timetable, and even many well-intentioned members lack much understanding of the issues.

Accordingly, Scottish legislation is essentially legislation passed mainly by Englishmen, made in the light of centrally determined policies, and adapted to Scottish conditions as far as knowledge, understanding and sympathy permit.

A good example of this is offered by the various Acts of the mid-1940s, which laid the foundation of the post-war British systems. The system in England and Wales was restructured by the Education Act of 1944 (the 'Butler Act'), passed by a Conservative-led coalition but adopting what had previously been a *Labour* policy of 'secondary education for all'.[2] It is sometimes said that 'Scotland followed suit' in the Education (Scotland) Acts of 1945 and 1946; but Scotland, as such, did nothing of the kind—the United Kingdom Parliament did so *on behalf of* Scotland, using the 1944 Act as a model. There were some differences in nomenclature, such as the use of the term 'public school' in the Scottish Act (meaning a public school, not a private one). There were administrative differences, such as assigning duties to the Secretary of State for Scotland rather than the Minister of Education. There were, inevitably, differences in financial arrangements, in the provisions for the teaching of religion, and so on. But a careful search through the two sets of legislation reveals few major differences of substance.[3]

There were one or two. The position of the denominational schools in Scotland was rather simpler than in England, largely because Catholic schools had been taken over completely by the secular system while leaving certain powers with the church; there was therefore no need for the more complex arrangements thought necessary in England. Again, the right of English local education authorities to charge fees in any of their schools was removed; but in Scotland this right was retained. (This anomaly may be explained by the fact that more Scottish Labour voters, particularly Catholics, sent their children to these schools than would have been the case in England. The voting habits of the various social groups in Scotland are similar to those in England, but not identical.)

But generally the connection between the English and Scottish Acts is clear enough, right down to the use of common rhetoric such as 'age, ability and aptitude'. Whatever the merits of any Act it must be doubted that the Education (Scotland) Acts were Scottish in any real sense; putting the country's name in brackets may be symbolically more appropriate than was ever intended. There have been minor or particular enactments, and another major consolidating Act in 1962, but it is really not surprising that many people are under the impression that the Scottish system also comes under the Education Act of 1944.

There have been occasions when a major dispute has made it clear where the real power lies, as in the case of the Scottish local authority fee-paying schools.

Whatever reasons the 1945 Labour Government may have had for letting them continue, its successor of 1964 took a different view, and moved to abolish what it saw as a system of subsidised privilege; local authorities charging fees in any of their schools now had to stop, and absorb them into the neighbourhood comprehensive system.

Trouble started again when the 1970-4 Conservative Government introduced legislation to restore to Scottish education authorities the right to charge fees. Although the House now had a Conservative majority, most of the Scots members were still Labour. Though the division was still on party lines, this situation did make it plain that the party composition of the *whole* House was being allowed to determine a specifically Scottish policy contrary to the views of most Scottish MPs.

To be sure, the Bill, being a Scottish one, had to go through the Scottish Grand Committee before coming back to the House for the final reading. But the Scottish Grand Committee, like any other Committee of the House, is selected to reflect the balance of the parties in the House as a whole, whatever the Scottish balance might be. As there was a shortage of Conservatives, a number of rather bewildered English colleagues had to be brought in to make up the required majority. As it turned out, it made little difference in the long run. The Bill eventually passed the Committee stage and became law. But it only *allowed* Scottish authorities to charge fees; it did not *compel* them to do so, and in the meantime local elections had returned in the authorities most affected (Edinburgh and Glasgow) Labour-dominated councils with no intention of using the restored powers. (They continued with the policy of integrating the former fee-paying schools into the non-selective system, thus precipitating lengthy legal wrangles with the Conservative Secretary of State for Scotland.) What emerged at the end of the whole business was not, after all, a substantial change from Labour policy, but a convincing demonstration of what specifically Scottish legislation can mean when party balance there and in England differ—a common enough situation. It was, after all, a change in *local* electoral fortunes, not any feature of the parliamentary system, that aborted the change in practice.

There is also legislation that applies to the whole of the United Kingdom anyway, but affects the different educational systems. One example of this was the Act of the 1970-4 Conservative Government forbidding local authorities to continue free provision of milk in schools, which was applied to Scotland as well as to England and Wales. This was the product of deliberate policy, and if the implications of including Scotland in a general Education Act were understood, this seems to have made little difference.

In another category comes general UK legislation which has administrative implications for the various parts, such as followed the acceptance of some of the Robbins Committee's recommendations on higher education.[4] Broadly, the argument resolved itself into a division between those favouring the creation of a separate ministry of higher education (which would take over, among other things, responsibility for the University Grants Committee) and those who preferred a single ministry to be responsible for all levels of formal education. The latter view prevailed, and the result was the Department of Education and Science. If it was realised at the time that the DES was not to be responsible for schools and non-university colleges in Scotland, it seems to have counted for little. The outcome was, certainly, a unified ministerial structure in England; but in Scotland it was an odd mixture, whereby the Secretary of State for Scotland was ultimately responsible for all school and college provision except the universities, these being the ultimate responsibility of the English DES. The UGC was given the function of acting as a cushion between the universities and government (with an effectiveness that is a matter of some controversy). In the case of the Open University, which eventually had more students in Scotland than four of the eight existing universities, the DES was put in *direct* control. Whether by design or sheer absent-mindedness, an important and influential part of the Scottish system was, in effect, attached to the English one. Not surprisingly, this anomalous situation was to become a subject of controversy in the discussions leading up to devolution in Scotland.

But there are other mechanisms than the purely legislative. Technically separate though they are, administrative systems under the same political control tend to work together and influence each other. How much consultation goes on between the DES and the Scottish and Welsh Education Departments is not always publicly stated; though, as we have seen in Chapter 3, it is likely to vary according to circumstances and the personalities involved. Further, when one considers how far civil service departments can influence policy, such collaboration is bound to increase interaction between systems. Admittedly, the function of the civil service is not to form policy but to carry it out; but it does have advisory functions, its members are usually specialists while the elected politicians in charge usually are not, and they are thus in a position to exert an influence on the shaping and interpretation of policy far beyond their legal powers. Governments come and go, but the departments remain. It is notable that in economic affairs and foreign relations, British policy remains remarkably consistent in spite of the great differences in the public positions of the parties which form governments. This is less obvious in education, but a similar built-in continuity exists none the less.

There must be a good deal of speculation here, as neither ministerial nor civil service discussions are normally made public. But it is worth considering the possibility that the Secretaries of State for Scotland and Wales (and, *a fortiori*, Northern Ireland) find that the multiplicity of their functions puts them in a weak position *vis-à-vis* the Secretary of State for Education and Science. It is possible that they, having many other things to attend to, rely heavily on their English colleagues and their own civil service departments. But we cannot be sure. One thing that does emerge clearly from a study of this kind is the dearth of firm information, as opposed to rumours and leaks, about the ways in which any governmental decisions are actually arrived at.

Economic and demographic mechanisms work alongside the political, but they can be powerful even in the absence of any political connection. This can be seen most vividly when we consider systems that are politically independent of the United Kingdom. The Republic of Ireland is the most obvious of these. Separate, and determined for many reasons to retain its distinctiveness, it is nevertheless open to influences from across the border, the Irish Sea and indeed the Atlantic. Political developments have shown how porous the border with Northern Ireland can be. In education, although there is little official contact between North and South, the two systems do make some of their decisions with an eye on each other. Apart from imponderables such as the long-standing practice of many Northern *Unionist* politicians of sending their children to schools in the Republic, there is the reservation of 20 per cent of places in Trinity College, Dublin, for students from Northern Ireland, and the long refusal in Northern Ireland to establish a faculty of veterinary medicine there, since the facilities in the Republic were adequate for Northern Irish needs as well. There are other influences, too, of a longer-standing kind. For much of its modern history, Irish education has been part of a wider British and more precisely English cultural area, with, for the upper class at any rate, English-modelled schools serving much the same social function as in England. Execrated though they were by Patrick Pearse in 'The Murder Machine'[5] and by many since as both nationally and socially alien, schools of this type continued to influence the Irish scene after independence. Further, the schools run by the Orders were not necessarily Irish in character; those run by the Jesuits, in particular, were strongly influenced by the intellectualism of the international order and, by the nineteenth century, by English concepts of social elitism as well. This, too, has been a continuing influence in modern Irish education.[6] A past connection through political union can survive, if the social forces are still in operation, after the political link has been severed.

On a much smaller scale, the Isle of Man and the Channel Islands, being politically independent of the United Kingdom in internal matters, maintain educational systems quite free of legislative control from Westminster, but are strongly influenced by the English system none the less. Examples of this are the building into a Manx Education Act of an English Education Department Code,[7] or the deliberate policy in Jersey and Guernsey of recruiting teachers from 'elsewhere', particularly from England, in order to develop the system. Both were quite deliberate decisions taken by authorities in no way under the political control of the English system. Obviously other factors must be at work, powerful enough to over-ride political independence.

Man and the Channel Islands do not, in fact, have complete educational systems at all. While they have some provision for further education, they have, as we have seen, no higher education at university or college of education level, and are thus particularly prone to English influence.

In this, the islands are a special case; but by similar mechanisms the spread of English norms is evident throughout the British Isles.

Before Scotland lost her independence and after Ireland recovered hers, both countries have been under pressure to pay heed to English practices and standards. Economic power has had a great deal to do with it. For centuries, England has enjoyed greater prosperity than Scotland, Wales or Ireland fairly consistently, partly because of richer natural resources—by the time Scotland's mineral wealth could be tapped for the Industrial Revolution, the Union with England had taken place—and partly because political instability was occasional in England, endemic in Scotland and Ireland. (Lest that be thought a matter for self-congratulation, it is worth pointing out that a great deal of this instability was the direct result of English interference over the centuries.) As for Ireland, independence did not untangle economic ties with the United Kingdom or weaken Ireland's dependence on British markets, as De Valera discovered when he tried to force Britain through economic warfare to remove some particularly obnoxious terms in the treaty that had partitioned the island. Even now, the Irish pound is tied to the pound sterling.

When British currency was decimalised in 1972, Irish currency did exactly the same, and coins became for the first time identical in weight and size as well as value to the British ones, only the designs being different. This was partly because the international standardisation of coin-operated machines made this desirable but also because it was probably cheaper for the British Royal Mint to produce coins in identical sizes. The same point can be conveyed by a glance at the shops in any Irish street. Many do bear the names of purely Irish firms, to be sure, but the bulk of the goods even there are of foreign provenance, while the familiar signs such as Woolworth and Esso (not to mention that fact that none of the cars in the streets is Irish) testify to the internationalisation of the Irish economy, and symbolise in visual form what the import-export and holdings figures make even clearer to the economically or statistically-minded. The same holds, *a fortiori*, in Scotland and Wales.

Of course, economic penetration of the smaller countries is not entirely English; as in England, there is ample evidence of the influx of goods, capital and branches of firms from the United States, Japan and several European countries, notably Germany—with, naturally, loss of control by the government of important sectors of the economy. But this trend is relatively recent; English penetration of the whole of the British Isles is of much longer standing.

This has created pressures for standardisation, in an economy which has become largely centralised. Quite apart from the effects of dramatic population movements, such as those following the Irish famine or the Highland Clearances in the nineteenth century, there is the quieter mobility that continues to the present. The more ambitious often have little choice other than between forgoing advancement or moving to where the power is; conversely there can be movement from England to senior posts in Dublin, Edinburgh, Glasgow or Swansea; and even when appointees to higher positions in government or industry are natives, they get there through a career structure essentially based on London.

There are countless examples of the educational effects of such pressures, past and present—the use of English GCE examinations in Irish and Scottish schools,[8] the introduction of Honours degrees to Scotland in the nineteenth century,[9] pressures for greater specialisation in the Scottish Certificate of Education, which often proves difficult to equate with the more specialised GCE, and of course the devaluation of the native Celtic languages and Lowland Scots as alleged cultural handicaps.

This might be called non-functional normalisation. Some adjustment of, say, examination structures may be functional and practical, while copying the exact terminology of one particular system is less obviously so. Again, the ability to speak and write a form of English comprehensible all over these islands is obviously useful, but to do so with the diphthongised vowels of the south is not. (Modern descendants of the anxious eighteenth-century Edinburghers sometimes still try to do this, with a resultant form that is accepted by neither nation.)[10] But the spread of norms from one system to another goes beyond the functional. One consequence of the mechanisms we are examining here is not just that they make for the borrowing of certain practices; they create a climate in which entire models are imported, whether they are functional in the receiving country or not.

Even nomenclatures can be affected. Many Scots, as we have seen, regularly talk about their children taking 'O levels' and 'A levels', 'direct grant schools', '11-plus', and are even heard to use 'public school' in the English sense. With the exception of the last, none of these terms has any validity in Scotland. The Ordinary *grade* of the Scottish Certificate of Education is certainly analogous to the GCE O level, but the specialist Advanced level is foreign to the Scottish system, which still traditionally preferred breadth to depth at this stage until the recent introduction of the CSYS. Scottish grant-aided schools were similar to English direct grant schools in many respects, but there were important differences, in particular the absence of any requirement on such schools in Scotland to make available a proportion of free places. Transfer to secondary school takes place in Scotland at 12, not 11. As for 'public school', this means in Scotland, as in America, a publicly provided school, not a private school of the kind that has acquired this label in England for largely forgotten historical reasons.

Much of this may be attributed to the greater familiarity of the English terms in the press and on the radio and television. It also happens that Scots who are aware of the inapplicability of the English terms tire of explaining the differences to the uncomprehending and, faced with the choice of being dubbed perpetual pedants or accepting the English terms as common usage, take the line of least resistance. This may seem a miniscule point, but is not. The names of things are important in influencing the way we think about the things. For example, the SCE differs from the GCE in philosophy as well as nomenclature; the Scottish 'Ordinary' degree is not a kind of 'failed Honours', but a general degree of a kind not common in England; and so on. To call the Scots thing by the English name for a similar but not identical thing is to invite misunderstanding of the thing itself. One possible outcome is simple confusion, and is common enough; but another is the taking over with the word itself the complex of associations and overtones that accompanies it. It is at least possible that one of the factors in the decline of esteem of the Scottish 'Ordinary' degree, or the anxiety about specialisation in the sixth year in secondary schools, was the existence of English things with the same or similar names, and a consequent tendency to look at the Scottish practice from the standpoint of a different system with a different set of assumptions.

The role of the media in spreading metropolitan norms repays study although, since much of its operation is at the level of the barely conscious, it is exceedingly difficult to quantify. But there is a case for regarding them as one of the most potent mechanisms of interaction between systems. Most people depend for what knowledge they have of education on limited sources of information—their own schooldays (or at any rate what they remember of them), possibly their children's schooling, and what they read or see on television. The first two may easily turn out to be special cases, given the considerable variety in educational practice in the United Kingdom. As for the third, it is reasonably safe to assume that relatively few teachers, let alone anyone else, follow closely the specifically educational programmes on television or read the non-advertising parts of the *Times Educational Supplement* or the *Scottish Educational Journal*. The general press is much more likely to be a source of information, or at least of impressions; and on economic grounds alone, given the relative size of the English and non-English markets, the newspapers, magazines, works of fiction and television plays are more likely to reflect an English model.

Oddly, this can happen even with material published in Scotland; the Thomson comics like the *Dandy* and *Beano*, so familiar to English and Irish readers, may be produced in Dundee, but they are aimed at a much wider readership. But this is not true of all the Thomson characters; Oor Wullie frequently receives the tawse in a classroom of a type more familiar in Scotland some decades ago (though there are still quite a few of them around), and he and his *Sunday Post* stablemates, the Broons, cling firmly to the speech and life-style of an archetypal Scottish working class. It is a nice question whether they are as remote from reality as other Thomson characters designed for an audience outside Scotland—Lord Snooty and his pals, the cane-wielding and mortar-board wearing headmasters, and the slightly more serious stories set in boarding schools with a strong 1920s flavour. One sees the attractions of the boarding-school story as a literary form: by keeping most of the action among youngsters with whom the children can identify, and by holding the outside world at a distance, it has the same advantages as the murder story set on a train or in a country house—definitions of form, a recognisable set of conventions, and the avoidance of complicated (and complicating) issues. Nevertheless, one side-effect is to familiarise a norm which, while wildly untypical of England in fact, is inescapably English in flavour. Orwell saw school stories as a way of selling upper-class norms to working-class children;[11] it could be argued that they go some way to selling English norms (of a sort) to the Scots, Irish and Welsh. At a more serious level, the great bulk of educational literature published in these islands is English in origin and reference. Intending teachers, though they may use *some* texts referring to their own countries, have rather more exposure to the problems of London and Liverpool than those of Glasgow or Aberdeen, Swansea or Belfast. It could be said that in many fields—curriculum development, for example—there is more work being done in England anyway; but the imbalance of educational publishing is such that English material is more commonly swallowed whole than related to the home situation.

As far as the content of school textbooks is concerned, however, all the smaller nations are affected. Complaints about the anglicisation of the content of Scottish and Welsh education are often met with pained protests that one can hardly teach Scottish algebra or Welsh physics. This is a fair reply as far as it goes, which is not very far. Culture-free the sciences, mathematics and the like may be, but the humanities and social sciences are another matter. Obviously, one can and does teach Scottish, Welsh and English history, for example; but (leaving aside Ireland for the moment, where partition has simplified the issues in the South and complicated them in the North) it is *English* history that dominates. Welsh and Scots children are taught some of their own history, usually in the primary school; but at the secondary stage, for the most part, they move over to British history. Textbooks of British history are in fact rare; usually they are texts of English history, mentioning Irish, Welsh or Scottish affairs only as and when they are relevant to developments in England.

Some of the ethnocentrism displayed is quite astonishing. There are histories of 'Tudor *Britain*'[12] (a phenomenon unknown to history) which interpret the importance of the Irish revolt purely in its contribution to the downfall of Essex; one relegates its account of the turmoil in Scotland during the Reformation to a chapter entitled 'Threats to England', and also manages to sustain a whole chapter on education without more than one reference to Scotland, and a minor passing reference at that.[13] The misnumbering of 'British' monarchs is so common as to excite no comment, and indeed follows official usage. There are also numerous gaffes of the 'England is an island' type. (John of Gaunt's dying speech from *Richard II* is a favourite, but of course Shakespeare was no geographer; he referred to England as an island, and gave Bohemia a seacoast.)[14] It is not necessary to believe that such textbooks are the work of diehard English nationalists. A great many English historians, like many English generally, seem to have great difficulty in grasping the fact that Britain and England are not the same thing, and write accordingly. The danger here is not, perhaps, so much that Welsh and Scottish children will be brainwashed into forgetting their identity; even the minimal dose of their own history may act as a partial corrective, and some of the gaffes are sufficiently (if unintentionally) offensive to remind them just what they are reading. English children, though, rarely have any such corrective, and thus acquire an anglocentric view which turns up again in the next generation of textbook authors, legislators, civil servants, teachers, and so forth. But the fact remains that non-English children also receive a diet of history that confounds 'British' with 'English', overwhelmingly so when and if they reach the stage of 'serious' study. Textbooks in other subjects may not lend themselves to quite such obvious bias, though the wary reader may find some surprising things in civics, geography and literature.

If the approach of such texts can be explained by the limited vision of so many English authors, the fact that they are used at all in the non-English countries is largely a matter of economics. From the publication of the King James Bible onwards, English material has reached a market beyond her frontiers; and at the same time the existence of an English market (and, later, an American and commonwealth market) has given Irish, Scots and Welsh authors some incentive to couch their material in an acceptable form.

Anglicisation is not complete, though considerable; but English dominance in publishing and the media tends to make even surviving distinctive characteristics look like deviations from an English norm.

The movement of people is as important as the movement of books and journals. Emigration has been a constant fact of life in Ireland, Scotland and Wales for centuries, reaching its most drastic point in the nineteenth century. In recent times, the drift of population to metropolitan centres has been normal in most societies, as witness the domination by Paris of the francophone world. Similar movements have been going on in the British Isles, both within the individual countries and within the area as a whole. There has been a dramatic shift of population from western Ireland to Dublin, from the Scottish Highlands to the Glasgow area; but there has also been a drift from Ireland, Scotland and Wales to England (as well as to North America and elsewhere), and within England itself to London and the south-east.

Ireland illustrates all these movements in particularly drastic form. In 1841 only 20 per cent of the population lived in towns. By 1971 the figure had risen to 59 per cent in the Republic and 55 per cent in Northern Ireland. Actually, the population of the towns rose only slightly during that time, for the greatest movement was out of Ireland altogether. The population of the whole island dropped from about 8 million in 1841 to just over 5 million in 1881, a decline which continued until 1946, when there were barely 4¼ million left; recovery since then has been slow, with the 1971 figure still under 5 million. Much of this fall in numbers can be attributed to deaths during the Famine, but in the years following, 1845-55, almost 2 million left for North America and Australia, and about three-quarters of a million for Britain. This trend continued throughout the century (about 70,000 a year between 1871 and 1891) and into the present one; only since the 1960s has there been any sign of recovery, though some emigration continues. One recent development with implications for the educational system is the higher proportion of women emigrants, particularly the better qualified, 'due to the economic problems which face a working woman in Ireland, where equality of pay and opportunity are only distant visions'.[15] Significantly, among recent Irish immigrants to Britain, about 20 per cent of the women have joined the professions, compared with some 2 per cent of the men.

Emigration is doubly a problem for the exporting areas, whether we are thinking of whole countries like Scotland or Wales, or of culturally distinctive areas within them, such as the Irish Gaeltacht or the Scottish Highlands. Most obviously, it means a loss of people, possibly to the point of loss of viability, in the areas of minority cultures. Ironically, a reversal of the process can have equally disruptive effects.

The oil boom, for instance, has led to some movement back into the Scottish Highlands, the north-east, and Shetland. In the case of Shetland, emigration had already been checked by a period of prosperity in fishing, knitwear and even crofting, and by the time these were running into difficulties the oil-related developments were able to take up the slack of unemployment that would otherwise have set the population exodus off again; and since many of the new immigrants are returning Shetlanders, it is possible that the island culture may survive the shock of having to cope with the role of the European Klondyke.

In the case of the western Highlands, the signs are more ominous; depopulation has gone so far that even a relatively small number of incomers can have an effect on what is left of the indigenous culture, so that even a few hundred non-Gaels working at the Loch Kishorn site are seen by many Highlanders as the final blow to their identity (though some are attracted by the possible economic gains, even if they do turn out to be short-lived). The forebodings may turn out to be unduly gloomy, but it does seem that after large-scale depopulation, sudden boom and large-scale immigration is not an unmixed blessing.

But the movement of population has implications for the whole educational system. It may not be as drastic in effect as on Man and the Channel Islands; but even a complete system, when many of its products have to seek work elsewhere, has to provide qualifications suitable for export. Wales has exported teachers, Scotland engineers and doctors, Ireland doctors and teachers (as well as labourers), in some cases as a direct consequence of government policy. Indeed, the medical faculty at Belfast was deliberately encouraged to 'overproduce' during the sixties in order to meet the needs of elsewhere. The need, therefore, to take the requirements of other systems into account is strong, and this applies to politically independent and administratively separate systems as well as those more closely tied to the English pattern.

A good example of this is the system of entry to higher education in the United Kingdom, and consequent pressures on the examination systems. There are still important differences, both in structure and philosophy, between the General Certificate of Education in England and Wales, and the Scottish Certificate of Education. Very broadly, and there is considerable controversy as to how far this is still true in practice, the GCE is a specialist qualification while the SCE still prefers a generalist approach. Actually, the GCE may assume but of course does not enforce, a broad curriculum up to O level (approximately age 16), changing over to specialist work in two or three A level subjects, usually related, for the next two or three years. The SCE maintains, if anything, a slightly narrower range of subjects up to O grade, but tends to keep a greater breadth thereafter.

Subject for subject, A level papers are generally thought to be about a year ahead of Higher papers, though overall the Scots at the end of their course make up in breadth what they lack in depth. Some take most of their Highers in the fifth year (about age 17), others accumulate them over the two years beyond O grade. For the first group, there is the possibility of going on to university straight from the fifth year, though few now do so; the Certificate of Sixth Year Studies (CSYS) was devised to provide a goal and focus for post-Higher work. It was not intended to be used as an A level, though it is roughly comparable in standard.

It can be seen, then, that in spite of a degree of uneasy convergence, Scottish and Anglo-Welsh examinations are not precisely comparable, and that these differences reflect differences in the curriculum of the upper secondary schools. Criteria for admission to university also differ, as do the procedures—students in Scotland are admitted to *faculties*, rather than to *departments* as is generally the rule in England. Differences in *specialist* standards on entry are offset by the longer course (four years) for the Honours degree in Scotland. Now, this matters little as long as Scots students go to Scottish universities and English students to English; but as soon as substantial numbers seek to cross the border, either way, there are bound to be difficulties over equivalences. Scottish universities have managed to cope with their considerable numbers of English applicants on the basis of their A levels, but for Scots wishing to go to England the position is more complicated—English universities, having a more specialised degree structure, make their judgements on individual subject passes rather than on students' overall performance. This raises the question of how to judge a group of Scottish Highers, to which there is no simple answer. The confusion is impressive; Oxford seems able to accept Highers on the same basis as A levels without much difficulty, while London astonishingly insists that they are acceptable only as the equivalent of O levels. Between these two extremes come various degrees of acceptability, some bringing CSYS into the equation, despite the original insistence that it should not be used in this way.[16]

The growth of a common UK career structure in higher education, particularly in the universities, likewise encourages a common norm. This, again, chiefly affects Scotland. The differences between Scottish and English universities are less than they were—indeed, Davie argues that the pass was sold during the nineteenth century—but can be summarised thus as far as the 'non-professional' faculties are concerned. As well as criteria for admission, the course structure itself is more 'generalist' in its philosophy in Scotland. Even after the introduction of

Honours degrees, a large proportion of students—about half as late as the 1960s—were still taking the general or 'Ordinary' degree, accumulating a number of courses over three years (two at Higher level) thus combining a spread of subjects with a certain amount of study in depth. It was not intended to be a 'failed Honours' course; but as McPherson has shown,[17] career considerations have strengthened the position of the Honours degree to the point where the 'Ordinary' is now usually taken by students not selected for Honours, or who feel that they are not up to the more demanding course. By the familiar mechanism of self-fulfilling prophecies, a course regarded as inferior can easily become inferior through attracting the less able or less ambitious students, resulting in devaluation of the generalist approach itself.

But the Scottish Honours degree retains a generalist element. The usual form has been for students to embark on the general course for two years, during which their potential Honours subject forms part of the curriculum; on admission to Honours at the end of the second year, they specialise in that subject for two years more. This principle has been eroded in recent years, with some departments insisting on earlier selection and different courses for Honours students.

The generalist approach is still under attack in the twentieth century as it was in the nineteenth. This can be attributed in part to the devaluation of the ordinary degree, but suspicions have been growing that the influx of academics from a more specialist system has a great deal to do with it. The movement of academic staff is not, of course, only one-way. Proportionately, more Scots academics may go to England than vice versa; but in absolute numbers, given the relative sizes of the two countries, the effect is very different. Scots academics in England are bound to be in a minority, but this is not true of English academics in Scotland; indeed, there are departments in Scottish universities where the entire teaching staff is English. This is not supposed to matter; but while the wandering Scots can hardly help being aware that they are in a different system, this is not necessarily true of the English. Many actually believe they are still in England; and though not all are as insensitive as this, relatively few are fully aware of and sensitive to the differences between the two systems. This is not surprising; few academics are educationists, comparative or otherwise, and they rarely feel the need to re-examine the assumptions with which they have grown up. During the mid-1970s a controversy sprang up in St Andrews over the fact that Scottish students failed in first-year science courses much more readily than English students, and investigation revealed some differential in other faculties and some other universities as well. Accusations and counter-accusations flew thick and fast; students complained that their English-trained teachers were basing their courses on assumptions of A level competence as the starting point, while some university spokesmen blamed the Scottish students for not working hard enough and the Scottish schools for not training students for independent study in depth. Actually, the evidence was not conclusive either way for, as McPherson pointed out, English students in St Andrews and Edinburgh were not typical of English students in general, whereas the Scottish students there were much more like their national average. The two groups were thus not strictly comparable. Nevertheless, it did emerge that many of the academics were judging their students and courses by criteria more appropriate to the English system.[18]

It can be seen from these various examples that both emigration and immigration pose problems for the smaller systems. On the whole, Scotland, Ireland and Wales are exporting systems; England, Man and the Channel Islands are importing systems; but in every case it is a two-way process, and we have seen that even small-scale immigration can have drastic effects. Greater cultural uniformity and mobility have been creating common patterns, in which, so far, the norms of the richest and most numerous system usually prevail.

Not always, however; interplay can work both ways, and there are circumstances where the lesser can influence the greater. For instance, pressure at governmental level may be exerted by someone other than the central authorities, given sufficiently energetic and persuasive individuals and a fluid situation. It is difficult to know how common this is; a great many decisions can be taken in circumstances of which we know little. But the very fact that one or two such instances are known demonstrates that when there is a common political structure, influences *can* come from minority as well as majority systems.

Individuals may also carry ideas from minority systems, which may prove acceptable if they seem to provide a possible solution to problems that are proving intractable within the framework of the majority system. Two fairly recent examples spring to mind in the university sector, namely, the foundation year at Keele and the credit system at the Open University, where attempts were being made to deal with problems for which the English system had no usable model and, as it happened, the Vice-Chancellors at the formative period were Scots. In Keele, the aim was to provide some link between the scientific, social and humanistic disciplines in a system where breadth of study and interdisciplinary work were becoming rare, at school level as well as university. The English system had nothing to offer here. Nor had the Scottish system in any precise way, but the familiarity of general courses leading on to Honours made it easier to escape from the idea that university work had to be specialised from the very beginning. (This is not to argue that the Scottish degree structure was the actual model used; the foundation course set out in the Harvard Report is a likelier candidate.[19] But an approach of this kind would make sense more easily to someone trained in the Scottish system.) Similarly, the Open University drew extensively on North American practice in establishing a system of taking degrees by an accumulation of course credits; but the presence of a Scots Vice-Chancellor, familiar with a similar system at his own former university, may well have helped the idea to gain acceptance. The Open University degree structure is more American than Scottish, but it is much closer to the Scottish than the English model. It operates, of course, throughout the United Kingdom, not just in England. Its attachment to the DES might have made it more English than anything else, but for the great differences in its function from that of any traditional system, a situation favouring the importation of ideas from any source. Altogether, important though size may be in determining the relative influence of England and the non-English countries, it is not an absolute determinant; in times of change and especially in the absence of appropriate English models, the usual pattern of influence can be reversed.

There are cases, too, where non-English practice may influence educational discussion at times of dissatisfaction with English practice, at least when the feasibility of change is being examined. There is some evidence that the different role played by the Scottish universities, as compared with Oxford and Cambridge, did make some contribution to the growth of certain universities in England in the nineteenth century.[20] More recently, the use by the Northern Irish government of the UGC as an advisory rather than a controlling body has been brought forward as an example of how a devolved system can have the advantages of a United Kingdom system without being English-dominated; though on the whole British incomprehension of anything Irish ensures that most use of Irish evidence in educational debate is less than enlightening. Again, while most of the rather muted debate on the problems of early specialisation in the English system is carried on in the abstract, there have been a few instances of reference to generalist systems, including Scotland.[21]

Finally, it has to be recognised that many changes are common responses to common problems, and that there is little specifically English or Scottish, Irish or Welsh about them. The pressures that led to the comprehensive reform of secondary schools, new approaches to curriculum and method in primary schools, the raising of the school-leaving age, the expansion of higher education and the re-examination of the relationship between the universities and other higher institutions are common to all the countries of the British Isles, and for that matter in Europe and beyond. Practically every European country has during the last two or three decades moved towards more open secondary and higher education. Within these islands by far the greatest amount of published material on these questions is English, or, very often, American. The flow of ideas from the Continent, while not negligible, is curtailed by the low level of linguistic competence in Britain. It is not surprising, therefore, that in working through these common problems the tendency is to think generally of the English way of approaching them, where this is distinctive at all. It is unfortunate, though, that the mechanisms already described make it difficult to tackle common problems with due regard for national differences where they *do* exist. It is also unfortunate that so little influence comes from anywhere else. For example, there is a need for more careful thought and action on the lifelong learning of adults. Some work has been done on this in Scotland and Wales, but not much; and English experience is of limited use, since not much has been done there either.[22] Far more thought has been given to this topic in other parts of Europe, the Soviet Union and North America; but rather little of it has penetrated these islands. While such barriers remain, England and the non-English countries alike are the losers.

But interaction has not been limited to within the British Isles. The training-grounds for young empire-builders aimed to turn out Britons who would obey the orders of their superiors, and *rule* natives of farflung countries, possibly teach them, but not necessarily understand them and certainly not identify with them or challenge the imperial relationship. Thus, British education was given an even more particularistic character when its world role was at its height—ironically, making it less susceptible to outside influences.

Equally ironical is the effect of the decline of empire since the Second World War, for it is arguable that international influences have been much stronger in the post-imperial period. The English 'public' schools have been left looking for a role—some of them emphasising an intellectualism not apparent in the imperial heyday but useful for entry to academic careers, politics, industry or government service, others taking on a clearer class role which has made them more vulnerable to political attack. But many 'state' schools have, thanks to immigration from former imperial territories, had to come to terms with languages, cultures and religions previously kept at arm's length. It would be a supreme irony if the English were taught to understand the Irish, Scots and Welsh now that they are more likely to meet an Urdu-speaker than hear Gaelic or Welsh spoken in the street.

Continuing Commonwealth connections also have a role to play. Many people come to Britain from formerly dependent territories for higher education. British institutions thus find themselves training a large proportion of the governing elites of the Third World, and may thus occasionally be induced to give some thought to their international role, and even learn from the experiences of Third World societies. Of course, there were some Indian and African students in Britain during the imperial period, but now they come as equals, not subjects, and are less inclined to accept the entire body of British cultures uncritically. After a long period of near-isolation, the aftermath of empire has given British education the chance of acquiring a more international frame of mind. There is also some movement of teaching staff; university teachers in particular still go to African and Asian universities, often for years, and on their return reinforce fields such as politics, anthropology, education, medicine, linguistics, geography and others where Commonwealth experience has a contribution to make. One should not make too much of this, and clearly British influence on the former Empire is still greater than the reverse; but it is at least possible that if the British systems, and the English in particular, ever become accustomed to thinking internationally, it will be in great measure due to the adjustments of the post-imperial period.

But influences from other sources have to be considered, particularly from North America and Europe. In some ways, the influence of the United States on Britain parallels that of England on Scotland, Ireland and Wales, and largely by the same mechanisms. Not the political and administrative ones, to be sure, but we do find the dominance of educational literature affecting the curriculum and teaching methods, especially in the primary school, though of course the curriculum of London University owed a great deal to Thomas Jefferson and his German-inspired plans for the University of Virginia.[23] The American origin of much 'progressive' teaching is not obvious, largely because these methods have, by and large, been adapted and naturalised since the 1920s. One of the ironies about the current American enthusiasm for the 'British primary school' is not merely that such schools, so admired by American observers, are not really typical, but that their admired features are themselves often of North American inspiration.

Then there is the influence of the constant interchange of academic personnel. There is a continual flow of university teachers and researchers both ways, carrying ideas and practices whether they migrate for long or short periods. Only a minority are involved, but the practice is growing, and there are places where having had American experience is close to becoming a professional qualification often known as BTA (Been to America). Among earlier influences of this kind can be cited the growth of the PhD degree, both in its inception (to provide visiting American scholars with something to show for their study periods in Britain) and in its increasing use as a filtering device for academic appointments. More recently we have modular teaching, the University of Stirling's semester system with, among other things, undergraduate teacher training, and the Open University's credit system. There are some signs that this influence continues. In some universities and colleges there are moves towards more part-time and external degree work, and possibly a more general system of transferable credits; and in discussions about this, the familiarity of a similar system in the United States is bound to influence the outcome.

The mass media also play a role in the North Atlantic cultural area not unlike that within the British Isles. The large number of American programmes shown on British and Irish television creates a familiarity with American speech, vocabulary and *mores*, some of which bid fair to become the norm; this can be seen in a hundred small ways, from the mid-Atlantic accents of the commercials to the dwindling number of people who wince at the use of 'hopefully', 'campus' or 'commuter'. In so far as they have a picture of higher education at all, more people in Britain during the last half-century got it from American campus movies than ever come into contact with home-based colleges or universities. This may not lead to the adoption of American norms, but it does make them seem less alien; and when other mechanisms favour American-inspired innovation, this familiarity makes it more acceptable. That this particular form of fiction is, as often as not, a caricature of American education is not of great importance, since it is general familiarity that counts, not the details.

Although sharing a common language (more or less) makes particularly easy the mobility of academics, students and published work between the British Isles and the United States, interaction with other countries should not be overlooked. During the nineteenth century many scholars, especially Scots, studied in Germany and the Netherlands, and often brought ideas home with them. Some of these proved difficult to transplant, such as the attempts to set up a *Privatdozent* system at the University of Glasgow in 1908,[24] but familiarity with the German generalist tradition did provide some counterbalance to the specialist pressures from England.* Likewise, the acceptability of technical and vocational education, particularly strong in nineteenth-century Germany (as witness the flourishing of the *technische Hochschulen* alongside the traditional universities), found an echo in Scotland at a time when even medicine was considered unworthy of academic study in Oxford and Cambridge. German influence underwent a dramatic decline in the war hysteria of 1914, when many universities (such as Edinburgh) sacked members of staff who were of German origin; but at its height it could almost be compared to American experience today.

*One significant figure in the history of Scottish pedagogy was R. R. Rusk, who entered university late, as a student teacher, took a German PhD in the long vacations while studying for his MA at Glasgow, and then proceeded to Cambridge to take one of the first BAs in psychology, while acting as a correspondence tutor to the future celebrated Professor Bartlett. He was once heard to define an educationist as 'a schoolteacher on his holidays'.

Mechanisms may account for the fact of influence, but not altogether the forms which it may take. By creating a climate favourable to assimilation, they encourage the modelling of whole institutional structures on those of another system, including quite irrelevant features. This may sometimes have practical considerations behind it; since educational systems can design new structures from first principles, it is only natural that when new needs are felt, they cast around for ideas from elsewhere. Thus, when various European countries sought to establish systems of public education during the late nineteenth century, they turned to those with some experience, so that practically every country on the Continent modelled its system on those of France or Germany. Other examples abound, such as the adoption by all Scandinavian countries of Grundtvig's idea of the folk high school,[25] the massive exportation of British and French models to Africa, or the modification of the French or German style of system in Eastern Europe after the Second World War on lines similar to those of the Soviet Union.[26]

But the use of models can extend to nomenclature, and to symbolic practices, which can lead to the import of assumptions along with the terminology. The effects are sometimes faintly comical. In Scotland, for instance, many secondary schools solemnly divide their pupils into 'houses', to which they are then expected to show and even feel loyalty on the playing field and in the classroom. In English boarding-schools, on which this system is based, 'houses' at least mean something; but in their Scottish copies, where they are totally arbitrary, it is difficult to give pupils any convincing reason for such identification. But there is more to this than the adoption of names. 'Houses' are not *only* an arguably convenient way of dividing a school into more manageable units, nor is their adoption merely copying a piece of chic from a socially exalted system. It means accepting, unexamined, the notion that youngsters should be encouraged to evince loyalty to a group in which they have been *put*, and which does not 'stand for' anything in particular; and, moreover, that they should feel hostility or at least rivalry towards other such groups. This is often justified in the name of 'team spirit'; but this is seldom defined, nor does it seem to be much considered that 'team spirit' may take sinister forms. The idea of forcing children into arbitrary identities and rivalries seems to have been examined but little; the existence of 'houses' in English boarding-schools has become a legitimation for fundamental organisational change in the quite different conditions of Scottish day-schools.

Elitist Models

One of the most obvious examples is the growth of elite schools in Scotland and Ireland. Until the nineteenth century there was no particular demand for them. The scope for class differentiation was limited in the smaller, poorer countries. We have already shown how social distancing took place in Edinburgh and how the more prosperous sections of society, busy anglicising their speech and manners, seized on English 'public' schools as the obvious model for the education of a social elite. The earliest of such schools was Edinburgh Academy, quite specifically designed to provide an English style of schooling for the sons of gentlemen. The middle-class takeover of the Edinburgh Merchant Company schools, hitherto orphanages, sometimes with primary schools attached, took the process a stage further; and the conversion of local town schools such as Glasgow High School or the Royal High in Edinburgh into selective fee-paying schools completed it. This was not a modelling on the English system in every respect, but it certainly became more than an increase in class stratification. Significantly, the independent schools and many of the grant-aided schools took English rather than Scottish examinations, aimed their pupils at Oxford and Cambridge rather than Glasgow or St Andrews, and followed English holidays with a regularity that suggests deliberate policy, despite the difficulties for families with children in both sectors.

Similar observations could be made in Ireland, Wales, Man and the Channel Islands, but Edinburgh provides a particularly striking example. Until the corporation selective schools were made comprehensive, over a quarter of the city's children were attending fee-paying schools of some kind. (This was the average for all age-groups; the figure rose to 70 per cent among those over 16.)[27] The 'creaming-off' effect on the rest of the school system can well be imagined; such was the flight of the middle-class parents that the selective schools operated a '4-plus' system, and whole areas of the city had, in effect, no public (as opposed to 'public') provision at all. As can so easily happen when models are adopted in this way, Edinburgh came to caricature certain aspects of the English system. Even the games played are an example of the process at work; the elite schools play rugby as opposed to (and to the exclusion of) Association football. Rugby may be a 'people's game' in Wales, but not in Scotland (other than in the Borders). Football is the national game; rugby is seen as the game of the English or the anglicised middle class, an assumption which the schools' preferences mirror exactly. Something of the same is true of Ireland, with the added political complication there of the existence of nationalist, Gaelic games. Indeed, the late President De Valera, otherwise an impeccable Gaelic nationalist, retained from his own anglicised schooldays a devotion to rugby which sometimes got him into bad odour with the Gaelic Athletic Association.

As for the universities, the adoption of elitist models is obvious enough. We have already seen the mechanisms, such as central financing and mobility of students and academics. The use of models ranges from the superficial to the fundamental, from matters like the nomenclature of degrees to assumptions about the specialist competence of first-year students and the primacy of the specialist Honours degree. The obtrusiveness of English models was particularly apparent in Trinity College, Dublin, specifically designed as an English-style institution, but in Scotland two of the 'ancient' universities, St Andrews and Edinburgh, have also taken on many features of English and particularly Oxford and Cambridge models. It must also be recognised that the expectations of the universities spill over into the schools. There is, of course, no machinery whereby the universities can *require* the schools to do anything at all; but if it becomes known, for instance, that a greater degree of specialist competence is expected of university entrants, the pressure on the school to meet these expectations is hard to resist. Not only do some academics call periodically for the introduction of something like the A level into Scotland—and many of the elite schools do A levels anyway—but also in 1975 the Scottish Universities Council on Entrance called for greater specialisation in secondary schools in order that students be more adequately prepared for university study, the standard of which is apparently believed to be absolute and immutable.[28] The impact of elitist models on the universities, therefore, affects more than the university entrants themselves. Given the tendency of schools to organise their work with an eye to the most prestigious courses, in this case the *potential* university entrants, far more than will ever see the inside of any higher institution, will be affected to some degree by changing assumptions about specialisation in the curriculum.

Powerful though they are, elitist models are not the only ones in use in these islands. The English CSE, for example, has recently provided a potent model, albeit ignored by the Scottish authorities so far. But England has usually been the recipient rather than the provider of non-elitist models. The University of London, for example, was originally not intended to reflect the Oxbridge model, but rather looked to the Royal High School of Edinburgh for precedent. (Universities and secondary schools were much less clearly differentiated in the nineteenth century than later.) Again, when the civic universities were set up in northern English cities, it was obvious that the models of Oxford and Cambridge were inappropriate and Scottish models were preferred. But it is in the nature of the use of models that more may be taken over than was intended, that incidental and possibly quite irrelevant practices may be imported as part of an educational and social package deal causing distortion of the imported model, or of the receiving system, or both.

This is not to argue that the use of models is inappropriate, or that political control is irrelevant in the face of other pressures. But it is important to appreciate that both have their limitations, and that there is a need for thorough analysis of the processes of interaction and innovation. Some of the mechanisms examined here may well continue, regardless of any action taken to check them or change their direction; and some of the models will continue to have an appeal. Life is too short to work out solutions from first principles every time. When the processes are fully understood, however—and we are still a long way from that—political action may provide the chance to ameliorate or adapt the workings of the non-governmental mechanisms (which may respond to economic if not educational pressure) and to consider what can sensibly be imported and what can not. By making the processes conscious rather than blind, it should be possible to use models without taking them over uncritically, side-effects and all. We shall be returning to this point later. Meanwhile, it is important to bear in mind the great variety of ways in which the various educational systems of these islands can influence one another, for gain or loss. But the process does not stop there, for the same mechanisms are at work *within* systems. It is to these internal differences that we now turn.

NOTES AND REFERENCES

1 John Prebble, *The Lion in the North* (Harmondsworth, Penguin, 1973), p. 288.
2 See Brian Holmes, *Problems in Education: A Comparative Approach* (London, Routledge & Kegan Paul, 1965), ch. 9, and Michael Parkinson, *The Labour Party and the Organization of Secondary Education 1918-1965* (London, Routledge & Kegan Paul, 1970).
3 Education Act, 1944 (7 & 8 Geo. VI, c. 31); Education (Scotland) Act, 1946 (9 & 10 Geo. V, c. 72); Education (Scotland) Act, 1962 (10 & 11 Eliz. II, c. 47). All HMSO.
4 *Higher Education. Report of the Committee appointed by the Prime Minister under the Chairmanship of Lord Robbins 1961-63* (Cmnd 2154) (London, HMSO, 1963). Robbins recommended a separate ministry of higher education but the government of the time determined on a unified DES, the decision being effective from 1 April 1964. For a discussion, see Richard Layard, John King, Claus Moser, *The Impact of Robbins* (Harmondsworth, Penguin, 1969).
5 'The Murder Machine', in *The Collected Works of Pádraic H. Pearse* (Dublin, Phoenix, 1916) pp. 5-50.
6 It is relevant to note that Trinity College Library, Dublin, remains a British copyright library despite independence and with the full approval of the British parliament.
7 See Chapter 5 for full treatment.
8 A number of independent schools in Scotland and Ireland enter their pupils for English GCE examinations rather than for those of their own countries, in order to make entry to English universities, especially Oxford and Cambridge, easier.
9 George Davie, *The Democratic Intellect* (Edinburgh, Edinburgh University Press, 1960).

10 See Chapter 5, note 27, and Alexander Law, op. cit., pp. 157-61.
11 George Orwell, 'Boys' weeklies', *Horizon*, no. 3, March 1940; reprinted in *Inside the Whale and Other Essays* (Harmondsworth, Penguin, 1962).
12 There are dozens of textbooks written under the delusion that the Tudors ruled *Britain* (a delusion often shared by the Tudors themselves). For a prize specimen, see Mary R. Price and C. E. L. Mather, *A Portrait of Britain under Tudors and Stuarts, 1485-1688* (Oxford University Press, 1954, 1969).
13 ibid.
14 Shakespeare also shifted Bohemia from Central Europe to more arid parts; see *The Winter's Tale*, III, iii 1-3:

Antigonus: Thou art perfect then our ship hath touch'd upon
the deserts of Bohemia?
Mariner: Ay, my lord, and fear
We have landed in ill time;

For John of Gaunt's notion of England as an island ('sceptr'd'), see *King Richard the Second*, II, i, 40 *ff*.
15 Ruth Dudley Edwards, *An Atlas of Irish History* (London, Methuen, 1973).
16 See, for example, the regulations of London University during the 1950s.
17 Andrew McPherson, 'Nobody wants an ordinary degree nowadays', *Times Educational Supplement*, 12 January 1973, p. 19.
18 Andrew McPherson, 'National differences in pedagogy and first year achievement at Edinburgh University', *Scottish Educational Studies*, vol. 7, no. 2, November 1975, pp. 49-66. At St Andrews, differential failure rates brought accusation of discrimination from the students and laziness from the Principal.
19 *General Education in a Free Society* (Harvard Committee, 1945).
20 See, for example, H. B. Charlton, *Portrait of a University* (Manchester) (Manchester University Press 1951), pp. 27-8.
21 See John Hajnal, *The Student Trap* (Harmondsworth, Penguin, 1972).
22 There has been some, as witness the Russell Report in England and Wales and the Alexander Report in Scotland; but it can hardly be said that the idea has made much impact in circles where decisions are made and money allocated.
23 Bellot, H. Hale, *University College, London* (University of London Press, 1929), pp. 9-11.
24 See motion adopted at the meeting of the General Council of Glasgow University held on 1 April 1908.
25 Thomas Rørdam, *The Danish Folk High Schools* (Det Danske Selskab, 1965).
26 See N. Grant, *Society, Schools and Progress in Eastern Europe* (Oxford, Pergamon, 1969), chs 5-8.
27 *Public Schools Commission, Vol. III* (London HMSO, 1970).
28 The SUCE memorandum preferred to talk in terms of greater subject *choice* in the senior classes, but the context made it clear that greater scope for specialism was envisaged.

Chapter 5

The Minorities: Islands and Languages

Mr Crabbe had, I presume, read very little about Scotland before that excursion. I believe he really never had known, until then, that a language radically distinct from the English, was still actually spoken within the island. And this recalls a scene of high merriment which occurred the very morning after his arrival. When he came down into the breakfast parlour, Sir Walter had not yet appeared there; and Mr. Crabbe had before him two or three portly personages all in the full Highland garb. These gentlemen, arrayed in a costume so novel, were talking in a language which he did not understand; so he never doubted that they were foreigners. The Celts, on their part, conceived Mr. Crabbe, dressed as he was in rather an old-fashioned style of clerical propriety, with buckles in his shoes for instance, to be some learned abbé, who had come on a pilgrimage to the shrine of Waverley; and the result was, that when, a little afterwards, Sir Walter and his family entered the room, they found your father and these worthy lairds hammering away, with pain and labour, to make themselves mutually understood, in most execrable French. Great was the relief, and potent the laughter, when the host interrupted their colloquy with his plain English 'Good-morning.'

The Life of George Crabbe, by his son
(World Classics edn, London, OUP, 1932, p. 264)

Distance lends simplicity to the view, even if the distance is not great. The Englishman who is well aware of differences between North and South is still likely to see the Scots, the Welsh, even the Irish, as much of a muchness. This may be less true of the minority nations. The Glaswegian who regards the forty-odd miles to Edinburgh as an immense distance psychologically *may* lump the English into one general category, but there is a good chance that the mass media and personal contact will have informed him that London, Liverpool and Lymington are not identical in their problems or their cultures.

Yet there is a sense in which England has a cohesion of identity that some of the other nations lack. Effective central government was established earlier, and the trend in England has been towards linguistic homogeneity, unlike in the other countries where the introduction of English has created internal divisions. There are great disparities in school provision in different parts of England, but it would be rash to attribute them to different cultures in north and south. Educational legislation has always been intended for the whole country; and any unevenness in its implementation is seen as the outcome of failure or deprivation, not cultural distinctiveness.

In the smaller nations it is otherwise. Scotland was internally divided during the Middle Ages and for a long time thereafter; the writ of the King of Scots might run in the Lowlands, but the Borders were only intermittently brought under the control of the Scottish government, usually by means of military expeditions.[1] The Highlands were linguistically and culturally quite distinct, and even more remote from central government control. They also constituted a large part of the country—roughly half the population of Scotland until the eighteenth century—which can be considered as outside the mainstream of the nation's educational development.[2] The much-acclaimed system of parish schools, which for a time put Scotland educationally well in the lead, was essentially a Lowland phenomenon.[3] The Highlands were hardly touched by it until, following the political collapse of Highland society after 1746, and the forced depopulation of the nineteenth century, the school system was used for what one author[4] called 'the teaching-out of Gaelic' and the destruction of Highland identity. The divide is still there, but the balance of population has altered drastically, with about 80 per cent now living in the Lowlands. The Highlands are nearly empty, and most of the remaining inhabitants are English speaking. Though the cultural differences remain, the most important contrasts are now those between remote and urban areas.

But other divisions are just as important to those standing close. It is customary to bracket the Highlands and the Isles together, but they do differ in some important respects. The Western Isles, largely because of their remoteness, have resisted anglicisation more successfully than the Highland mainland. The decision of the Western Isles Regional Council, *Comhairle nan Eilean*,[5] to pursue a completely bilingual policy, was not a move to make the Isles more different, but an attempt to preserve something of their Highland identity. What distinguishes the Isles from the Highlands is not cultural (except that they are *more* Highland); the problems they share with other island areas—the inaccessibility of outlying parts, dependence on weather for communication, and the difficulty of providing schooling on small islands with aging and declining populations, can be independent of cultural considerations.

This can be seen in the Northern Isles, Orkney and Shetland. Unlike the Hebrides, they have never been 'Celtic'. The Western Isles were for a time under Norse rule, but remained 'Celtic' in population and language; but the people of the Northern Isles were totally Norse in origin. The Hebrides were regained for Scotland by Alexander III in 1263, but Orkney and Shetland remained part of the Kingdom of Norway until the sixteenth century, when they were turned over in settlement of a debt. The people are still conscious of a separate identity, and are almost as reluctant to be called Scots as the Scots are to be called English. But there is no linguistic separation; the Norse dialects have died out and been replaced by a form of English more like Scots than anything else. Some of their problems are similar to those of the Western Isles. They have small populations scattered over several islands, making various special arrangements necessary. Shetland, for example, has a population of less than 19,000, of whom just under 3,500 are at school. Since these pupils are spread over several islands, some of them sparsely populated and difficult to reach, it is not possible to provide the full range of schooling except in Lerwick. Many primary schools have only one or two teachers, and there are seven four-year high schools, three on the northern islands of Unst, Yell and Whalsay and four on the Shetland mainland, taking pupils up to the age of 16. But since most of these are too small to provide much in the way of even O grade SCE courses, pupils who intend taking these have to transfer at the age of 14 to the only six-year comprehensive, the Anderson High School in Lerwick, living in hostels or lodgings. Although transfer is by free choice—there is no selection at 14-plus—this procedure has obvious drawbacks in requiring early decision and distorting the composition of the four-year schools; but the geography of the islands leaves very little choice.[6] In Orkney, with the population of some 17,000 the problems and their solutions are similar.[7]

Both groups of islands are remote from the centres of government, whether British or Scottish—it is easier, and cheaper, to fly from Edinburgh to London than to Shetland; they are, however, spared the problems of population decline, thanks to recent prosperity of their basic industries (and now oil) and a reversal of the drift to the mainland cities. Orcadians and Shetlanders who seek higher education still have to go to the Scottish mainland (or, as they put it, just 'to Scotland'), and there are limits to the prospects for graduate employment back on the islands. Many therefore have to stay away; hence the assertion that Orkney's chief exports are butter and professors.[8] But most come back if they can. In teaching, for instance, both directors of education report that they have more applications from islanders than they can possibly gratify.

The depopulation trend seems to have been reversed, largely because of the oil boom. But the blessings are not unmixed; as in the Western Isles, many view the influx with mixed feelings. While welcoming the prosperity, they also fear that their way of life may be dislocated beyond remedy.[9] Societies as small as this are highly vulnerable. Even a slight rise or fall in the school population makes all the difference to the practical organisation of the system. Similarly, even small-scale boom and slump, immigration and emigration, can have disproportionate effects. For the present, the unexpected bonus of oil has brought to the Northern Isles prosperity that has enabled them to cope rather well with the problems bequeathed by geography and history but it would not take much of a change to push the economy into a decline again. Unlike the Western Isles, they no longer have a language to lose; but they have a great many other things, which temper enjoyment of the present favourable turn of events with the knowledge that they live much more on a knife-edge than the peoples of more central and populous areas.

The Lowlands have their internal differences too, containing farming country as well as industrial areas, and they in turn can be strikingly different from Aberdeen and the North-East, the Borders, or Galloway. Even the two main centres of population, Glasgow and Edinburgh, are almost as different as the constant stream of half-serious witticisms would lead one to believe. Half the population of Scotland lives in Strathclyde, mostly in or near Glasgow, a city sorely plagued by overcrowding, urban decay, dying heavy industry and one of the highest rates of unemployment in the country. Many of the vast housing schemes on the periphery lack any social amenities, and have degenerated into new slums that lack the sense of community of the old ones. Popular mythology notwithstanding, Glasgow does not consist entirely of rotting tenements and bleak housing estates, littered with broken bottles and sprayed with gang slogans; but much of it does, and many Glasgow children receive their schooling in conditions that other parts of Scotland find barely credible. Edinburgh, likewise, is not all Georgian New Town and elegant suburbs; the Athens of the North has some ravaged housing estates as bad as anything in Glasgow, and odorous slums as well. But these features are less prominent. Living standards are undoubtedly higher, a greater proportion of the people work in the professions, and there has been a substantial influx (particularly of English) since the eighteenth century. Linked with this is the unusually high proportion of fee-paying schools, which pose problems of quite another kind to the city's school system.

In Wales, the most obvious internal differences are between the industrial south and the rural north, but there are cultural differences as well.[10] South Wales (where most of the population now lives) is largely English-speaking. In the less populous north and west, however, Welsh is still commonly used, and appears to be on the increase after a long period of decline; although only 11 per cent of the people of Glamorgan speak the language, for example, the figure in Merioneth is near the three-quarters mark. The parallel with Scotland is tempting, but should not be pushed too far. In Wales, the majority of the population were Welsh speaking until the turn of the century, over 280,000 speaking nothing else. But Scotland has not been a totally Celtic country since the eleventh century; Gaelic dominance lasted only briefly in Lothian and the south-east, yielding to anglicising pressure in the Lowlands until it was pushed into the Highlands and the Isles. During most of the medieval and modern period, the Scottish Lowlands spoke a variant of English, and had little to do with the Gaelic world.[11] In Wales, there never has been the feeling that the native language is somehow alien; but in much of Scotland just such an attitude prevailed until recently.

Few could fail to be aware of the differences within Ireland. Some are painfully obvious and have, unlike other divisions in these islands, been the occasion of bloodshed in modern times. Appalling though their consequences are, and extensively analysed in all the mass media, they are still liable to be misinterpreted and oversimplified. Although the conflict has its origins in a cultural divide between Irish natives and British settlers, symbolised by their adherence to Catholicism and Protestantism respectively, which in turn was the basis for Partition, it is not just a question of North versus South or Protestant versus Catholic, convenient though it is for many on both sides to present it in these terms. That there is a political division is obvious enough; what it implies is less so. The commonly-used labels 'Ulster' and 'Eire' in themselves are not really accurate; three of Ulster's nine countries are within the Republic,[12] and *Éire* is simply the Irish for Ireland. Northern Ireland itself is not the Protestant area, but the area where Protestants are numerically dominant; and although a great many northern Catholics do identify with the Republic, not all do. (It is worth recalling the hostility of the Catholic church to the nationalist movement before independence.) By the same token, there are Protestants in the Republic who have no sympathy with Northern unionism at all, and who play a part in Irish society out of all proportion to their numbers—two of the Republic's presidents have been Protestants.[13] Although government policy and public opinion in the South are sympathetic to the Northern Catholics and favour (eventual) reunification of the islands, public support for any faction of the IRA is minute, government is actively hostile to it, and advocacy of reunification is generally lukewarm. No Irish government wants to be landed with a million hostile Protestants.[14]

It can be doubted that the basic division is religious at all. As Liam de Paor has shrewdly pointed out, none of the protagonists seems at all interested in *converting* anyone.[15] The essential divide is socio-economic, with religion serving as a label.

As well as seeking to extirpate Gaelic culture through the school system, James VI and I also sought to cut off the Gaels of Scotland from those in Ireland by settling Scots and English Protestants in Ulster. These inevitably became a dominant class, feeling alien from, and superior to, the native Irish whom they supplanted. There are interesting parallels between this situation and that of settler populations in parts of Southern Africa, with the important difference that the descendants of the settlers in Ulster form a definite majority in one part of the island, and have been there long enough to develop an identity and culture of their own. For all the Union flags and royal portraits, the Northern Protestant *ambiance* seems quite foreign to most people in Britain itself.[16] Everyone is paying a high price for James's venture into social engineering and the denominational decisions of Northern Ireland's education are in many ways more significant than in the South.[17]

In the Republic, much more important than the Protestant/Catholic difference is the difference between the east and the west, in particular between anglophone and increasingly cosmopolitan Dublin and the remote, rural, conservative *Gaeltachta* (Irish-speaking areas). Over the whole country there is a constant shift of population from east to west, from country to city, which widens the gap. Thus, a cultural difference is emphasised by the contrast between rural depopulation and urban congestion, each presenting its own educational problems.

The island systems have special problems, some of which have been looked at briefly. Different though they are in many ways, Scotland's Celtic and Norse islands share the effects of emigration, but there are island systems where the political pressures at least are absent. Orkney, Shetland and the Western Isles are part of Scotland, but Man and the Channel Islands are not strictly speaking part of the United Kingdom at all. They are as independent as the Republic of Ireland, except that they recognise the British sovereign as head of state and leave defence and external affairs to the British government. In education, as in other internal matters, their autonomy is complete. Whether this guarantees cultural independence in practice is another matter.

The Isle of Man,[18] though at various times ruled by Norse, Scots and English, was Celtic in population, with a language closely related to Irish or Scots Gaelic. Written Manx did not appear until 1610, with spelling conventions based on English. The educational system grew under the shadow of English domination, exercised through the Anglican church under a succession of energetic bishops of Sodor and Man. One of these (Philips, a Welshman) is credited with setting Manx in writing, but another (Barrow, bishop from 1663 to 1671) was determined to replace it with English. In his view, 'the best way of cure [of the 'looseness and viciousness' of the people] would be to acquaint the people with the English tongue, so that they might be in a capacity to read catechisms and books of devotion; and for this purpose to set up an English school in every parish, and withal, to fit the children for higher learning, in a grammar school, which was also necessary'. It took a long time. The power of the church declined in the mid-eighteenth century, and with it declined the educational system, with a temporary recovery during the time of William IV, until rescued by legislation in the late nineteenth century.

Meanwhile, the language had survived Barrow's efforts. Bishop Wilson, who had learned Manx for preaching, noted in 1698 that 'The English is not understood by two-thirds of the Island, though there is an English school in every parish; so hard is it to change the language of a whole country'. His successor, Hildesley, tolerated and encouraged the language, but by this time the townspeople were completely anglicised and were at best indifferent to it. He obtained money from the SPCK (which took a tolerant view of Gaelic in Scotland also) for translations into Manx; but the language of the school system remained English which, together with urbanisation and increasing outside contact, gave that language a near-monopoly. By the mid-nineteenth century Manx was rarely used in the courts and was ignored by the schools. By 1961 the number of speakers was down to 165 in a population of some 50,000. There is some evidence that the number is rising again, due largely to the efforts of a few revivalists, and it is offered in two schools as part of 'local studies'. But this is a long way from general use, and it seems that the point of no return may have been reached.

The alignment of the church which developed education on Man ensured that it would never be Manx in the linguistic sense. Hildesley remarked, 'This, I believe, is the only country in the world that is ashamed of, and even inclined to extirpate, if it could, its own native tongue'. He was wrong; similar attitudes, under pressure of similar social and political developments, were to be found sooner or later in all the Celtic areas.[19] They, nevertheless, managed to retain some kind of distinct character. It is worth asking if legal independence has made this true of Man.

Legislatively and administratively independent though it is, Man has closely modelled its Education Acts on those passed at Westminster. State intervention dates from the Act of 1872, which followed the English Act of 1870 so closely as to incorporate the code of the English Education Department. A commentary of 1900 explains:

> In this way education in the Island is saved from becoming local in its character and from falling below the standard prevailing in England. The Manx schools are, in effect, included in the great system governed by the Education Department at Whitehall. The same subjects are taught in them, the same inspectors visit them, and they are compelled

> to attain the same standards of efficiency as the English and Welsh schools.[20]

The assumptions implicit in this statement are familiar enough. The prestige of the English model is equated with scholastic superiority, and equality with sameness. Similar logical lapses have gained currency in Scotland and Ireland also, in spite of their systems' greater size and resilience, and are still to be found in the 1970s. It is not surprising that a small system like Man should prove even more vulnerable.

The pattern of following England has continued. Not in every detail: comprehensive education was effected in 1948 without controversy; raising of the school-leaving age, by contrast, has lagged behind the mainland systems. English practice prevails even in the dominance of the 'public' schools, which some 10 per cent of the island's children attend. Cameron-Jones and Kelly, while recognising this trend, see a growing mood of Manx identity in recent years; the proportion of teachers who are Manx themselves has risen from almost none to about 70 per cent, and the revival of interest in island language and culture may indicate a trend. But, as we have seen, Manx education is incomplete at a vital point; having virtually no higher educational provision, it is bound to be a semi-detached part of the English system. As Cameron-Jones and Kelly point out,

> These forms of control are of a rather different order from Barrow's imposition, on Manx children, of English as a necessary sub-goal to spiritual salvation. But they derive, no less than Barrow's measures did, from the ascendancy of a powerful though benevolent neighbour.[21]

Some may be less sure about the benevolence, but of the power there is little doubt. For all its independence, the smallness of Man's population and the absence of a higher educational sector ensure that English influence is overwhelming.

Similar mechanisms have been at work in the Channel Islands.[22] Geographically, they are much closer to France than England, and their history and culture show strong French influence. Politically, they are independent, the bailiwicks of Jersey and Guernsey having complete control of internal affairs, including education. One might expect to find distinctive systems with a blend of English and French characteristics, but on the whole, one does not: primary schools follow the English pattern, and in secondary schools a conservative version, with 11-plus selection and a large independent sector. No less than Man, the Channel Islands are an extension of the English system, even in the absence of any political machinery to enforce this. The reasons seem to be similar. There is considerable immigration from Britain; since there are high property qualifications for residence, incomers are likely to import upper-class and generally conservative English norms. Again, there are colleges of further education, but no university or other higher provision, not surprising in a total population of approximately 13,000. For higher study, there are some scholarships to Caen or Grenoble, but most go to Britain (usually England), so that here too the schools have to meet the appropriate entrance requirements, and are in turn staffed by teachers trained in England and likely to work to English assumptions. In fact, according to Pickering,

> The policy in both bailiwicks is to recruit teachers from Britain and elsewhere as far as possible and very few island-born teachers until they have had considerable experience elsewhere. This is considered to be to the advantage of teachers and pupils alike. The native inhabitants would appear to be rather parochial through habit, custom and intermarriage.[23]

There are some interesting assumptions here, not least that the norm of a small society is 'parochial' while that of a large one is not. Not that Jersey and Guernsey have been subjected to the arrogance that came in with many teachers to Ireland or the Scottish Highlands; it is clear that many incoming teachers have considerable liking for the islanders, and may even feel that they embody qualities now lost in England. It is equally clear that the Islands rely on England for their teaching force and are thus subject, for all their independence, to English norms, generally in a conservative version.

It would seem, then, that in the case of the smaller island systems the degree of political independence is of limited relevance, and that there is a size below which populations cannot fall and retain genuine autonomy without at any rate a level of sophisticated planning that has, so far, been lacking. In the case of the island systems, geography makes their peculiar position obvious enough. But similar questions have to be asked about minorities within minority systems. It should perhaps be stressed that the major problem is not with dialects of English, but with the position of the Celtic languages *vis-à-vis* English of any kind. Time was, of course, when in England itself various regional dialects enjoyed parity of esteem, but for all the vigour of popular culture in the north and west, the standard form has not been seriously challenged within England. Scots is another matter.[24] It did not, of course, develop as a corrupt form of southern English (whatever impression later spelling conventions may give),[25] but as a separate form of the Anglian speech current as far south as Yorkshire. Its use as an official, court and literary language survived even the Union of the Parliaments in 1707, but by the middle to late eighteenth century it was being ousted by southern standard. It survives as the medium for a vigorous literature (especially poetry),[26] and as spoken vernacular in various parts of the country. But it has no modern standard form, and apart from the specific study of Scottish literature has no place in the teaching process—on the contrary, efforts are generally made to eradicate Scotticisms from children's speech in favour of the standard form.[27] This provincialisation of Scots, needless to say, has nothing to do with its intrinsic characteristics; it was the normal language of instruction in the schools up to the eighteenth century; it stemmed, ironically enough, from its closeness to southern English. When the King James Bible appeared, it was used in Scotland as well as England, as it was comprehensible enough to require no separate translation. Although there were signs of English influence before this (Knox's Scots contains a good many anglicisms),[28] the Authorised Version probably did more to weaken the position of Scots than anything else, and the growth of a reading market in standard English continued the process. It is quite likely that the eighteenth-century philosophers in Edinburgh *spoke* Scots, but they wrote in a form that would be acceptable elsewhere in the English-speaking world.[29]

The problems of the indigenous minority languages are of a different order. Apart from Brittany, these islands are the last refuge of the Celtic family of languages, once spoken over most of northern and central Europe.[30] As mentioned earlier, Britain was a Celtic island before the Roman invasion, and so remained after the Romans left. Its inhabitants (with the possible exception of the Picts in the far north)[31] spoke Brythonic or 'P-Celtic',[32] from which are descended modern Welsh, the virtually extinct Cornish[33] and its close relative Breton (brought to France by refugees from the Saxon invasions of Britain). Another branch of the family, known as Goidelic or 'Q-Celtic', seems to have developed in Ireland, where it became the medium of one of the richest cultures in northern Europe. This was carried to Britain after the departure of the Romans—temporarily to Wales, more permanently to western Scotland, where settlers from Dal Riata in Ulster founded a kingdom of the same name in Argyll. They called themselves Féni, but were more widely known by the Latin name Scotti. By a mixture of settlement, conquest and dynastic marriage, they eventually came to control all of ancient Caledonia (even the south-eastern part where Angles had over-run the native British), giving their name to the country in the process. Their language was long regarded as simply a variant of Irish, though by the sixteenth century it had developed significant differences. Even now, Scots Gaelic has enough in common with Irish, especially as spoken in Donegal, to make mutual comprehension possible after a little practice. Manx belongs to this branch of Celtic.[34]

The Celtic languages have all been subject to repression, sometimes legal and sometimes scholastic. In Ireland, this was the effect of English conquest. The earlier Norman settlers had been assimilated into Gaelic society, becoming *Hiberniores ipsis Hiberniis*, more Irish than the Irish themselves.[35] The Tudors, however, were determined to put a stop to this, and initiated a policy of systematic destruction of Irish Gaelic society, culture and language. It had been tried before; in 1366, the English-dominated Kilkenny Parliament had pronounced thus:

> All Englishmen and the Irish dwelling among them must use English surnames, speak English, and follow English customs. If any Englishman, or Irishman dwelling among the English, use Irish speech, he shall be attainted and his lands go to his lord till he undertake to adopt and use English. They may not entertain or make gifts to Irish minstrels, rhymers or story-tellers.[36]

The statutes were widely ignored, English actually having lost ground by 1500, but in 1541 the Dublin Parliament returned to the offensive:

> Be it enacted that every person or persons, the king's true subjects inhabiting this land of Ireland ... to the utmost of their power, cunning and knowledge, shall use and speak commonly the English tongue and language and shall bring up his children in such places where they shall or may have occasion to learn the English tongue, language order and condition.[37]

By the end of Elizabeth Tudor's reign, the authority of Parliament had spread over the whole island, and this time the policy was effectively prosecuted. Irish chiefs were expelled, poets were killed or imprisoned, manuscripts were burned, and the sons of Irish nobles were legally kidnapped (made wards of court) and brought up to English language, manners and allegiance. Contemporary English writers took it for granted that the language had to be exterminated to make political conquest permanent (and assumed that this was self-evidently desirable). Edmund Spenser put it thus: 'It hath ever been the use of the conquerors to despise the language of the conquered, and force them by all means to learn his.... The speech being Irish, the heart must needs be Irish.'[38] What prescription began, urbanisation and English schools continued. By the nineteenth century Irish had fallen out of use in the towns and among the educated classes, and was increasingly regarded as the language of the more backward peasantry, and as such something of a handicap. As in Scotland and Wales, many of the clergy discouraged the native tongue as a hindrance to learning English, which their parishioners would need to work outside the country. This view was taken by some of the nationalist leaders, even O'Connell, a fluent Irish speaker himself:

'Although the Irish language is connected with many recollections that twine around the hearts of Irishmen, yet the superior utility of the English tongue, as the medium of modern communication, is so great that I can witness without a sigh the gradual disuse of Irish.'[39] Rejection of the native tongue even by natives themselves became increasingly common during the nineteenth century in all the Celtic countries, and still exists today.

What finally killed off Irish as the customary language even of the peasantry, however, was not the English but a virus that destroyed the potato crop on which most of the people depended. When the blight struck in 1845, the population of Ireland stood at about 8½ million; by 1851 starvation and emigration had brought it down to little over 6½ million, and the decline continued to the middle of the present century. It was just over 4¼ million in 1961, since when it has recovered slightly.[40] But this unique population collapse does not tell the whole story, for its effects were not evenly spread. What is now Northern Ireland fared better—whereas the population of the present Republic is still well under half its 1841 figure, that of Northern Ireland is down by only 7 per cent. But it was the west that suffered worst of all; in Connacht, for example, the population fell by 72 per cent, and is still falling. As it was in the west that Irish was in general use, the effects were devastating. In 1851 the proportion of Irish speakers was only 25 per cent; by 1911 it was 12 per cent; and for the rest of the century the habitual use of Irish has shrunk to the Gaeltachta, tiny toeholds on the west coast where numbers continue to fall despite governmental economic aid.[41] In theory, 27 per cent of the population of the Republic can speak Irish, but this is of the school-learned variety.[42] If the figure were limited to native speakers, it would be more like 1 per cent.

Welsh[43] has been more fortunate. Political conquest, at first, did not produce an all-out onslaught on the language. Edward I killed the poets as a source of disaffection, but also felt it expedient to promise that his son would be brought up to speak Welsh (a promise that does not appear to have been kept). It was the Act of Union of 1536 that really began the attack. By this incorporation of Wales into England, Welsh was denied any official status in the courts or in any public connection. The Anglican church and the connection of all patronage with London erected English as the language of power, prestige and loyalty, doing much to further the Act's declared intention 'to utterly extirp' what was regarded as no more than 'diverse sinister usages'.

Not surprisingly, the familiar argument that the native language must be a handicap gained ground, and could be astonishingly violent, as in this *Times* editorial of the mid-nineteenth century:

> The Welsh language is the curse of Wales; its prevalence and ignorance of English have excluded and even now exclude the Welsh people from the civilisation of their English neighbours. An Eisteddfod is one of the most mischievous and selfish pieces of sentimentalism that could possibly be perpetrated. It is simply a foolish interference in the natural progress of civilisation and prosperity. If it is desirable that all the Welsh should speak English, it is monstrous folly to encourage them in a loving fondness for their old language. The sooner all Welsh specialities disappear from the face of the earth, the better.

Nor was this opinion held only by the hysterical, the insensitive, and the arrogant. Matthew Arnold, who had shown in his writings some appreciation of Celtic literature, took this view:

> It must always be the desire of the government to render its dominions, as far as possible, homogeneous. Sooner or later, the differences of language between England and Wales will probably be effaced ... an event which is socially and politically so desirable.[44]

Many Welshmen agreed, and accepted that the state system of education established in 1870 would be conducted entirely in English. But active suppression played its part too, as Thomas points out:

> Teachers used, and parents acquiesced in the use of, the notorious 'Welsh Not' so that their children might the sooner acquire English. The 'Not' was a stick or board hung round the neck of a child speaking Welsh. The child was allowed to pass it to someone else heard speaking the language, and at the end of the day whoever was in possession was punished. References to the 'Not' can be found throughout the nineteenth century, and almost exact parallels existed in Brittany and Provence.[45]

(They existed in Scotland too, and lasted longer. The *maide crochaidh* was still reported to be in use on Lewis as late as 1930.)[46]

What saved Welsh from decline on the scale suffered by the other Celtic languages was a religious development. Being Protestant after the Reformation, Wales did not have its language identified with Catholicism by a hostile government, as happened in Ireland and Scotland, so that the moves to 'extirp' it were pursued less vigorously. Further, the nonconformist chapels were not interested in anglicising the country. Welsh was the language of the people, and they were much more concerned to bring the people to salvation through reading Scripture than to raise the social tone of their congregation. A network of Sunday schools was established to teach children and adults to read and discuss in Welsh. According to a report of 1845 a fifth of the population were attending these schools, and 'the younger portion of the labouring classes in Wales can generally read, or are in the course of learning to read, the Scriptures in their mother tongue'.[47] By the time of the 1870 Act, literacy in Welsh was well established, and was thus more able to resist the anglicising effect of the new schools. Moreover, a flourishing literary and musical culture grew up which, if not invented by the chapels, was clearly fostered by them.

But, although these developments put Welsh in a stronger position than Irish, it could not totally resist other pressures. As Thomas puts it,

> This whole area of activity can be regarded as a kind of counter-culture. What people learned was to be for the good of their souls or for the immediate instruction and entertainment of the local community. It was not, and being in Welsh *could* not be geared to geting on, rising socially, becoming richer. Herein, in retrospect, lies its great attraction, but also, as it turned out, its weakness.[48]

It was not just the state schools that put pressure on Welsh, not even merely the fact that the grammar schools, the instruments of mobility, were English. Wales was opened up by the railways, which made communication with England easier than within Wales. English newspapers became more available and more intelligible, industrialisation changed the social patterns of south Wales, and even the successes of Welsh education served to encourage emigration as so often happens when educational advance outstrips economic development. The process accelerated during the twentieth century; in 1900 about half the population spoke Welsh, but by the 1960s it was down to less than half that figure.[49]

Demographic and economic trends, together with hostility and straight repression, have wrought havoc with the Celtic tongues, but it would be unfair to attribute this *entirely* to English action. In Scotland, the first conscious steps against Gaelic were taken by the government at a time when the country was politically independent. Gaelic differs from the other Celtic languages. It has not been the language of the whole country since the early Middle Ages, it has long been perfectly possible to assert Scottish identity without feeling for the language. When Scotland had been hammered into a nation by the Wars of Independence, it had become a polyglot country. Admittedly, most of Bruce's army at Bannockburn was Gaelic speaking, and the language was still in general use in Galloway and Fife as well as the Highlands; but the towns had been anglicised, and the centres of power were to shift more and more to the central Lowlands during the next turbulent centuries. James IV was apparently the last King of Scots to speak Gaelic,[50] and by the reign of his great-grandson the Highlands were considered outside the mainstream of Scots society; the term 'Scottis' was used to describe the Anglian dialect of the Lowlands, Gaelic being commonly labelled 'Irish'—linguistically accurately enough but making it clear that the Gaels were regarded by the government as not really Scots at all. Scarcely touched by the Reformation, they were seen as a menace to church and state alike. The Statutes of Iona (1609) required the chiefs send their sons to school in the Lowlands where they 'may be found able sufficiently to speik, reid and wryte Englische'.[51] The Act of the Privy Council of 1616 went further:

> Forasmekle as the kingis Majestie haveing a speciall care and regaird that the trew religioun be advanceit and establisheit in all the pairtis of this kingdome, and that all his Majesties subjectis, especiallie the youth, be exercised and trayned up in civilitie, godliness, knowledge and learning, that the vulgar Inglishe toung be universallie plantit, and the Irishe language, which is one of the cheif and principall causis of the continewance of barbaritie and incivilitie amongis the inhabitantis of the Iles and Heylandis, may be abolisheit and removit; and quhairas thair is no means more powerfull to further this his Majesties princelie regaird and porpois than the establisheing of scooles in the particular parrocheis of this kingdome ... thairfore the kingis Majestie has thocht it necessary and expedient that in everie severall porroche of this kingdome where convenient means may be had for interteyning a scoole, that a scoole sall be establisheit, and a fitt persone appointit to teache the same.[52]

This was not new, but a reinforcement of earlier attempts, from 1568 onwards, to establish schools in the Highlands and the Borders. Not much came of this at the time, largely because the parish school system was not effectively established in the Highlands. But, as MacKinnon has pointed out, the Ulster Plantations (and the smaller ones in Kintyre) did separate Scottish from Irish Gaeldom: 'As the links with Ireland were broken, Gaelic Scotland was thrown upon its own resources and then drawn into the cultural system of Lowland Scotland'.[53] The attack was to be resumed intermittently. For instance, after the revolution of 1688 the rents from the bishoprics of Argyll and Dunkeld were diverted 'for the erecting of English schools for rooting out the Irish language and other pious uses'. Again, this was relatively ineffective, and ironically the seventeenth and eighteenth centuries saw a flowering of Gaelic literature. But the intention was clear enough, evidence of what one poet called *mi-rún mór nan Gall*, the great malice of the Lowlander.[54]

The onslaught was intensified during the eighteenth century. As in Ireland during Tudor times, the real body-blow was the collapse of the political base of Gaelic society (in the 1745 Jacobite rising) and the repressive legislation that followed it, pursued with vigour and brutality for the following decades. (The clans which supported the Hanoverians were no less affected than the Jacobites.) Into the vacuum stepped the Society for the Propagation of Christian Knowledge which, apart from arithmetic, taught little but English language and Presbyterian religion. It also, for a time, managed to prevent the publication of a Gaelic Bible. Dr Samuel Johnson wrote in 1765:

> There remains only their [the Highlanders'] language and their poverty. Their language is attacked on every side. Schools are erected in which only English is taught and there were lately some who thought it reasonable to refuse them a version of the Holy Scriptures, that they might have no monument of their mother tongue.[55]

Johnson's complaint had some effect; Gaelic was admitted as a medium in the SPCK schools (though not the parish schools) in the following year, coinciding with the appearance of a Gaelic New Testament. But even a partial change of heart by the SPCK came too late. In 1762 the first 'great sheep' had been introduced in Easter Ross, and by 1790 landowners were clearing the land of people to make way for sheep. The Highland Clearances had begun, and were to continue into the 1850s and beyond.[56]

Although meantime opinion had been shifting in favour of Gaelic, and more schools had been set up to teach in it, the Gaels themselves were all but removed from most of the homeland. The board schools set up under the Education (Scotland) Act of 1872 used English exclusively, and, by taking over the SPCK schools as well, ensured that the 'teaching-out' of Gaelic would continue. Children, as in Wales, were beaten for speaking the language[57] and many parents were persuaded that it was a handicap; there are many accounts of Gaels working in the Lowlands concealing their knowledge of the language lest they suffer discrimination. There was some respite: the Gaelic Society of Inverness and the Educational Institute of Scotland pressed for Gaelic in the schools during the 1870s, and the foundation of An Comunn Gàidhealach (The Highland Association) did something to provide a focus for agitation as well as encouraging cultural activities, but could do little to reverse the trend set in motion by population movements and public policy (though it is possible that it saved the language from dying out completely). In 1901, Gaelic was still spoken as the main language in the western and central Highlands as well as the Isles; by 1961, it had retreated to the Isles alone, plus a few mainland footholds. With continued emigration from these areas and the dominance of English in public affairs, it seemed only a matter of time before Gaelic went the way of Manx and Cornish;

70,000 speakers out of 5 million Scots is a weak basis for the survival of any language; especially when the great majority of those are bilingual.[58]

Of the Celtic languages, Irish alone has had strenuous governmental support in more recent times.[59] Although the Revival movement had begun earlier, it was only in 1922 that the Free State government made Irish compulsory in their national (i.e. primary) schools. This was extended to the secondary sector in 1928-9 by making it compulsory in the Leaving Certificate. It became a requirement for all entrants to the civil service, and has been assiduously fostered in the press, radio, television, and minor things like signposts. At one level, the policy has had some success; about 20 per cent of the population have some command of the language, it is still widely studied at a serious level, and elements of it have entered into English, possibly giving it some symbolic validity in public affairs. But its aim to restore Irish as the customary speech of the people is generally accepted, even by its advocates, to have failed. Even before the turn of the century, 99 per cent of the people *could* speak English, and 85 per cent could not speak Irish. The work of the Gaelic League—language classes, propaganda, summer schools in the Irish-speaking areas—'had neither saved Irish in the Gaeltacht nor established it to any considerable extent in the 'Galltacht' in the first twenty-five years of its existence. As Brian Ó Cuív has observed:

> The restoration of Irish requires firstly that the language be learned and secondly that it be used as a normal means of communication. The first can hardly be achieved without good teaching, aided by text-books, dictionaries, grammars and so on that are ancillary to learning a language. For the second an act of will is necessary in addition to an adequate knowledge on the part of its users.[60]

The first is in principle solvable, though it is widely agreed that one reason for the failure of the language policy has been a generally low level of teaching. Even now, the pass standards for Irish in the Leaving Certificate are much lower than for any other subject (only about 1 per cent fail).[61] There is also some evidence, presented by John Macnamara[62] in a book that caused a storm of controversy in the Republic, that attainment in other subjects suffers from time given to Irish, particularly when it is used as a teaching medium for children whose first language is English. These defects are not seriously denied; whether they are curable within a policy favouring Irish is less clear. It is only fair to mention that some of the criticism of Macnamara's findings is sober and analytical, and makes a less gloomy view possible; apart from detailed criticisms of testing procedures there is the more fundamental objection that he did not allow for *other* possible factors behind the relatively low scores of the Irish pupils, such as the time given to religious teaching. This, of course, would have been at least as controversial.

Although the vast majority now live in English-speaking areas, the remaining areas where Irish is the normal language have an important bearing on the whole policy, for it is here that forces beyond government control are most obvious. As Ó Cuív puts it:

> It has always been accepted that the Gaeltacht is essential. It is not only the sole surviving body of people among whom Irish has never ceased to be the traditional language, but it is also the source from which learners can acquire ability to speak Irish naturally. (But) the Commission on the Restoration of the Irish Language has pointed to the possibility of the Gaeltacht being wiped out in a single generation should a decrease comparable to that since 1926 occur within the next thirty years. The Commission has also said that if the Gaeltacht were allowed to disappear, the will to preserve and spread the Irish language would probably vanish with it. Hence it follows that the struggle for Irish must be won before the end of this century if we are to preserve our national integrity.[63]

But the Gaeltacht continues to dwindle. In 1956 it was redefined to cover places where most of the population spoke Irish, and then contained 85,700 people; in 1961 the number was down to 79,323, and a decade later to 70,568. The reason was basically economic: 'Despite government grants, the younger generation do not wish to be restricted by their language to an extremely limited range of jobs or locations.'[64] It could be added that many people from Gaeltacht have complained at being unable to use Irish in Dublin, for all its official standing. The Gaeltacht, like its Scottish counterpart, would seem a weak base for the recovery of the language.

It is in this context that many see compulsion as the only hope. Ó Cuív, while fully aware of the dangers says, 'Today we have no choice. The only hope for the survival of Irish is to have it taught generally in our schools.'[65] Some have gone so far as to insist that the eventual aim must be the *replacement* of English by Irish, but although some have taken up the slogan *Bás don Bhéarla* (Death to English), this is a view overwhelmingly rejected by government and public opinion alike: 'It is not the Government's intention that English should be discarded, but rather that the use of Irish should be progressively extended.'[66]

But even compulsory bilingualism has come under heavy attack in recent years. The Language Freedom Movement spoke for a great many Irish in agitating against compulsion.[67] Following the 1973 general election, the new Fine Gael-Labour coalition decided to drop required

Irish in the schools, a move not contested by the Fianna Fáil party, hitherto the strongest advocate of compulsion. This was not a move against the language; Richard Burke, the new Minister of Education, himself a fluent Irish speaker, admitted that compulsion led to mere 'tokenism', not effective revival, and that it had caused resentment, harming the language rather than helping it.[68] Voluntarism (combined with support, of course) is being tried instead.

It might just possibly work. There have been signs—little more than straws in the wind, but something—that genuine interest is on the increase. There has been a growth of self-sponsored adult classes, reported to be flourishing even in the working-class housing estate of Ballymun.[69] Republican ideology may play a part in this, though learning a rather difficult language is not to be dismissed as a mere gesture. Nor is support for Irish exclusively Republican or Catholic. One Orange Lodge in Belfast has fostered the language and used it on its banners to make the point that Irish is not the property of the Catholic church, and a well-known Protestant grammar school in Belfast has been experiencing something of a revival.[70] These are exceptional cases; Orange Lodges are much more inclined to stress their Britishness than their Irishness, and Northern Protestant schools rarely have anything to do with Irish at all—this is almost exclusive to the Northern Irish universities and the Catholic schools (where the absence of official commitment means that the same standards are applied to Irish as to everything else, thus producing a markedly greater competence than one usually finds in the schools of the Republic, particularly in oral work).

A report conducted in 1975 for the Irish government on public attitudes to the languages underlines both the problems and the possibilities. Most people want Irish to be spoken, but few speak it themselves or are willing to learn it. (Only 6 per cent are given as *fluent* speakers, much fewer than the more generous estimates of the 1971 census). As Dr Joshua Fishman of New York, consultant to the project, told a reporter, 'The vast bulk of the population are quite content to see Irish in its current fringe, symbolic role ... People don't want to see it die but they don't want to go through any sharp pain in connection with it. You can't have a painless revival of a language.'

This is neither surprising nor encouraging. What does give some hope is the finding about the attitudes of different age-groups. Contrary to the widespread expectation that Irish is most highly regarded by the elderly and conservative, the survey finds that the 17-22 age-group, stimulated in part by the rise of an Irish language folksong revival, is the most committed. This does not diminish the effect of depopulation in the Gaeltacht, but it suggests that Irish may after all have a role to play that compulsion has, on the whole, failed to provide.

Revival in Wales has not had the same strenuous backing, though in view of the Irish experience many feel that this is no bad thing for the language. But it does have a much stronger base, and it is more identifiable with the nation as a whole than either of the main Goidelic tongues; the slogan *Cenedl heb iaith, cenedl heb galon* (A country without a language is a country without a heart) arguably carries more conviction than the equivalent elsewhere. It could also be argued that the use of Welsh on radio and television is more effective than Gaelic of either variety. It gets a more generous time allocation than Scottish Gaelic, and some Irish commentators have made a point that it has the advantage of using a form of language widely understood and alive in a way that the 'Irish Newspeak' of RTE is not.[71] Against the signpost-demolitions of the Welsh Language Society, protesting against the preference given to English, can be set the quieter work of Urdd Gobaith Cymru, the Welsh youth movement, which has 50,000 members, runs a national youth Eisteddfod, publishes magazines and brings young people from different parts of Wales together in holiday camps and similar activities.

More significant is the development of Welsh-language and bilingual schools.[72] The first private Welsh primary school was opened in 1939 at Aberystwyth, local authorities following suit in 1947. Bilingual secondary schools, where most subjects are taught in Welsh but some in English, have been slower to develop, but th follow logically from the Welsh primary schools. Interestingly, they been set up in mainly English-speaking areas, to the annoyance of many English-speaking immigrants, and have a good reputation for academic standards and modern methods, thus disposing of fears that the use of the language in formal education need be connected with backwardness. Ironically, such developments are less readily accepted in rural Welsh-speaking areas; the very remoteness and conservatism, which kept them Welsh speaking while other areas were anglicised, now makes them suspicious of attempts to use the language scholastically. The growth of support in the English-speaking areas, secure enough to reject the notion that Welsh need be the badge of backwardness, may be the best hope for the survival and revival of the language in a modern Wales.

It is worth stressing, too, that central government policy, once so hostile, has moved through tentative tolerance to positive support. The Gittins Committee, though finding a third of the parents of primary school children indifferent (not hostile) on the language issue, recommended a fully bilingual education throughout Wales. This was accepted by the Secretary of State for Education and Science, who was then still responsible for schools in Wales, in the circular of 1969. This 'declaration of intent' was accompanied by some practical measures, such as making extra teachers available, approving more Welsh schools, and encouraging experimental bilingual schools in mainly English-speaking areas which could 'serve as growth points for bilingual education'. There are difficulties and dangers. The existence of a Welsh-speaking professional middle class has played an important part in the survival of the language so far, but it is not an unmixed blessing; Welsh speakers in anglophone towns tend to be middle class, and this can give rise to tensions in what is intended to be a comprehensive system. Further, in some English-speaking enclaves in predominantly Welsh counties (Bangor, for example) the authorities have been accused of pushing Welsh to the exclusion of any other educational consideration. Complaints about the 'Taffia' apart, there is some evidence that over-strenuous fostering of the language before all else is producing some of the resentment that caused so much trouble in Ireland, and could be similarly counter-productive. Whether these dangers can be averted remains to be seen. The number of Welsh speakers was still falling at the last census, and although there are signs of a revival they have yet to be quantified. With these reservations it can be hazarded that Welsh, having declined less and been persecuted less, has a better chance than its Celtic cousins.

In Scotland, the situation is more complicated. Here again official repression has been replaced by encouragement, if rather lukewarmly. As in Ireland, the Gáidhealtachd accounts for a tiny fraction of the population, subject to the same pressures; but unlike Ireland, Scotland as a whole has no particular commitment to Gaelic. But there may be a change in public attitudes. The 1961 census returned some 80,000 as Gaelic speakers, and it was expected that the 1974 census would show a further decline of around 10,000; instead, there was an increase of about 8,000. The first reaction was that the computer must have been wrong; the results certainly seemed odd in view of the continuing decline of the Gáidhealtachd.[73] What had not been expected was the revival of interest, and a rise in numbers learning the language, even in the Lowlands; and there has been some reawakening in the Gáidhealtachd itself. Skye, for example, is marginal; most of the Isle is Gaelic-speaking, but in Portree, the main town, most are monoglot in English. The High School primary department uses English as the teaching medium, but gives the children *blasad Gáidhlig* (a taste of Gaelic). At the beginning of secondary school, pupils can choose between French and Gaelic, and in 1974, for the first time, most chose Gaelic. Not all were native speakers; there are separate classes for the 'learners' paper in the Scottish Certificate of Education. Nor did all the 'speakers' choose Gaelic—with two languages already they had the chance of learning a third, and many took it.[74] Developments like this, and the new bilingual policy of Comhairle nan Eilean, may indicate a recovery in native areas.

But it is the growth of interest in the Lowlands that is potentially more encouraging, not because the numbers are as yet significant but because it illustrates a possibly important trend.[75] One must not exaggerate their importance, but enrolment in evening classes and, more important, persistence in study, is on the increase in unlikely places like Glasgow, Edinburgh and Stirling. Some Lowland secondary schools offer Gaelic, and report an increase in the number of pupils taking it, either as a separate subject or as part of a course in Scottish studies. Many of the people concerned are of Highland origin, and follow a pattern observed by Fishman among the grandchildren of immigrants in the United States. But many are Lowlanders, or even English who have settled in Scotland and come to identify with the country.

It may be doubted how far these new learners become really proficient. Some become enthusiasts and attain a fair fluency. There are no hard data on this, but personal impression suggests that a great many fall well below this standard. They can hardly be said to be *using* the language except for symbolic purposes. But even this is an enormous change from the past two centuries, a complete reversal of the attitudes which led Gaels to be ashamed of their language. There is even a tendency to use a minimal knowledge of Gaelic as a badge of Scottishness. This is familiar enough in Ireland and Wales, but in Scotland it is new. This, by itself, is hardly likely to arrest its decline, but by changing attitudes towards the language it makes its survival marginally more likely.

Apart from the economic, political and demographic trends already discussed, there are several factors working against a major revival of the Celtic languages. The most obvious is the strong position of English as a major international language. Hardly anyone suggests that English should be replaced; it is too obviously useful for that.

Again, one hardly even *needs* to use the languages as one may have to use foreign tongues, the most effective way of learning beyond the elementary stage. Also, the Celtic languages are not easy. This is not necessarily fatal, but many feel that the effort could be more usefully spent on German, Russian or Arabic.

There are some cases elsewhere of successful language-revival movements that have given heart to the supporters of the Celtic tongues. The revival of Finnish in the nineteenth century, its establishment as an official and literary language, complete with a national epic, *Kalevala*, is often cited. So is the development of 'Nynorsk' (New Norwegian) as a means of throwing off dependence on Danish. In modern times, we have witnessed the revival of Hebrew, apparently against all the odds, as 'the customary and habitual language'.

There is some encouragement in these cases, though less than some would urge. Finnish was certainly a despised peasant language that the educated and urban population were rejecting in favour of Swedish. It is also true that national self-assertion, particularly on the part of intellectuals, gave it prestige in its own homeland and made it the touchstone of national identity. It was, however, much more widely spoken than even Welsh was at the turn of the century, and thus had a stronger base. Nynorsk is a somewhat different case, having been constructed deliberately out of the various country dialects which were felt to be more authentically Norwegian than the Dano-Norwegian known as *riksmål* (court speech). Actually, there is a good deal of confusion in Norwegian language, too complex to be gone into here; but it would be rash to assert that Nynorsk has really replaced *riksmål* in educated usage, or that it is always distinguishable from regional forms. (It is said that every Norwegian can speak at least three languages, of which at least two are Norwegian.) The issue generates a great deal of heat; but fortunately all forms are close enough to be mutually comprehensible.

Hebrew is a special case. It has been argued that what enabled it to re-establish itself was its espousal by an admired elite, who were emulated by the Israeli population to the extent of either learning it themselves or at least having their children learn it. This analysis gives great comfort to Celtic revivalists, who point out that just such considerations helped English to oust Welsh and Gaelic, and could presumably work the other way. There is a good deal in this, but there is a practical factor too. The new State of Israel was populated by Jews from all over the world, speaking Yiddish, Ladino, German, Russian, Romanian, Arabic, English and a host of other languages. Hebrew was not only the language of Jewish religion and cultural identity; it was the only possible common medium available. It thus met a practical as well as a cultural need, and survived the disapproval of the ultra-orthodox. None of the Celtic languages is in this position, or likely to be. The other language revivals may, therefore, give some encouragement to Welsh and Gaelic, but it would be unwise to read *too* much into them.

It is sometimes asserted that the Celtic languages may be all very well for rural life or high poetry, but will hardly do for a world of science and international communications. What, it is asked, is the Gaelic for television or the Welsh for bicycle? The answers — *telebhisean* and *beisicl* — are easily taken as evidence that the Celtic languages are unable to cope with modern life without English borrowings.

This is hardly a serious argument. What, after all, are the *English* words for bicycle and television? English has in its day borrowed extensively from French, Latin, Greek and less copiously from other sources, an extremely common linguistic device. There are some purists who insist on seeking native roots and produce compounds that no one understands, but on the whole the process of taking words as needed goes on naturally enough. There are special difficulties in some areas—Gaelic Scotland for example—where words, even whole phrases, are taken from English without being adapted to the borrowing language. This can have a distorting effect. MacKinnon quotes a telling example from a cartoon in the Gaelic magazine *Gairm*, where the chiarman of a deadlocked committee is shown as saying: 'Tha na h-*opinions* an so cho bheil agus cu *varied* e *impossible clear decision* a dheanamh anns a' chuis.'[76] One hardly needs to know any Gaelic to get the gist, but a monoglot Gael might be totally at a loss. But this is not an intrinsic quality of the language; it is not long since educated English speakers were using French and Latin in much the same way.

There may be some force in the claims of other languages on the learner's time, especially when international contacts are becoming more important. But earlier anti-Celtic policies seemed to be based on the assumption that bilingualism was impossible, which modern experience does not bear out. Given the opportunity and motivation, most people are better at learning languages than used to be thought possible. Further, people learn languages for different purposes. If a language, however few its speakers, is a part of the life of a community, particularly if it is a developing entity and not a relic, then it has a function that need not interfere with the learning of English and foreign languages as well. It may even help by encouraging a sensitivity to language in general.

More positively, one can argue that there is a value in having a language of one's own, part of one's identity, and not necessarily inimical to other languages or to a wider identity—all of us can, and do, identify at different levels. There is the conservationist argument, weak when it seems tied up with mere conservatism, stronger when expressed as a reluctance to see something unique and often rich die through indifference and neglect. But the more articulate spokesmen for the minority languages are not interested in mere preservation, but want to see them develop in their changing societies. To argue that reviving these languages is retrogressive is to assume that progress must mean assimilation to English ways. It is easy to see why this seemed inevitable from the seventeenth to nineteenth centuries, but it is an assumption that more people, taking an international as well as a national view, are coming to reject.

The prospect for the survival and development of the minority languages in education and public affairs is still doubtful; especially in the case of Irish and Scots Gaelic, it is possible that the process has already gone too far. The figures which seem to show a recovery are incomplete and open to question. It does seem, though, that attitudes have changed, particularly among the young. As Dr Fishman has pointed out in the Irish case, there is a gap between favouring the survival of a language and actually doing something about it, such as learning or speaking it; but at least the climate of opinion is more propitious for the Celtic languages than it has been for a long time. This is true even among many who do not themselves know the languages, possibly in growing awareness of the need to come to terms with cultural pluralism at home or abroad.

NOTES AND REFERENCES

1 For a lively account of Border turbulence, see George MacDonald Fraser, *The Steel Bonnets* (London, Pan, 1972).
2 T. C. Smout, *A History of the Scottish People, 1560-1830* (London, Fontana, 1972), pp. 240 *ff.* (Useful generally on Scottish social history, as well as for the particular references given here.)
3 ibid., pp. 81 *ff.*
4 Menneth MacKinnon, *The Lion's Tongue* (Inverness, Club Leabhar, 1974), pp. 54 *ff.*
5 See Steven Rae, 'Gaelic and Comhairle nan Eilan', *New Edinburgh Review*, no. 33, pp. 4-10.
6 Discussions with R. A. B. Barnes, Director of Education for Shetland, Lerwick, September 1975.
7 Discussions with Alex Bain, Director of Education for Orkney, Kirkwall, September 1975.
8 A common Orkney saying, with some basis in fact.
9 John McGrath, in *The Cheviot, the Stag and the Black, Black Oil* makes effective dramatic use of the warning, 'The West is next in line'. It should be pointed out that apprehension of destruction of unique cultures is found among both radicals and traditionalists.
10 See, e.g. Ned Thomas, 'Education in Wales', in R. E. Bell, G. Fowler and K. Little (eds), *Education in Great Britain and Ireland* (London, Routledge & Kegan Paul, 1973), pp. 14-19 and J. R. Webster, 'Curriculum development in Wales', in ibid., pp. 85-7; G. Morgan, *The Dragon's Tongue* (Caerdydd, Triskel Press 1966), *passim*; Tony Heath, 'Wales: a nation gives tongue', *New Society*, 20 November 1975, pp. 418-19.
11 MacKinnon, op. cit. See also H. M. Chadwick, *Early Scotland* (Cambridge, CUP, 1949); G. Menzies (ed.), *Who Are the Scots?* (London, BBC, 1971); K. H. Jackson, *Language and History in Early Britain* (Edinburgh, Edinburgh University Press, 1953); and T. C. Smout, op. cit.
12 Cavan, Donegal and Monaghan. Donegal's position makes even the term 'Northern Ireland' geographically dubious.
13 Douglas Hyde and Erskine Childers.
14 For an unusually *public* repudiation of the traditional policy on reunification, see Conor Cruise O'Brien, *States of Ireland* (London, Hutchinson, 1972).
15 Liam de Paor, *Divided Ulster* (Harmondsworth, Penguin, 1970).
16 A good example is to be found in the bewilderment of British Conservatives at the views expressed by their erstwhile political allies, the Ulster Unionists, in Belfast and Westminster in recent years.
17 Margaret Sutherland, 'Education in Northern Ireland', in Bell, Fowler and Little, op. cit., pp. 19-26.
18 Margot Cameron-Jones and Dollin Kelly, 'Education in the Isle of Man', in Bell, Fowler and Little, op. cit., pp. 26-31.
19 Thomas, loc. cit., and MacKinnon, loc. cit.
20 A. W. Moore, *A History of the Isle of Man* (London, Unwin, 1900); cit. Cameron-Jones and Kelly, loc. cit., p. 28.

21 ibid., pp. 27-9.
22 Dora M. Pickering, 'Education in the Channel Islands', in Bell, Fowler and Little, op. cit., pp. 31-8.
23 ibid., p. 34.
24 J. D. McClure (ed.), *The Scots Language in Education* (Aberdeen, Aberdeen College of Education and Association of Scottish Literary Studies, 1974).
25 Some Scots writers use apostrophes to show where a letter would be missing if the words were English—e.g. awa', gi'e, lo'e, wa', etc. This was not the practice in earlier written Scots, but caught on because of the assumption that the English spelling had to be the 'norm'. So it was—for English.
26 Notably Hugh MacDiarmid, whose international reputation is much greater than his UK reputation.
27 John T. Low, 'The Scots language in the contemporary situation', in McClure, op. cit., pp. 17-27. 'Scots tended to be associated with slang, or slovenly language or socially unacceptable speech forms.' This applies to vocabulary and grammatical forms rather than pronunciation; on the whole, Scots pronunciation remained acceptable if not too obviously regional. There are exceptions; attempts by certain groups in Glasgow and Edinburgh at 'eliminating the internal "R" sounds and lifting or diphthongising the vowels' have given rise to the extraordinary phonetic hibrids known (after long-established middle-class districts) as 'Kelvinsaide' and 'Moaningsaide' (i.e. Kelvinside and Morningside) respectively. (For non-Scots readers, Maggie Smith's performance as Jean Brodie provides a brilliant illustration of the latter.) Generally, however, what most teachers encourage, and speak themselves, is 'standard' English with a definitely Scots vowel-pattern.
28 Knox was accused in his time of 'knapping soudron' (speaking southern). He regularly wrote 'churche' for 'kirk'.
29 Donald J. Withrington, 'Scots in education: a historical retrospect', in McClure, op. cit., pp. 9-16. One of the present authors has had a mild experience of the same thing, having had 'outwith' replaced by 'outside' (not *quite* the same) by a publisher's editor.
30 For fuller treatment of the early history of the Celtic languages, see David Greene, 'The Celtic languages', in Joseph Raftery (ed.), *The Celts* (Dublin, Mercier, 1964), pp. 9-22; Myles Dillon and Nora Chadwick, *The Celtic Realms* (London, Cardinal, 1973) pp. 257-97.
31 The Picts of northern Scotland present something of a problem, owing to the scarcity of written material. What kind of Celtic language they spoke, and whether it was Celtic at all, is a matter of controversy. See Isabel Henderson, 'The problem of the Picts', in G. Menzies, op. cit., pp. 51-65.
32 'P. Celtic' and 'Q Celtic' are terms sometimes used to differentiate the two main Celtic language groups, otherwise Brythonic and Goidelic respectively; they refer to one of the more obvious sound-changes, whereby Goidelic Q (modern C) corresponds to Brythonic P, as in the pairs; Gaelic *ceann*, Welsh *pen* (head); Irish *ceithair*, Welsh *pedwar* (four), etc. Some Celticists have recently questioned the usefulness of this classification as a historical indication of language change, however.

33 Cornish died out as a spoken language in the eighteenth century, but has been revived in modern times by enthusiasts. A. S. D. Smith (Corradar), Rev. E. G. Retallack Hooper (Talek), *The Story of the Cornish Language* (Camborne, An Lef Kernewek, 1969).
34 The Manx word for the language is *Gaelck*.
35 A great many Irish names of Norman origin, like Burke and Fitzgerald, date from this period. A similar process in Scotland, though the penetration was peaceful there, has produced such clan names as Grant and Fraser, as well as well-known Lowland names, notably Bruce.
36 An tAthair Tomás ó Fiaich, 'The language and political history', in Brian Ó Cuív, (ed.), *A View of the Irish Language* (Dublin, Stationery Office, 1969), p. 102.
37 ibid., p. 104.
38 ibid.
39 Brian Ó Cuív, 'Irish in the Modern World', in Ó Cuív, op. cit., p. 123.
40 For a clear and detailed exposition of population trends, see Ruth Dudley Edwards, *An Atlas of Irish History* (London, Methuen, 1973), Section XI, pp. 209-29.
41 Ó Cuív, loc. cit.
42 The figures for competence in Irish vary from 20 to 27 per cent, but since the criteria are not precise it is hard to be sure what to make of them. The actual range of competence among non-native Irish speakers varies greatly, but the proportion of the population who can be said to have a 'tolerable fluency' is probably nearer the 20 per cent mark, perhaps less.
43 See Thomas, loc. cit.
44 Thomas, loc. cit., p. 14-15.
45 ibid., p. 16.
46 MacKinnon, op. cit., p. 55.
47 Report of the National Schools Society, 1845; cit. Thomas, loc. cit., p. 15.
48 ibid., p. 18.
49 Heath, loc. cit., and Thomas, loc. cit.
50 Don Pedro de Ayala, Spanish Ambassador, reported in 1498 that James IV 'speaks the following languages: Latin, very well; French, German, Flemish, Italian and Spanish.... The king speaks, besides, the language of the savages who live in some parts of Scotland and on the Islands'. W. C. Drikinson, G. Donaldson and I. Milne (eds), *A Source Book of Scottish History, Vol. II, 1424 to 1567* (Edinburgh, Nelson, 1963), p. 3.
51 MacKinnon, op. cit., pp. 34-55.
52 ibid., pp. 35-6.
53 ibid., p. 37.
54 Alasdair mac Mhaighistir Alasdair (Alasdair MacDonald), an eighteenth-century bard, put his view of the position of Gaelic thus:

Mhair i fós
Is cha téid a gloir air chall
Dh'aindeoin gó
Is mioruin mhóir nan Gall.

(It continues yet and its glory shall not become lost despite the vilification and the great malice of the Lowlanders.) Cit. MacKinnon, op. cit., p. 30.

55 Letter from Johnson, 1766; cit. MacKinnon, op. cit., p. 41.
56 John Prebble, *The Highland Clearances* (Harmondsworth, Penguin, 1972).
57 One such was the father of one of the present authors, in Lochaber at the turn of the century. The teacher was a Highlander also.
58 MacKinnon, op. cit.
59 Tomás Ó hAilin, 'Irish revival movements', in Ó Cuív, op. cit., pp. 91-100.
60 Ó Cuív, loc. cit., p. 129.
61 John Horgan, 'Education in the Republic of Ireland', in Bell, Fowler and Little, op. cit., pp. 35-42. Also report in the *Irish Times*, 13 April 1972.
62 John Macnamara, *Bilingualism and Primary Education* (Edinburgh, Edinburgh University Press, 1966).
63 Ó Cuív, loc. cit. See also Caoimhin Ó Danachair, 'The Gaeltacht', in Ó Cuív, op. cit., pp. 112-21.
64 Dudley Edwards, op. cit.
65 Ó Cuív, loc. cit., p. 130.
66 Ó Cuív, loc. cit., p. 131.
67 e.g. reports in the *Irish Times* 9 June 1971 and 10 October 1972.
68 Discussions with Richard Burke, T. D., Minister for Education, Dublin, February 1975.
69 'Setting up a Gaeltacht in Ballymun', *Irish Times*, 16 June 1972.
70 'Teaching Irish in the North', *Irish Times*, 7 January 1971.
71 Anthony Weir, 'Irish Newspeak', in Bell, Fowler and Little, op. cit., pp. 90-1. (RTE = Radio Telefis Eireann.)
72 Thomas, loc. cit.
73 MacKinnon, op. cit.
74 Discussions with headmaster and head of Gaelic department, Portree High School, Isle of Skye, 1974.
75 Iain Mac Cuinn and Iain Mac Aonguis, 'Gaidhlig air Gallachd Alba', *The Weekend Scotsman*, 6 December 1975, p. 7.
76 MacKinnon, op. cit. Rough translation, if necessary: 'The opinions here are so many and varied it is impossible to take a clear decision on the matter.' Needless to say, Gaelic does have words for those given here in English.

Chapter 6

The Professionals

One of the most important but one of the least emphasised developments in education during the past hundred years has been the growing tendency towards specialisation among professional educators. In the mid-ninteenth century, it was assumed that any figure who had to do with education would normally be able to participate in far more sectors and play far more roles than would be the case nowadays. The secondary public schools in England shared a career structure with the Church of England and with the colleges of Oxford and Cambridge. Thomas Arnold was able to combine the post of headmaster of Rugby with that of a professor of history at Oxford, as well as with an active career as an author and public leader in religious and political circles.[1] Lenin's father was able to combine his role as a regional administrator of education with that of a devoted classroom teacher who specialised in helping individual children who were in difficulties.[2] The Educational Institute of Scotland, the most long-established of the teachers' associations within the British Isles, was able in its early years to gather into its fold not merely primary and secondary teachers, but also professors in the universities and technical teachers of all kinds.

By 1970 however, all this was changed. In Ireland, Wales and England as much as in Scotland, a growing sense of professionality had imposed a new rigidity on the system. A primary teacher tended to be a primary teacher for life, a secondary teacher a secondary teacher for life and if one wished to teach 'education' in a university not only did this involve a considerable degree of specialisation in the study of one's subject matter, it also usually meant the renouncing of any career within the secondary sector or within administration and politics. In Scotland, for example, the common habit of appointing secondary teachers to the headships of primary schools came to be more and more frowned upon by teachers' representatives as an infringement of primary teacher 'professionalism' as if teaching were no longer a single profession.

There was a growing confusion between 'areas of responsibility' or 'career structures' on the one hand and 'professional life' on the other. Doctors, architects and lawyers could move in and out of university teaching with comparative ease and, so far as time allowed the picking up of new expertise, could move from one sector of their profession to another without seeming anti-professional in the eyes of their organisations; not so with educationalists. In particular, just as parents were excluded by many teachers from the school's decision-making process, so teachers were kept at arm's length by their educationalist colleagues, the administrators. Indeed, these two groups of professionals usually faced each other across that fence in the style of employers and employees, and only rarely saw each other as fellow labourers engaged in the pursuit of educational aims.

It was, of course, true that many of the administrators were initially recruited from among the ranks of the teachers, but rarely if ever did they return to those ranks in later stages of their career except, perhaps, to become headteachers; and headteachers themselves were, as a group, coming to be segregated more and more from the remainder of the same teaching profession. All these groups, class-teachers, administrators, headteachers happily joined in the same rhetoric of 'partnership' at their annual conference or in the newspapers, but often seemed in their heart of hearts to regard themselves, if not as enemies, at least as rivals in a struggle for influence and resources. Thus, when the Schools Council was established in England and Wales in the early 1960s in order to encourage curriculum development and to oversee the organisation of public examinations, there was a great insistence from the organisations representing the mass of classroom teachers that their fellow professionals from the administrative service should always be outnumbered on the Council's committees by 'serving teachers' who were felt to be closer to and more knowledgeable about the educational task than those who held the purse strings.

This newly stratified and sectorised educational profession, or, as one should perhaps more accurately call it, professional world, with all its inner tensions and demarcation disputes, has been one of the most potent of influences in imposing a greater degree of uniformity upon education within the islands as a whole, for nothing produces uniformity more readily than the fear of being beaten in a race, of being done down in comparison with one's neighbours. In Ireland, particularly in the Republic, such a political process has proceeded less quickly, for, as we have seen, the influence of the religious orders, forming a separate professional and career structure in themselves, has tended to confuse the situation so far as professionalisation is concerned.[3] Moreover, in the Republic of Ireland, as no general local education authorities have been established, this has tended to discourage the development of a large administrative profession outside the central civil service. But elsewhere in the British Isles many educational professions now exist side by side[4] and have developed career structures that tend more and more to ignore national boundaries.

This is particularly true of the educational academics and administrators, who move freely between England, Scotland and Wales with no appreciable difficulty. It is true that movement is more difficult for primary and secondary teachers, particularly where Scotland is concerned, but even in these sectors migration is by no means impossible and has grown considerably in recent years. Although it is still far from common for English students to begin their post-secondary studies in Scottish colleges of education, many English students are found in Scottish universities,[5] and often move on to a local college for their postgraduate teacher training.

The other most significant development since the Second World War has been the growing assertiveness of the teachers themselves in relation to government and to their employers who, in the case of the United Kingdom, are usually the local education authorities. Teachers, often in the face of opposition from politicians and administrators, have successfully demanded more and more places, not only on the education committees of their authorities, but also on the various advisory bodies which service central and local government. In England and Wales, their greatest achievement has been perhaps the gaining of hegemony on the Schools Council for Curriculum and Examinations, while in Scotland their professional achievement has perhaps been even greater with the establishment of the General Teaching Council, which also has a built-in teacher majority and while it is true that doubt has been cast on the effectiveness of both bodies, the acceptance of the principle of teacher control marks a considerable political breakthrough for the school-based professionals. It also involves a considerable curbing of the powers of the administrative professionals and of the elected representatives of the population as a whole.

Moreover this movement continues. There is a growing agitation in Scotland for greater teacher representation on curriculum bodies there and for the establishment of a GTC, not only in England but also in the Irish Republic where considerable alterations have been made in recent years to the governing bodies of its educational institutions, partly in order to allow a greater direct representation for teacher opinion.

On the other hand, much of this teacher control can remain a mere figment of the fevered imagination of the trade union official. Representation does not necessarily lead to power. It assumes, for example, a homogeneity of teacher opinion which is rarely obtainable and far too often teacher representatives are too divided among themselves to have any distinctive influence on political developments. Single representatives from the various fragmented sectors of the teaching profession are unlikely to be able to represent efficiently the views and feelings of all their fellow professionals throughout the country. On some so-called representative bodies for the United Kingdom one place may, for example, have been allocated to teachers of physical education and the single member admitted under that head may be a Welsh female primary teacher. It is clearly impossible for her to represent not only all her Welsh colleagues but also her English, Scottish and Northern Irish colleagues, just as it is also clearly impossible for her to represent adequately the views of secondary (or male) teachers of physical education. When such difficulties are recognised and the membership increased accordingly, then the committee all too soon becomes unwieldy and too easily allows its power to pass back into the hands of the full-time officials who service such committees and who largely ignore their findings unless these are backed up by a considerable head of political steam.

For similar reasons, it is in fact the professional administrators in the education world rather than the teachers who have moved farthest towards gaining power and influence over the elected representatives who pay the educational bills. Yet even their professional sector is fragmented; and there is a clear division of career structure between the national civil servants and inspectors employed in the central government departments on the one hand and the officials, inspectors and advisers employed by the local education authority on the other, while at both central and local level there is a further division between the pure administrators (often members of a general, administrative rather than purely educational profession) and the inspectorate, the psychologists, the social workers or the advisers (many of them ex-teachers) on the other; and while all these groups of educationalists do in the main work happily together, pressures can sometimes produce clashes between them far greater than the clashes between authority and teachers or between teachers and parents.

In the past the power of the local administrators has tended to vary, for until the changes in local administration structure during the 1970s the size of local education authorities could itself vary enormously. Some of the areas controlled by local education authorities, like that of the Inner London Education Authority, had a population greater than that of either of the Irish states, or indeed of Wales. On the other hand, some Scottish authorities, like Shetland or Kirkcudbright, had populations of less than 20,000. Yet, theoretically, the professionals in charge of the education services in each of these areas were equal in rank and professional status. Certainly they were equal in their legal autonomy, though of course the range of resources available to them must have acted as a hidden mediator of their actual authority.

Even with the changes of the 1970s, whose primary intention was to even out just such anomalies, they have not disappeared altogether. In Scotland the head of the education service in the Strathclyde region finds himself providing services for a population of 2½ million, while his equally autonomous colleague in the Dumfries and Galloway region to the south is responsible for a population of little over 100,000, while in the so-called Island authorities of Orkney, Shetland and the Western Isles, equally autonomous so far as education is concerned, the populations are considerably smaller.

In England and Wales, and Northern Ireland, some of these extreme differences have now disappeared. No English authority is now as small as Dumfries and Galloway, while none (except Inner London) is anywhere near the size of Strathclyde. But even where the authorities *are* similar in size, the actual power exercised by the professional administration may vary considerably, depending not merely on their own personalities and political skills but also on the personalities of their political masters, and on the procedures already established within an authority. There is, for example, considerable variation in the powers of the chief education officer now that most local authorities have adopted 'corporate planning' procedures covering education along with other departments. Some of the new chief executives of these 'corporate planning' authorities still leave a great deal to the initiative of the chief education officer, but some have stripped him of his major decision-making powers, especially where physical planning is concerned. For, as we have already noted, one of the major characteristics of British educational legislation has been its lack of precision over devolution of powers, particularly in defining the relative roles of the various parties involved in its administration. Until the legislation of 1976, authorities in England had to provide secondary education for all but were free to organise that secondary education on comprehensive or selective lines, as they thought fit. The only sanctions available to central government in this matter, as in as many others, were financial rather than statutory and even financial sanctions were rarely used for political purposes before the 1970s.

On the other hand, even the more specific 1944 rules placing responsibility for the curriculum in the hands of local education authorities or, by delegation, in the hands of the governors or managers of English and Welsh schools, have largely been ignored in the face of the rhetoric and challenge of the teacher organisations, who quite spuriously claim an unbroken 'tradition' of teacher autonomy in such matters and have succeeded in creating a public assumption that matters of curriculum are really a matter for headteachers who should tolerate no 'lay' interference in their arrangements. An experienced member of the board of governors of a large comprehensive school in Cheshire for example, appearing on television in 1975, denied all knowledge of the legal rights that he and his colleagues undoubtedly had to control the curriculum within the school of which they had charge.[6] Thus the delegated autonomy of the local education authority was being restricted by the unwritten laws of professional assertion quite as much as by a central fiat.

But this assertion of teacher autonomy *vis-à-vis* the local authority is very much the exception. Normally most teachers, and especially most headteachers, feel themselves in a very real sense to be at the mercy, not so much of their education committees, as of those committees' permanent administrators and advisers. Even where such officials or such committees have no legal or moral powers to interfere in a school's affairs they can always wield the hidden sanctions bestowed on them by their position as controllers of patronage and finance within an authority. The headmaster of a small rural school looking for better things is hardly likely to clash too readily with those who alone can promote his interests at the education offices. Thus the power wielded by local officials and advisers has grown considerably in a situation where financial and administrative questions have become more complex than in previous decades. Local education officials, like the central officials who bestow on them more and more autonomy (with strict financial limits!) have developed a professional mystique far stronger than that of the teachers themselves, whose attempts to act collectively are more obviously tainted with the simple and honourable self-seeking of trade unionism than are the stealthier but equally effective moves of the professional administrators.

Legally, of course, the latter remain servants rather than masters. Theoretically they are meant to be at the beck and call of 'amateur' committees, the politicians who ultimately control their finances and have a total right of veto over their actions; but, like the powerful professional butlers in Victorian households, their powers of intimidation both upwards and downwards are immense and very often even the most active politicians will be wary of interfering in the affairs of their educational directorate, unless some major matter of political principle of expediency is involved.

This is not to say that the professional administrators do not take their role as servant seriously. So did the butlers. But there are limits to the interference which they are willing to tolerate and, armed as they now are with highly sophisticated planning procedures, often giving the impression of being designed to save the ratepayers' or the taxpayers' money, hold over their political masters grows more and more considerable and few politicians will choose to cross swords with them in matters beyond their own amateur expertise. In England in particular, it is very often the Director of Education who receives the knighthood or the CBE, rather than his chairman or indeed the Whitehall official who is meant to have ultimate oversight of both their operations. Many such local education officials have managed successfully to play off teachers and parents against their political masters to their own great advantage. Moreover, they often have a status as international figures making them just as much at home (or, indeed sometimes more at home) in the Sweden of Husén or the teachers' colleges of New York State as in their own county hall. This again is awe-inspiring and means that few teachers, let alone politicians, will lightly bandy words with them on complex and controversial issues.

The role of the local administrator is remarkably similar in all parts of the United Kingdom, despite the marginal differences in his powers and in the legislative framework of the country in which he operates. Indeed there is considerable career mobility within this sector of the educational world.

Like the administrator, the inspector or adviser is also a fount of honour, a person whose advice is sought when probationary teachers or promotions are the issue or when financial encouragements are being discussed. On the other hand he is far more concerned than the administrator with the direct pedagogical concerns of the class-teacher and would be expected to be closer to him professionally than to the administrator as such, whose concerns naturally run to supply questions and budgetary manipulations rather than to classroom dynamics or techniques for teaching reading. This cleavage is particularly true at national level. There the 'pure' administrator is usually a general civil servant rather than a professional educationalist and in the course of his career he could probably deal just as readily with agriculture, transport or the arbitration service. At local level, the 'pure' administrator may be just as much an educational expert as his adviser colleagues and the visiting Inspectorate. Nevertheless, in all parts of the British Isles, the Inspectorate has developed its own peculiar career structure, and while there is considerably more movement in and out of the Inspectorate 'profession'—in from teaching proper and out to the universities or to the vaguer world of research projects which has mushroomed during the 1960s—most teachers still regard inspectors and advisers as one of 'them', rather than as one of 'us'. Indeed the normal primary teacher may sometimes feel far more professional solidarity with the teacher of sixth-form physics than he does with the sometimes intimidating lady who, he believes, comes round ostensibly to advise him but really to check up on his grasp of new mathematics teaching. This enduring feeling that the inspector really *is* an inspector and not the teacher's friend that he would now claim to be (and sometimes is) has endured particularly in both parts of Ireland where the more centralised nature of the systems has encouraged this feeling. To some extent it is also true of Scotland where centralisation of curriculum thinking is also greater than in England, though the greater degree of migration between Scotland and England in this professional sector has tended to blur the differences between the two countries.

In very recent years the growing reluctance to use the term 'inspector' at local level and the encouragement of the notion of the 'adviser' as the teacher's friend has been accompanied by a playing down of his role as fount of honour; but suspicion dies hard, and the growth of the curriculum movement has given advisers new scope for bestowing favours.

There has also been, perhaps, a failure of confidence on the part of the national Inspectorate, who have been so concerned to play down their policing role within the system that they are all too often (and unfairly) seen as parasites, lacking close ties with individual schools and teachers, more useful as observers of the scene for British Council tours or Royal Commissions than as dynamic interveners or change agents in the actual educational systems of the British Isles themselves. It is no accident that, like some administrators, the more articulate members of the Inspectorate are better known in the United States and Australia than they are in England and Wales and the international conference circuit has sometimes become a more congenial stamping ground than actual classrooms which can too easily merely become places for gathering 'material' for use at conferences or on lecture tours. Symptomatic of this decline in confidence is the virtual disappearance of the old General Inspection of Institutions which took place on a regular basis at least once a decade and embraced the work of every class and every teacher in the institution. Small wonder that talk increases of the disappearance of the British Inspectorate being imminent to be replaced by professional 'change agents' and technical researchers, though it is only fair to add that administrators continue to see the Inspectorate as performing a vital informational and animative function.

The tone of some of our comments so far will indeed have horrified some leaders of the administrative profession, as indeed they will have horrified many leaders of the teaching profession who, as we have said, see the education system not as a battlefield but as a wonderful opportunity for partnership between the various parties involved in 'the great enterprise of education'. Yet, in reality, the various professional groups are not so much partners as participants in a situation which can change rapidly from peace to war and in which alliances can change just as rapidly. Thus, over teachers' salaries, local and national government will join in fighting the claims of the teachers; over cuts in general local spending, the teachers will join local officials against Whitehall; while in certain local quarrels the teachers will turn to Whitehall for support against a set of local 'tyrants'.

There is of course nothing unique in such a triangle. There are similar sets of checks and balances throughout government but they can cause tensions which are profoundly anti-educational and often extremely costly in both time and money.

At a local level, perhaps the greatest easing of continuing mistrust has come through the development of teachers' centres as an offshoot of the curriculum movement of the 1960s. The provision of such centres is not mandatory though it has suddenly become almost universal—at least in England and Wales. To some extent the poor physical facilities in some of them (in 1974 the Blackburn centre still had no lavatory) have been the result of their hasty establishment but most of them now boast discussion rooms and libraries along with stocks of curriculum project packs and other hardware. Some have a full-time professional staff to advise on the use of equipment and to encourage the discussion of curriculum problems generally. They have obviously been a major breakthrough in the professional development of British teachers. Moreover on the comparatively neutral ground of the centres, teacher and adviser can meet as professional equals far more easily than in the situation of the actual classroom and there is no doubt that such a development has helped considerably, not merely with the work of curriculum change, but with the personal counselling of teachers, not too easily done in the presence of children or within the strict constraints of the school timetable. Certainly both parties—teachers and advisers—seem to have achieved great professional stimulus and increased prestige from participation in this particular experiment and it is difficult to see how it would ever have developed, had there not been for many years a growing sense of a very specialised professionalism among LEA advisers.

However, the actual class-teachers remain the largest and dominant professional group concerned with education; and despite the greater claims to press coverage that can be made by individual academics, inspectors or administrators, there is no doubt that none of the governments of the British Isles could long withstand the united demands of the teaching profession itself. However the truth is, of course, that as we said earlier, such united demands are rarely if ever articulated because the profession is rarely, if ever, actually united. It is disunited for example, about intersector rivalries—to such an extent that until recently, the words 'middle school' could never be mentioned in Scotland, so great was the threat it seemed to pose to the career structures in both primary and secondary schools. It is disunited in its views on educational organisation—hence the internal disruption over the raising of the school-leaving age to 16, supported enthusiastically by the English NUT but as vehemently opposed by its Scottish equivalent, the EIS. It is divided on ideological lines—hence the dispute within the profession over comprehensive schooling. It is even divided about salary claims and working conditions—in particular, over the rights of women, the optimum size of classes and over forms of punishment.

Nowadays the vast majority of teachers of 4-year-olds in nursery schools, teachers of university candidates in sixth forms and teachers of physical education to 12-year-old delinquents would at least admit to being members of the same profession. Yet even this was not always so.

Until very recently, teachers in the English public schools and indeed teachers in most grammar schools would always refer to themselves as schoolmasters or schoolmistresses rather than as schoolteachers, a term if not of approbrium, at least of condescension reserved for teachers in the elementary schools, who (in the case of England and Wales at least) would be unlikely to have university degrees and would be likely to be socially inferior both personally and in terms of the pupils they taught. It is true that this dichotomy was never so extreme in the case of the Scottish and Irish teaching professions, yet even among them there was considerable prejudice against the 'non-academics'—such teachers as those of physical education and art and music—who even now are sometimes not even allowed in Northern Ireland to take their tea-break in the same room as their more intellectually exalted colleagues.

This obsession with pecking order is one of the few really long-standing traditions of British education, especially in England. Not only did the public and grammar schoolteachers in the early nineteenth century despise their elementary school contemporaries, they were just as likely to despise many of their own colleagues. At Shrewsbury School, for example, at the beginning of the nineteenth century, teachers of subjects other than classics were, whether graduates or not, forbidden to wear academic dress, thus demonstrating their intellectual and social inferiority—even if they were teachers of mathematics, a discipline already so respectable at Cambridge that it had been the subject of the first British Honours degree.[7]

With the spread of grammar school education at the end of the nineteenth century, earlier attitudes were weakened, particularly as the curriculum, even in the most prestigious public schools, was considerably widened, and the position of teachers of 'modern' subjects was legitimated. But the cleavage between grammar school (i.e. 'academic') teachers and the rest remained, so that even with the coming of comprehensive secondary education, the old academic grammar school union for men, the Assistant Masters' Association, has held its grip on graduate teachers in the secondary sector. Indeed within some comprehensive schools, the closer proximity of non-graduate colleagues has made some conservative graduates even more aware of their superior status than previously.

In Scotland there never was any such great cleavage, yet even there the English example has in recent decades proved to be powerful. It is true that the largest teachers' organisation in Scotland, the Educational Institute of Scotland, has maintained a wider spread of teachers from all categories than has its nearest English or Irish equivalents, the National Union of Teachers and the Irish National Teachers' Organisation. Nevertheless, perhaps the most significant event in its recent history has been the breaking away from the parent body of a considerable Scottish

Secondary Teachers' Association, and of a smaller body representing Honours graduates. The creation of these bodies was the natural consequence of professional events during the 1920s and 1930s.

The EIS had for long advocated an all-graduate profession and in the 1920s they were willing to accept a government decision which may well have been less an altruistic gesture of goodwill to the profession than a cynical use of the teachers' own rhetoric as a device for cutting down the number of unemployed teachers on the labour market. Whatever the government's motives, the EIS accepted a regulation demanding graduation of all secondary and all male teachers with the exception of the 'despised' specialists in PE, music and art. This was a considerable step forward in the eyes of those demanding for teaching the status of medicine or dentistry, but it was certainly calculated to drive a wedge for the first time between Scottish primary and secondary teachers, and, to some extent, between men and women. On the other hand it did avoid reproducing the even more destructive English dichotomy between those teaching the academic streams in the secondary sector and those teaching the remainder i.e. the majority of children.

Fortunately, recent economic pressures have not produced any noticeable resurgence of another earlier cause of tension—the differential treatment of male and female teachers in the career structure and the salary scales. At least two unions, the (English and Welsh) National Association of Schoolmasters and the Scottish Schoolmasters' Association were at one time particularly concerned with the defence of male careers against the inroads of the female who was usually considered a short term interloper stealing rewards that should rightly go to the 'breadwinner' (i.e. the male). It is symptomatic of changing attitudes to women in the profession that such attitudes are now rarely heard and even these organisations now tend to emphasise other issues of concern to both sexes, such as indiscipline and the defence of corporal punishment. Indeed, they have united their efforts with that of a specifically female union, the Women Teacher's Association.

The NAS and SSA have been, incidentally, the first major teachers' unions outside the grammar school and post-secondary school sectors to decide (in 1975) to operate on an all-Great-Britain basis and this reflects a further change. Previously, discussions between teachers and government took place strictly within national boundaries. Even unions such as the AMA with members in all parts of the United Kingdom negotiated separately with the DES, the SED and the Northern Ireland government, but in 1975 the Houghton Report on teachers' salaries covered, for once, all sectors[8] in all parts of the kingdom. Although its recommendations differed for Scotland from those for England, Wales and Northern Ireland, the procedure was a reflection of the growing geographical mobility of teachers within the British Isles and the resultant intolerance of differentials. The Houghton decisions may have a more unifying effect on the profession throughout the United Kingdom than is at present realised. The operating union between the NAS and SSA may be the first fruits of this.

But teachers' organisations are not merely concerned with salaries. They are concerned also with the more intangible 'badges' of true professional status. Those badges which have been widely regarded as characteristic of true high professionalism include: widespread university graduation (with the high social status that it brings); control of entry, training and discipline by the profession itself; professional autonomy in decision making at work; and, more recently, the building up of a respectable body of academic work and research related to the profession's needs.

The most general achievement of these aims has probably occurred in Scotland. As we noted earlier, it is now some fifty years since graduation was made mandatory there for most male and secondary teachers; and although this rule has to some extent been relaxed, in that a small number of male teachers have recently been admitted to primary positions without university graduation, this temporary anomaly is unlikely to continue in view of the growing tendency of primary teachers to take the new B.Ed degree during their training. A great deal has been made by the professional organisations of the exceptional opportunity the B.Ed course gives for developing a curriculum where professional and purely academic studies are satisfactorily integrated, thus making it superior as a form of professional training to the commoner method of graduate entry, a three- or four-year university course followed a year of post-graduate training. The strength of teacher rhetoric on the subject has encouraged the SED to make at least one tentative statement implying that eventually only those holding the 'integrated' B.Ed might at some later date be eligible for graduate teaching posts in Scotland. The implications of this statement for the whole teaching profession as well as for the universities (some of whose arts faculties are more than half full of budding teachers) are so massive that they have largely been ignored by those who would otherwise find them too horrifying to contemplate and it is doubtful if it was really ever meant to apply to secondary schools.

Scottish universities have never been good or consistent at working out a permanent policy so far as the teaching profession is concerned. Many professors and lecturers (especially those of English origin) have been reluctant to admit to the fact that so many of their graduates take up the widely despised job of teaching. In fact, in some faculties, a clear majority of students end up as teachers and, as we noted earlier, the Scottish universities provide a general education for many future teachers who in England and Wales would seek their general education elsewhere.

Nevertheless, despite such prejudices, university studies in the educational field were earlier developed in the Scottish universities and on a larger scale than was the case in most other British universities save London. The first two chairs of education in the British Isles were established at Edinburgh and St Andrews in 1876 and postgraduate specialist Honours degrees in education (now the M.Ed) were founded at all four 'ancient' Scottish universities during the First World War. The classes conducted for these degrees at Edinburgh, Glasgow and Aberdeen[9] became the largest single source of trained manpower for the administrative and psychological services of both England and Scotland in the years preceding 1970 and it was in Edinburgh (at Moray House) that a professor and his assistants developed the tests used by the majority of British authorities in the secondary selection examination.

Not that such activities were always welcomed by the universities concerned. The education degree at Glasgow was instituted by the Principal, the Court and the General Council of Graduates in the teeth of opposition from the Senatus (the body ostensibly in charge of academic policy and the main organ of professorial opinion) while both Glasgow and Aberdeen failed to appoint professors of education until well after most other British universities. (Indeed, the first holders of these chairs are still in office.)

Such reluctance is partly explained by the fact that, early in this century, the Scottish universities (unlike those elsewhere in the British Isles) had shed the responsibility for the money-spinning task of training graduates, a duty undertaken in Scotland by the colleges following the introduction of compulsory training in 1906. University departments attracted therefore only a small band of voluntary students. Educational studies were thus financially unattractive to the university authorities, who often shared a lingering theological and philosophical prejudice against education as an academic subject. However, in the period after 1945, even such voluntary studies, apparently paying off well for students in terms of professional promotion, began to prove more popular and highly profitable for the institutions concerned.

The most spectacular breakthrough was perhaps at the new university of Stirling where, in the 1960s, a (by Scottish standards) revolutionary style of teacher training was imported, owing much to American models. Symptomatically, it created grave suspicion in Scottish professional circles now more obsessed with 'qualifications' than with pedagogy. Qualified graduate teachers would leave Stirling two or three months earlier than graduates elsewhere. Regardless of the course's quality, this was 'dilution' and it was viewed with grave suspicion by teachers on the General Teaching Council.

This General Teaching Council was modelled to some extent on the General Medical Council, the General Dental Council and other national bodies which have been entrusted by Parliament with the task of registering fully trained professionals. It now decides not only who should be included in the professional register of teachers, but who should be expelled from the register for 'unprofessional conduct'. It also advises the secretary of state on the teaching programmes in colleges of education and carries out a regular visitation not only of all such colleges, but also of any Scottish university that undertakes teacher training (so far, only Stirling). From time to time it also acts as an advisory body to the secretary of state, not just on matters of teacher training, but on general matters of educational interest. Superficially, therefore, it does appear to have gained actual control of the profession to an extent not yet paralleled by any body in England, Wales or Ireland. Nevertheless its claims sometimes disguise the reality. It may for example be the sole body responsible for the registration and certification of all teachers in Scotland, but it does not have power under the legislation to decide whether registration is necessary for participation in the state's educational system and, indeed, during the first period of its operation, secondary teachers did not need to be so registered. A decision on whether registration is necessary for employment in local authority schools is still a decision for the secretary of state, who has not yet given such a ruling, for example, in the field of further education. Its writ does not run in independent schools or in the universities and this in itself casts doubt on its registration as being truly parallel with that in medicine or the legal system.

In addition, lacking any form of independent research and information services, the GTC is all too often dependent on the principals of the education colleges and on the civil servants and inspectors in attendance for the detailed information on which its decision making is based, so that, far from being an extra estate of the educational realm, it can sometimes be seen as yet another stamping ground for the non-teacher establishment. Moreover, the 'crimes' for which it can take disciplinary action do not include straight professional inefficiency or scandalous behaviour towards colleagues or employers; they are usually crimes of a moral nature that have already been dealt with in ordinary courts of law or in the offices of education authorities. All too often, deregistration is a mere formality reflecting the Council's lack of real teeth and self-sufficiency. Given the usual divisions in the ranks of teachers themselves, the non-teacher members of the Council can all too readily have their way by operating a simple system of divide and rule.[10]

In addition, leaders of teacher opinion elsewhere in the British Isles have other misgivings about the Scottish General Teaching Council. In particular, they mistrust the fact that teacher organisations with their massive membership and strong research organisations do not have seats on the Council as of right. Thus, the elected members, elected from a general list and not as delegates of their individual organisations, sometimes feel, like an MP, somewhat inhibited about putting too forcefully the official view of the union which has sponsored their candidacy. At the same time the domination of the electorate by the advice of the major groupings means that the smaller bodies find it difficult to get representation at all and neither large nor small unions are fully satisfied. English teacher organisations value far more highly their place as of right on the Schools Council where the views and research of the NUT are particularly significant. Direct election by teachers in the style of the Scottish GTC is an experiment unlikely to be repeated elsewhere. The trend seems to be towards a greater dependence on a system of nomination to the membership of national consultative bodies. The School Broadcasting Council, for example, the main advisory body on educational broadcasting for the BBC, depended until recently on the informal *ad hoc* recruitment of interested individuals. The NUT, the AMA and others have now successfully achieved the right of nomination to certain vacancies and its membership is even more class-teacher based than that of the Schools Council itself. But, whatever the moves in Great Britain to improve the professional status of teachers, there can be little doubt that Irish teachers have lagged behind in almost every area and this is not simply a function of home rule and the unavailability of British money. Even under British rule, Irish teachers were paid considerably less than their colleagues elsewhere in the British Isles. This was partly, in the case of elementary schools for example, because of decisions by the British Treasury, but it was true also in the secondary sector where, like English clergymen headmasters, the religious orders were not interested in higher professional status and where state intervention was slower to develop than in Britain. Even nowadays the majority of academically oriented secondary schools, both North and South, are independent or semi-independent, and in the period before Partition, academic education was universally provided (except in a small handful of public institutions and charity schools) either by private entrepreneurs or by the religious orders.

Following the Second World War, the Northern Ireland situation moved appreciably closer to that of England with the establishment of well-financed, selective secondary institutions under local authority control and the status and requirements of those teaching in such institutions rose accordingly. In the Republic the organisation of secondary education remained, so far as the vocational schools were concerned, largely as it had been in the 1930s, while in the case of the academic second-level schools, it remained largely as it had been in Victorian times. Until secondary education was made available to all by the O'Malley changes in the 1960s there were no pressures to improve either the career conditions or the professional standards of the teachers involved and this situation was particularly depressing for the lay teacher in a school run by a religious order.

Not only were lay teachers in such schools often bearing the burden of most of the teaching, but their conditions of service and chances of promotion were considerably depressed by the willingness of the religious, bound by their vows of poverty, not only to live on a pittance but to ignore career structures completely. Lay teachers were greatly incensed by the fact that the highest posts in many schools were permanently closed to them, regardless of their superior qualifications or their demonstrated skill as teachers.

This was not entirely the fault of the orders themselves; they could genuinely claim that they were not motivated by personal ambition but were satisfying parents who on the whole preferred the religious to remain in a commanding position in order to set the 'tone' of the school.

By a strange political irony, the situation of the graduate teacher was made worse in the Republic by a financial anomaly. Until the 1960s colleges of education there were able to offer far better scholarships than the university sector and they therefore attracted the cream of a particular year-group. Thus the personal status of non-graduates destined to teach in elementary schools could on occasions be professionally greater than that of the graduates themselves. It was ironically the case (although it was not to be deplored) that the academically most able teachers were thus being directed towards the teaching of the younger and less able pupils, always in Britain the mark of inferior status. The Irish teachers were thus accidentally following the pattern of those prestigious professions, such as medicine and law, which accord higher status to those capable of tackling the most formidable professional tasks rather than to those in possession of merely theoretical knowledge, however distinguished.

Since the provision of free second-level education for all in the Republic during the 1960s, the situation of the secondary teachers has improved considerably and in the new comprehensive and community schools, where overall control by the religious has usually been eliminated, their prospects are considerably brightened. But the conflicts of interest in Irish education between the religious and the lay-teachers as well as between different sectors and denominations has taken a great toll in terms of the fragmentation of teacher organisations. In Northern Ireland, in particular, this fragmentation has until recently, stifled the growth of any sense of common professional purpose.[11]

Of all the groupings in the islands, the Educational Institute of Scotland can claim to have had at one time the widest spread of membership among sectors and sexes and the greatest sense of professional unity but, as we have seen, even it has now acquired a formidable rival in the Scottish Secondary Teachers' Association, though it is neither so academically elitist as the Assistant Masters' and Mistresses' Associations in England (for not all secondary teachers are grammar school teachers) nor is it in any way divisive on sexual or denominational grounds. In Scotland also, the headteachers, although they have their own organisations, do not perhaps accord them quite as much significance as do the English or Irish headteachers who are not always also members of some other more general, professional association. This is partly explained historically by the fact that the dominant headteacher as head of an institutional hierarchy (now, for many years, a familiar Scottish figure) was nevertheless a late importation into Scotland from England. Until the nineteenth century, the headmaster or, as he is very often called, the rector of a Scottish high school was at best like the old-style principal of a Scottish university, simply *primus inter pares*, where each subject department in the High School of Dundee had a rector of its own with no overarching organisation to link their work together.[12]

This sense of non-hierarchy has lingered on. Significantly, even now, the Scottish teachers probably enjoy greater independence in the classroom than their English colleagues. They are, for example, usually allowed to administer corporal punishment autonomously without reference to any higher authority, in contrast to the English school where the infliction of corporal punishment is usually reserved to the headteacher or his deputy. Indeed, attempts by Scottish local authorities to limit this power have usually been ignored even in the infant departments of primary schools. It is the issue on which many Scottish teachers feel their professional rights to rest most strongly and the continued classroom use of the 'tawse' provides one of the few examples of the survival of a national style of pedagogy in a classroom more and more dominated by international models and theory, as mediated by the colleges, the universities and the advisory service. To them curricular autonomy seems a far less important issue.

One of the most interesting developments in British and Irish education since the war has been this growing uniformity so often resulting from the influences of the colleges and universities, and one would have expected to see in a partnership between the teaching profession and such institutions the most fruitful field for the expansion of educational research. In Ireland, this has been so. No major research organisation or organisation for the development of curriculum has grown up anywhere outside the universities and colleges with which the teachers' centres have a close relationship. In the Republic, the major research centre has been in the largest of the education colleges, St Patrick's at Drumcondra, and in an all-Ireland curriculum centre has been established in Trinity College. In Northern Ireland, curriculum research in particular has been centred in the New University of Ulster at Coleraine and in the Educational Institute at Queen's University, Belfast, and its constituent colleges.

In England and Wales a great deal of educational research and the publication of its findings does of course also take place within the university and college sector. However, a far more central influence is exerted by non-university organisations such as the Schools Council (with its satellites, the Ford and Nuffield Foundations) as well as by the National Foundation for Educational Research, started significantly on the initiative not of the teachers' unions but of the other professionals, those in the local education authorities.

In Scotland, on the other hand, the Scottish Council for Research in Education which began its work more than a quarter of a century before its English counterpart, was a genuine product of partnership between the main teachers union, the EIS (which provided it with premises and a nucleus of operations in its own research committee) and the new education authority officials who took office during the 1920s. It is possible to read too much significance into this. In fact, the EIS's interest in research was largely prompted by the enthusiasms of a single university member, William Boyd, who sparked off little enthusiasm among teachers' leaders themselves. However, in the case of the SCRE as well as of the NFER, autonomy from both government and university remains and direct links with non-college/university professionals have been maintained. Whether their work is sufficiently integrated with the training of teachers remains an open question and an increasingly important one now that all British teachers within the state sector have to undergo such training.

To the outsider it may seem strange for us to be referring to the presence or absence of such teacher training because in most countries of the world a course of training has for long been assumed to be the *sine qua non* of entry to the teaching profession, but it is worth remembering how recently such training became compulsory in the English and Welsh systems, where university graduates have universally been allowed to embark on secondary teaching without professional training, and where many thousands of untrained graduates are still working their way through the system.

In England and Wales, the training of non-graduates has for long been compulsory, but observing the dichotomy we noticed earlier between academic and non-academic teachers, the government for a long time assumed that university experience in itself constituted sufficient training for the grammar school teacher whose main concern, it was felt, was with knowledge rather than with pedagogy. It is in fact a classic example of the way in which a single United Kingdom government and parliament can expediently operate on quite different principles in relation to the various educational systems under its control, for in Scotland such views have been anathema for the whole of this century.

Although English universities have provided a postgraduate training year for potential teachers in secondary schools for almost a hundred years, it has never been compulsory. Indeed many of the more elitist secondary teachers have in the past prided themselves on the avoidance of such a course which they felt was not only irrelevant to their needs, but full of dangerous pseudo-scientific claptrap likely to lead them into follies. The psychological content of such courses was particularly mistrusted while, for some, even to undertake such a course was to identify themselves in some way with the socially less exalted elementary 'teachers' undergoing their compulsory training for working-class elementary schools.

Certainly the distaste for professional teacher training among certain sectors of public life in England and Wales is still a strong one. As recently as 1970, a Member of Parliament forming part of a parliamentary Select Committee on teacher education actually informed a delegation from the General Teaching Council for Scotland that he had deliberately chosen to send his children to a fee-paying private school, not for snobbish reasons, but because they would be protected from the ministrations of trained teachers, who, he felt, were imbued with far too many dangerous ideas.

Nevertheless, such prejudices have now all but disappeared and in the 1970s not only has the training of new graduates in England and Wales become universal (save for the all too rare scientists and mathematicians) but there has been a cry for an increase in the length of the three-year training course for non-graduates, in order to bring it into line with the four years of preparation undertaken by graduates. Moreover with the development of the B.Ed degree as a qualification for teachers in both the primary and secondary sector, it is conceivable that by 1980 all new teachers recruited in England and Wales *will* be graduates and the situation is likely to be very similar in Northern Ireland.

In Scotland, as we have seen, training has been universally insisted on for a much longer period and, although political circumstances and teacher shortages caused some relaxation of the regulations after the Second World War, one of the first acts of the new GTC was to insist on crash courses for all those in posts who had avoided such training plus the expulsion from the profession of those who were unable or unwilling to undertake such courses. On the other hand, the Scottish approach to the B.Ed degree has been much less wholehearted. On the whole the integration of studies between university and college has been considerably less adventurous than in England and a much more rigid line has usually been drawn between 'purely' professional and 'purely' academic studies in the arrangement of the syllabus. The hand of the supervising university has been heavy and all too often the contents of the graduate's one-year training course have simply been laid discretely alongside an ordinary degree course mirroring that taken by the generality of students. But there have been exceptions—at Dundee for example, where a more typically English model has been followed. This enables students to begin their course of study as ordinary non-graduating trainees in a college, with the option of changing over to a university-style B.Ed course half way through their period of training, while at Stirling University, as we have already noted, there has been an attempt to reintroduce teacher training into the actual undergraduate course within the university itself, thus reviving a Scottish notion of 'concurrent training' that had died out in the interwar years.

However, throughout the United Kingdom, teacher training remains in something of a melting pot. In England and Wales, many colleges of education have already disappeared, some without trace, others by visible incorporation into local universities and polytechnics or by incorporation into larger colleges of higher education which are able to launch far more ambitious programmes. Some have been converted into more specialised agencies for the in-service training of teachers—a process to which governments have for long paid lip-service and which has still to be organised on the formal basis promised in recent government White Papers.

But, as yet, there has been no move to make compulsory any further period of retraining once the intial training and probationary years are at an end. The information and formal skills teachers have acquired by the age of 22 are still all too often assumed to be adequate for a professional lifetime.

There is, however, another group of professionals who have a special interest in bringing teachers up to date—professionals who perform a vital task in creating the climate of educational opinion within a country but are largely neglected in most assessments of national systems of education, namely, the educational journalists. One of the reasons why they have been neglected by British and Irish writers is that they are still comparatively rare figures in the islands. Clearly, a turning point in the development of their profession and indeed in the history of education as a whole was the founding in 1910 of an *Educational Supplement* by *The Times* of London. The *TES* has remained, along with its more recent offspring of the 1970s, the *Times Higher Education Supplement*, the key journal of British education—at least in so far as the general body of professionals, teachers and administrators are concerned. Each group has its own specialist journal or newsletter—Birmingham researchers, Catholic primary teachers, educational psychologists—but only in the pages of the *TES* have all their interests usually come together in a form equally accessible to laymen.

But despite its obvious services to education, the *TES* has accidentally done some harm, for its very efficiency has tended to make *The Times* itself and most other English newspapers assume that educational matters were being covered adequately outside their own pages and has thus reduced the number of columns which those papers now feel it necessary to devote to the less sensational aspects of national educational news. Where they do have a *full-time* education reporter—and many daily newspapers (like BBC radio and television) do *not* have one—he is usually given far less regular or prominent space for his stories than is the case in many other countries (compare the regular education pages in *Le Monde* or *Die Welt* for example with those in *The Times* or the *Scotsman*) and his services are all too often used on a major scale only at times of major scandal or political controversy—when a teacher seduces a pupil or when a local authority defies the central government. The only exception to this rule among English national papers is, perhaps, the *Guardian* but it is notoriously a paper with a wide readership among teachers themselves. Parents and politicians in general read other papers and thus make little contact with educational news except in times of crisis, scandal or controversy. Coverage in serious national periodicals (with the exception of *New Society* which specialises in the social services) is equally fitful and is often far more sensational and superficial than is their treatment of other matters. In fact, English readers (with some justification) have come to regard education as a dull, even distasteful subject and are reluctant even to buy cheap paperbacks dealing with the subject in an entertaining way, as the disastrous fall of more than one publishing venture has demonstrated. Yet, in deploring this, one must admit that the weekly reading even of the *TES* can sometimes be an awful chore—not because of journalistic ineptitude on the part of the staff but because of the dullness of so many worthy but jargon-ridden outside contributions and because of the necessary inclusion of so many speeches and conference papers high on rhetoric and short on realism and humanity, which lose whatever flavour and palatability they may have once possessed in the subsequent summarising.

Until the 1960s, because of its high standards and comprehensive coverage, the *TES* tended to dominate educational journalism throughout the British Isles, but during the past decade there has been a growing sense of journalist independence in Scotland and the Irish Republic. Since 1965 a special Scottish edition of the *TES* has been prepared in Edinburgh with many pages of exclusively Scottish material, that give it an altogether distinctive flavour in comparison with its English counterpart. Indeed, to its regular readers it has become a quite separate newspaper making its own contribution to Scottish national life. For example, it, rather than a daily newspaper, mounted the first major national conference on Scottish devolution and it is probably due to the *TESS*'s growing influence that at least one Scottish national paper, the *Scotsman*, felt the need to appoint its own full-time education correspondent, whose material often gains far greater prominence in the news pages of his paper than that given to similar material produced by English colleagues. This renaissance of Scottish educational journalism is partly of course an offshoot of a general national revival and the consequent refurbishing and re-examination of native institutions but it reflects also a revival of educational discussion within an educational profession and a society that had become too smug and self-congragulatory over its own achievements.

The revival of educational journalism in Ireland during the 1960s was even more spectacular—not so much in Belfast where English influence was then at its strongest (and where the *TES* remained supreme) as in Dublin where the leading newspaper, the *Irish Times*, began regularly to employ a number of its leading journalists on education stories and in 1971 actually launched a separate weekly, the *Education Times*, in *TES* style, catering for educational interests in the North as well as in the Repbulic. Alas, by 1976 it was dead. In the smaller field of Irish education it found it economically difficult to equal the *TES* success and, more sinisterly, it may have formed too great a threat to the influence, if not the circulation, of certain teachers' union newspapers that were trying to sell outside their own immediate ranks. It may even have been too radical for a general Irish audience. But while it existed it was far more independent of vested interest in its editorial line than any educational journal in the British Isles apart from the *Times* publications themselves.

It is of course possible to exaggerate the political and educational influence of such journals. Cynics suggest with some justification, that their circulation is maintained only because of their classified advertisements. The *TES*, in particular, has become the major medium for the advertising of all educational posts by local authorities. Certainly more applicants for posts in primary and secondary education have seen the original advertisements in its columns than in the columns of the daily press. Some people despair of the whole way in which educational opinion is formed within the British Isles. Often it seems to be formed by a small group of leading academics (at present mainly sociologists) who dominate thinking in the colleges and university departments or by a small body of officials in government and teachers' unions who are themselves dominated ideologically by those same academics but place their common ideology in a more realistic economic and professional framework; thus two groups, scholars and bureaucrats, form an educational establishment which may make its major decisions behind doors closed not just to the general public but to their fellow professionals. The elected representatives and union members who are supposed to be controlling these 'experts' all too often, through feelings of technical inadequacy and ignorance, abandon their protests.

This is no doubt an exaggeration but in the absence of vigorous journalism it can be dangerously near the mark. Certainly a small group of professors seem to exercise an almost eighteenth-century system of patronage over academic and administrative posts while a small group of civil servants and union officials seem to decide far too much educational policy in private with little outcry from the press or from political parties. There has, it is true, been an outcry over comprehensive secondary schooling and the abolition of the direct-grant schools but there the whole class structure of English society was threatened. There has been little discussion even during such controversies, of what actually *happens* in grammar schools or the suitability of certain teaching styles for academically able children.

There are widespread rhetorical skirmishes about 'good' schools, 'standards' and 'equal opportunity' but little discussion of pedagogy as such.

Moreover, the internationalisation of educational scholarship and of the academic profession have done much to dilute the strength and self-confidence of public opinion on educational issues particularly in Ireland. All too often, those both lay and professional who disagree with international figures such as Bruner, Bernstein or Piaget are afraid to enter public debate for fear of appearing narrow and parochial.

This awe in which certain figures are held has even inhibited local discussion in an ostensibly scholarly context. Significantly, the *Irish Journal of Education*, founded in the 1960s for the publication of work of high scholarship, at first felt it necessary to commission work almost exclusively from outside the country. In the name of 'standards', Irish scholarship was admitted only with great caution. Its Scottish contemporary, *Scottish Educational Studies*, met a different problem. Unlike the Irish journal it was founded by the Scottish universities with the specific intention of providing a publishing vehicle for Scottish writing and the treatment of Scottish topics, for which English-based journals naturally could not always provide much space. It aimed therefore at publishing mainly Scottish work but some of the most distinguished Scottish scholars did not wish to compromise themselves by writing for such a Scottish (i.e. 'parochial') journal.

Such authoritarianism is, however, dying. *Scottish Educational Studies* now finds it less difficult to collect material. Its major problem remains that of learned journals in small countries everywhere—how to maintain an adequate circulation and income in the age of the photocopying machine when one library copy of an article can suffice for a thousand students as well as for a staff who in former years might well have bought copies for themselves. Thus it is even more significant that a journal based in Aberdeen College of Education—*Education in the North*—has achieved not only a remarkably high status in Scottish professional circles for both scholarship and relevance to classroom life but also a wide circulation, especially among teachers who welcome a journal actually dealing with education and not with the rather different political problems (usually to do with finance) which provide the only exciting talking points in most journals produced by the teachers' unions.

The success of *Education in the North* and the resurgence of educational journalism in Ireland and Scotland suggest that the creating of a climate of educational opinion which transcends and stretches beyond the boundaries of the various educational professions may become possible, so that in turn decision making may pass back away from the coteries of leading scholars and administrators, if not to the teachers, at least to the politicians who, in democracies, represent those to whom the schools are supposed to belong. The distaste for educational journalists already being displayed by the authorities not only in London but in Edinburgh and Dublin suggests that their work may be hastening this process.

NOTES AND REFERENCES

1 T. W. Bamford, *The Rise of the Public Schools* (London, Nelson, 1967) *passim.*
2 Edmund Wilson, *To the Finland Station* (London, Macmillan, 1972) p. 418.
3 Some religious orders merely appoint one of their own number as a temporary headmaster, *primus inter pares*, and establish no career structure in the normal sense.
4 These include not just teachers and administrators, but psychologists, speech therapists, lab technicians, etc.
5 At Aberdeen (where the incidence of budding teachers is highest) over 1,000 students out of a total of some 4,500 in 1973/4 were ordinarily resident in England and Wales (Hansard 18 December 1975, Written Answer cols 764/5).
6 In a curiously mystical compromise, the Inner London Authority has suggested that managers 'exercise oversight of the conduct and curriculum of the school' while the headteacher 'controls' them. (See Appendix VII of *William Tyndale Junior and Infants Schools Public Inquiry—A report to the Inner London Education Authority by Robin Auld QC* (London, ILEA, 1976).
7 V. Ogilvie, *The English Public School* (London, Batsford, 1957), p. 173.
8 Except, alas, for university teachers!
9 Although St Andrews instituted the degree, there were no graduates for over thirty years.

10 See the article by R. Bell, 'Lessons of the Scottish GTC', in the *Times Educational Supplement*, 22 January 1971.

11 In Northern Ireland, there are still some twelve teacher organisations representing denominational as well as sector groupings.

12 S. J. Curtis, op. cit., pp. 540-1.

Chapter 7

Devolution in a Wider World

What force or guile could not subdue
  Thro' many warlike ages
Is wrought now by a coward few
  For hireling traitor's wages.
The English steel we could disdain,
  Secure in valour's station:
But English gold has been our bane—
  Such a parcel of rogues in a nation.[1]

Put in less contentious language than Burns's declaration, economic power can be much more effective than military action. Admittedly, he was reflecting on the part played by bribery in securing a majority in the Scottish parliament for the Union of 1707, but the general point can be taken further than that; economic forces can achieve assimilation beyond the power even of political control, as we have seen in the case of relations between the Irish Republic and the United Kingdom. Whatever the political structures, the modes of the richer, larger and stronger have tended to prevail in any kind of union or association. This has been obvious within Britain ever since that shrewd Welshman, Henry VII, married his daughter Margaret to James IV, King of Scots. When warned that this could ultimately bring a Scot to the English throne, he is said to have replied that there was nothing to worry about, since the greater would always absorb the lesser. And so it turned out. When James's great-grandson, James VI, inherited the throne of England, he promptly departed for his newer, richer kingdom which then became his main concern. The later Stuarts hardly noticed Scotland at all except as a nuisance or a refuge in times of trouble, with disastrous consequences.

Political links undoubtedly played their part. The crowns were united in 1603 and the parliaments in 1707, but other forces were more effective agents of assimilation. Gaelic culture was broken politically at Culloden but it was the Highland Clearances that destroyed its population base.[2] As for the rest of Scotland, it was economic power, not conquest, that drew the country further towards England.[3] Wales had been politically assimilated long before, lacking even those distinctive institutions, such as the legal system, that Scotland managed to retain. Ireland was taken over during a much longer period culminating in the Union of 1801—to discover, much later, that political union is easier to dismantle than economic and cultural dependence. Ever since becoming a unified country, England has been richest and largest of all the island neighbours, and has been a dominant force among them even when not attempting direct control—not that such restraint was common. Given England's strength, expansionist policy and hostility towards any deviation from English ways, it is all the more remarkable that Scotland, Ireland and Wales managed to retain any identity at all. Quite apart from politics, the pressures of demography and economics have, up to recent times, favoured the greater absorbing the lesser.

In this, education is not unique, but shares the experience of other institutions in the interaction of societies of such unequal weight. There has been some resistance, attributable to the existence of a longer-established school system, as in Scotland, or as in Wales, a vigorous and stubborn language and culture, or a deep-seated religious commitment, as in Ireland—though, as we have seen, these have been able only to slow down assimilation, not halt it.[4] We have seen *some* cases in which the lesser influenced the greater, and there could be others—one can imagine, for example, English cities with large immigrant populations making good use of Welsh experience of bilingual education.

On the whole, however, the trend has been towards increasing assimilation of the content, structure and even the ethos of education. There have been cases of what would nowadays be called 'nationalist backlash', and sometimes political developments have led to divergence, as when the partition of Ireland created two distinctive school systems out of a formerly unified one.[5] Even in these cases, however, pressure to assimilate is likely to reassert itself. Even in administratively distinctive Scotland or the politically independent Republic of Ireland, the need for some degree of co-ordination and interchange, and the demand for skills and qualifications marketable abroad, favours their falling into line with the biggest and most powerful member of the multinational complex, namely, England.

There exists an educational equivalent of 'social Darwinism'—not by any means confined to the English—that regards this process as inevitable, even desirable. But, common though the approval of an unsubtle anglicisation may be, this is not the only current of opinion that sees uniformity as desirable. A few years ago, the head of a well-known grant-aided school in Edinburgh spoke of his 'personal frustration at the eternal wrangle between Scots and English enthusiasts for their own tradition in education—a wrangle consisting of odious and almost entirely irrelevant comparisons'. He went on to expand his point thus:

> There is one major point that must be mentioned, and while it may be unpopular to suggest that this is worth examination, we cannot really afford socially and economically to go on ignoring it indefinitely. I refer to the increasing importance of parental, and therefore of course, pupil, mobility in our educational planning. Promotion for large numbers of people now depends on a willingness to move readily—and, in many cases, frequently—from area to area, and from one education authority to another. It is a tragic paradox for these families that in a period of increasing population mobility we have made it more rather than less difficult for children to change schools. For, as responsible parents soon discover, a change of school almost always involves a change of systems. How much longer will they have to put up with the present frustrating differences between, for example, the English and Scottish patterns of education? Indeed, why should they be expected to? How much longer can heads of schools and their staffs be expected to go on wasting valuable time acclimatising children to the changes they face when crossing the border in either direction, or indeed when crossing education authority boundaries? How much longer can we ask children who change schools to pay a heavy price to uphold national traditions in England and Scotland—traditions supposedly maintained for the sake of the very pupils who suffer from them?[6]

Roger Young was not saying that Scotland should simply fall into line with England. Among other suggestions for the reform of education in Britain, he urged:

> The English and Scottish systems of education should be unified, *not* in the sense of one swallowing up the other but in the sense of creating a *new* system common to both countries. Whatever the glories of either in the past, the present barriers between the two systems created by their differences will be intolerable in the 1970s and 1980s.[7]

During the discussion, Young remarked that under modern conditions it made no more sense to have different school systems than different railway gauges in the two countries. Inevitably, some were heard to suggest that this might not be such a bad idea; but some of the Scots as well as English agreed that national differences were a thing of the past, and should be done away with.

But a number of doubts arise. Some account must be taken of the time when this proposal was put forward, before devolution was even a governmental promise; it seemed more natural then in many quarters to think of the United Kingdom (or at any rate Great Britain) in unitary terms than it has become since. It was also before the United Kingdom joined the Common Market; although discussions had been dragging on (and off) for some time, the implications of entry were not in the forefront of many people's thinking. Few, so far, had grasped the point that there could be a wider international dimension to these arguments, such as the one about parental mobility.

Also, the constant references to 'tradition' and 'past glories' (and this is still very common) suggest that Mr Young, like so many of the unionist persuasion, does not fully comprehend the nature of the differences he condemns. The assumption appears to be that although Scotland and England were once different countries, they are now so much alike that the remaining differences have become an irrelevant nuisance. This is disputable, however; the present arguments about education within Scotland and Wales—and England too—are not all that much concerned with 'past glories', real or imagined, except in so far as they are relevant to the current situation; they are about the desirability of small countries, with their own identities and problems, being able to tackle these problems with reference to their own conditions and needs, rather than those of the English south-east.

It is necessary to make this last point, because for all the disclaimers of any idea of letting one system swallow up the other, the pressures we have been looking at so far favour just such a development; and even if it were possible to construct an all-British system, this would probably be a single event—an educational Act of Union, as it were. But societies change, and school systems change with them. Unless it were possible to set up an administrative and political structure that could continue indefinitely to give due weight to the experience and needs of the non-English countries, assimilation to the English norm would be inevitable. It *might* be possible to create such a structure; but experience so far suggests otherwise. There is little point in protesting that a unified system would not become essentially English when so many Englishmen believe that this has happened already. Trivial and irrational though it may seem, it remains true that many (perhaps most) English have still not managed to grasp that Britain and England are not the same thing.

It would be interesting to conduct an attitude survey on this; but meantime there are plenty of signs, familiar to Scots and Welshmen but probably not even noticed by most English, which in itself suggests that understanding of the differences is rare. We have mentioned a few of them already, such as the odd belief that England is an island, but there are many more, petty yet indicative—the use of the Union flag by English football supporters even in matches against Scotland, or of its design linked with exhortations to pick an English apple; the numbering of British sovereigns according to English usage, resulting in the bad arithmetic and (to some Scots) national offensiveness of such titles as William III, Edward VII, Edward VIII and Elizabeth II,[8] the persistent reference to the whole of the UK as England, even by people long resident in Scotland; the puzzled surprise, amusement, embarrassment or even indignation when Scots or Welshmen decline to be called English; and so on in a hundred little ways, enough to make the non-English extremely sceptical about the ability of the English to think in genuinely British terms at all. To dismiss objections like these as 'nationalist' or 'parochialist' is to misunderstand the issue. In education as in much else, most Scots see the choice not as between being Scottish or British, but between being Scottish or English and prefer, incredible though it seems to many, to be themselves rather than a copy of someone else. Until there is evidence some major shift in English thinking, therefore (and even the 1975 White Paper on devolution showed little sign of it),[9] the prospects of a unified system being anything but English are far from good.

It could be argued that this might as well happen anyway. Young makes much of the effect of the differences between systems on the children of mobile parents; and we have seen how mobility, or even the prospect of it, affects the content and structure of educational systems in any case. Among those who regard this as sufficient ground for assimilation, some would want to take steps to *make* it happen. More commonly, however, what is advocated is to *let* it happen, since the tide appears to be running in that direction. Most of the trends we have observed so far seem to support this view; as usual, however, things are not quite as simple as that.

For one thing, there are other factors working in the other direction; some concern education in particular, some concern broader social issues. Among these are the economic troubles of the United Kingdom, and possible changes in population movement. On the economic side, North Sea oil is much discussed. This raises alarm in quarters where the oil is regarded as the potential saviour of the United Kingdom generally. But it would be as well not to make too much of this, either as an electoral boost for the SNP or as the agent of economic recovery. Many Scots, while welcoming even such prosperity as has come from oil exploitation so far, are apprehensive about the long-term effects on Scottish society, economy and environment. More significant in the long run, perhaps, is the effect on Scottish attitudes of the economic recession, which has cast doubts on former assumptions about the unshakable power and wealth of England, and increased willingness to consider alternative futures for Scotland.[10] This is linked with the complex phenomenon generally described as a resurgence of national consciousness. This goes much deeper than arguments about oil revenues or the implications of voting for the SNP or Plaid Cymru. It takes different forms, of course. In Scotland it has shown itself partly in willingness to vote nationalist, though there is considerable evidence that—so far, at any rate—this does not indicate a desire for total separation from the UK.

At the same time, there is evidence[11] that the majority of Scots think of themselves as Scots first and British (if at all) second, though many would be hard put to it to say precisely what this meant. (So would most people, of course, including the English.) Some fall back on historical experience, real or fancied, others on those institutions which survived assimilation in 1707—the legal system, the church, the educational system—as pointers to national identity. If this seems rather vague, it is none the less real for all that; and if much of the attempt to define 'Scottishness' comes down to an insistence on not being English, this is hardly surprising either, since the most obvious theme throughout Scottish history has been the danger of the southern neighbour bringing that identity to an end. Much of the resurgence of national awareness can be attributed to frustration at English failure to recognise that the Scots exist in their own right.

There is a cultural dimension as well, particularly in Wales, where devolutionary sentiment is apparently much weaker in spite of (or, it could be, because of) the persistence of a more distinct linguistic and cultural identity.[12] In Scotland, as has already been observed, there has been some revival of interest in Gaelic (the *Scotsman* has started printing articles in it, and thousands in the Lowlands are putting themselves to the considerable trouble of learning it),[13] in Highland music, dress, literature and the like. This may be little more than symbolic, and historically associated with part of the country rather than the whole. But the population of Scotland is much more mixed than it was in the eighteenth century; the Highland Clearances led to the settlement of large numbers of Highlanders in the Lowlands, as a glance at the telephone directory of any Lowland town will confirm, and many have retained some feeling of connection with their ancestral lands and culture. Paradoxically, the destruction of Highland society did much to end the Highland-Lowland polarisation; it emptied the Highlands, but partly Celticised the Lowlands and, as we have seen, 'Balmorality' continued this process. What used to be regarded as the marks of the Gael only are now more commonly seen as belonging to Scotland as a whole. Though it is important not to exaggerate this, it is one element in the increased sense of identity in the face of a long history of assimilation.

In one sense, however, it is possible to argue that much of this renewed awareness is the effect rather than the cause of resistance to assimilation. It is perhaps a cliche to say yet again that there is a widespread mood of disillusion with central government, a feeling of remoteness and even alienation, a lack of involvement and contact with the centres of decision making, but being a cliche does not make it untrue. In England, this delusion often takes the form of a flight from politics altogether; in

Scotland, the existence of a historically distinct identity provides a focus for this disenchantment, however difficult to define this identity may be. This may be one reason for the lack of enthusiasm for devolution in Shetland, even more remote from Edinburgh than Edinburgh is from London. In Scotland, the present climate of opinion and remoteness from the centre reinforce national awareness in resisting assimilation into a larger and essentially English unit.

The growing interdependence of nation states in the modern world—emphasised by the recent confirmation of membership of the EEC—has made it clear that Britain is not an autonomous unit anyway. The fact that we are members of a wider community becomes daily more obvious in countless ways, from political developments to the range of goods in the shops to trivia like Eurovision song contests and the antics of the *jeux sans frontières*. At the same time, Brussels is even more remote than London, Europe (even Western Europe) is too big to identify with fully; thus, the corollary of greater internationalism is the reinforcement of the more immediate identity—Irish, Scots, Welsh or whatever—to provide a base from which to relate to the wider world.

At one time, it seemed that being British could provide such a base, particularly when the Empire still existed, with the nations of the British Isles as controlling partners. But Britain is rather too large and heterogeneous for that, and in any case there has never been any sign that England was prepared to submerge *her* identity in any way; quite the contrary. On top of this comes increasing awareness of the wider world, and at least the possibility of other kinds of grouping.

Similarly, the realisation that neither Britain nor the United Kingdom is a self-contained unit deals a serious blow to the notion of inevitable assimilation to a single pattern, when there are so many others to relate to as well. The obvious absurdity of the proposition that one has to be *either* British or European casts further doubts on the notion that one has to choose between being Scots, or Welsh, *or* British. (Indeed, many Northern Irish Protestants claim *triple* identity.) Once the possibility of plural identity is admitted, it can be exercised on several levels at once. By showing a wider universe, modern internationalism has given national identity a relevance that seemed to be lacking in the world of the unitary and separate nation-state. Culturally as well as politically, the broadening of our horizons has made the smaller, more immediate unit a viable concept again. In education as in other things, then, uncritical assimilation to the nearest big neighbour begins to look unnecessary and undesirable. What if *they* turn out to be 'parochial' in the international context? Internationalism on the present scale makes minorities of us all, a new and salutary experience for some.

In this context, the prospect of devolution within Great Britain has given rise to a number of questions too far-reaching to be disposed of once and for all by White Papers, draft Bills, or any other device for settling the precise powers of the several parliaments or assemblies. In the continuing discussions, it needs to be asked whether *any* model can guarantee the preservation and development of identity against the economic and demographical trends that have so long been working towards uniformity in these islands. We have already observed that even complete separation is no guarantee of national or cultural integrity if the other forces are sufficiently strong. Arguably, Man and the Channel Islands are a special case, being small in population, lacking any higher education facilities and having a long history of home-based anglicisation. But even the Republic of Ireland, with its whole range of educational facilities, a population of viable size, a patriotic ideology of self-sufficiency, and strenuous government support for the Irish language, has continued to be strongly influenced by English models. What applies to Ireland can obviously apply to even semi-autonomous Scotland and Wales.

Does this mean, then, that the fact and the form of devolution are irrelevant to the chances of maintaining national distinctiveness? For a number of reasons, we think this unlikely. As has already been observed, political links, while not the only mechanism of assimilation, certainly form an important one. Returning control of education to the smaller nations does not guarantee anything—it depends on what they do with it—but it does at least give power to do something if the will is there. It can at least stop the habit of modelling legislation on English enactments, relating it instead to the particular needs of the countries in question, particularly if a greater degree of openness and consultation can be built into the system—something which the smallness of a country does not guarantee, but does make more possible.

Further, control over one's own institutions provides the opportunity to reorganise them in ways not necessarily determined by United Kingdom politics at large. Both England and Scotland, for example, have had systems of higher education in which the universities have been ranged on one side and the various colleges on the other. Yet the 1975 White Paper blithely proposed that half the Scottish higher system could be left, after devolution, in the hands of the London ministry.

But this confusion, and the probable persistence of anglicisation, cannot be said to prove the ineffectiveness of political control as such; it rather shows the limitations of fragmented control. With the universities firmly inside the Scottish system, the assembly would at least have the option of moving towards greater integration of the educational system, with the universities playing an important role; such a system could hardly help being more responsive to Scotland's problems and needs than the fragmented one which the White Paper proposed to preserve. Many of the other mechanisms, such as the movement of personnel, would presumably continue, as they have in the Irish Republic, but with less overwhelming effect in an identifiably Scottish system. The mere fact of overwhelming effect in an identifiably Scottish system. The mere fact of devolution guarantees nothing; but an adequate degree of it can make it possible to have a real impact on the Scottish system as a whole.

More generally, it is at least possible that political devolution could have some effect on economic and demographic pressures. Again, this is not guaranteed, but the possibility is introduced of checking the drift of senior personnel to London if the seats of government are in Edinburgh and Cardiff; and, with a bit of luck, it might be possible to check the larger population drift. Ireland did not manage this until very recently, but there are signs now that London is no longer quite the magnet it was to so many Irish, Scots or Welsh. As all governments have found in recent years, the powers even of nation states to influence economic and demographic developments is limited. But this does not mean that they are totally non-existent; and political autonomy does give some opportunity to influence events, and modify the social pressures on education that we have been examining.

Inevitably, voices are raised asking whether it matters much anyway, whether it would not be better to allow what appears to be a natural process to run its course. Whether one is thinking of the minority languages, the distinctive institutions, or anything else that makes Ireland, Scotland, Wales, Man, Jersey or Guernsey different from England, some are bound to urge that these are relics of the past that might as well be allowed to die out. If the cultures and educational systems of the small countries are so vulnerable to normal social change, are they worth preserving at all, let alone developing?

We take the view that they are; some of our reasons may be dismissed as sentimental, others would have to be conceded as practical even by those who reject them. One reason is our welcoming human variety. To take an apparently trivial example: neither of the authors of this book is Irish, but both visit the country fairly frequently, and actually enjoy going where people speak differently (some in a different language), where the post-boxes are green instead of red, where the buses are labelled in Irish and the street-signs are bilingual, where they drink whiskey instead of whisky, and the money is different in appearance if not in value, and where there is a smell of turf smoke even in the city streets—a few of the things that contribute to that 'sense of place' without which, we feel, there is not much point in going anywhere. More seriously, we welcome the extent to which the Irish seek to tackle their educational problems without continual reference to what is done in Britain. This does *not* imply uncritical approval of anything done in Irish society, politics or education; we reserve the right to be as critical of their system as of our own; what we do reject is the notion that anything is open to criticism just *because* it is different, an attitude extremely common in metropolitan cultures from classical Greece to modern

America or France.[14] Admittedly, this is a personal preference, unlikely to appeal to the large numbers who regard their own way of doing anything as a norm for the entire human race. We make this point of clarifying acceptance of *other* people's identity out of a dislike of grey uniformity among peoples as among individuals, and to anticipate the criticism that our concern for the identity of minorities is somehow narrowly nationalistic or parochial. Having made the point, which will appeal or not according to temperament and one's view of the world, we pass on to the practical arguments.

One of these is still concerned with variety, but in a different way. It can hardly be said that educational thinking suffers from an excess of good ideas. Even if it were possible to commission 'experts' to work out 'correct' solutions to our present problems, and to prevail upon the authorities to implement them swiftly, we are still left with the gathering speed of social change and an exponential rate of obsolescence of knowledge. We cannot know with any certainty what children at school today will need to know in twenty years' time, or what social pressures our educational systems will have to take account of.[15] We do know, however, that it is not always feasible to meet every new problem by working out solutions from first principles; we need to look around, with of course due allowance for differences of context, at what other systems are trying. We need variety as a source of ideas, just as surely as living species need a varied gene-pool to remain viable. If only for that reason, the swallowing of the several cultures and systems of these islands would be a loss to the English as well as to the Irish, Scots and Welsh.

More immediately, it has to be recognised that assimilation is rarely planned or even conscious, but tends to proceed by prestige, habit or absent-mindedness. There can also be problems of timing. Educational change can rarely be instantaneous; even the most revolutionary systems, backed up by maximum political power, usually have to work with existing buildings and teachers, and even with some of the older attitudes and assumptions. *Some* governments can introduce change, legally, at the stroke of a pen, but in the classroom it takes much longer to effect; the educational history of the USSR, for example, gives many examples of time-lag lasting over decades.[16] In systems with less central control, such as these of Great Britain, the process can be very slow indeed.

Now, if one system bases its policies on the practices of another, this takes time to effect; but, since societies keep changing, and educational realities with them, there is always the danger that by the time the imitation has been carried through, things have moved on in the country from which it was borrowed. Northern Ireland under the Stormont system provides a good example of this.[17] The policy of keeping 'step in step' with Britain meant, among other things, painstakingly erecting a secondary school system based on 11-plus selection of the English type, and completing this just in time for the idea to become discredited in the country of origin. More hypothetically, if the lobby pressing for more specialisation in Scottish secondary schools should prevail, drawing its models from English practice, this would take some time to effect—long enough, as likely as not, for opinion in England to have swung towards a more generalist approach, even using obsolescent Scottish models.[18] Uncritical assimilation can be a recipe for perpetual obsolescence.

Further, it can be questioned whether it is wise to base any educational system too closely on someone else's. This is not to deny that there can be useful borrowings; whatever disquiet is felt in Scotland about the SCE O grade examination now, it was in its earlier years a useful bridging of the gap between potential 'Highers' candidates and the rest; and although it was not quite a straight copy of the GCE O level, that was qute clearly in the minds of the Working Party which recommended it.[19] But the crucial point was that the innovation was argued for on the basis of Scottish needs, not from any desire to 'bring the system into line' with England. Where this crucial condition is not observed, adoption of the modes of another system can be unhelpful, and even destructive.

The world is full of examples of this kind of thing, many of them grotesque. Before the francophone states of West Africa became independent, schools there followed the official French curriculum in detail, so that children in Guiné and Dahomey were informed that their ancestors had come from across the Alps, and that they were tall people with blue eyes and fair hair. British school systems are less uniform and centralist than the French; nevertheless, in colonial Nigeria children learned a great deal more about Henry VIII and his marital problems than about Dan Fodio and the Fulani *jihād*. Similarly, uncritical copying of Soviet material in Eastern Europe after the war produced some odd results, of which books on nature study listing birds not found west of the Vistula were only the most picturesque examples.[20] Many of these non-functional borrowings might be said to have done little harm. But the effects are hard to predict. In the 1920s, for example, the Soviet Union was going through a phase of determined modernism, to sever ties with anything redolent of the tsarist régime. In education, some of the innovations were derived from indigenous traditions, such as nineteenth-century intellectual liberalism, and of course there were attempts to put some of Marx's ideas, such as work-related 'polytechnical' education, into practice. But there was also extensive borrowing from the West, and in particular from the United States; inevitably, much of this was ill-digested and chaotic in its effects at a time when the country was in desperate need of technologists, technicians, teachers, doctors, skilled workers of all kinds, and general literacy. It would be less than just to lay all the early failures at the door of Western progressive methods, but the indiscriminate adoption of practices developed in quite different circumstances did little for the efficiency of the system. It was all the easier, then, for Stalin to reimpose the whole set of traditional methods and content, and push Soviet schools into a conservative cast from which they have only recently begun to emerge.[21] This is an extreme case, but a useful reminder that educational practices are not always an exportable commodity.

Of course the practice in countries facing similar problems can be enlightening in the consideration of one's own, provided that due attention is paid to differences of context. What can all too easily happen, however, when the pattern of uncritical assimilation is set, is that the practices of the majority or dominant system are applied whether appropriate or not.

Not that the differences in these islands are anything like as wide as in the United States and the Soviet Union of the 1920s. But they do exist, and any educational system that fails to take account of them is not fully serving the needs of the society in which it functions. The same point could be made, if to a lesser degree, *within* systems, where the variety can be substantial. There is a limit to the extent to which one can reasonably go; but the internal differences within the countries of these islands are sufficient to justify building flexibility and variety into national systems, rather than assuming that national norms, whether emanating from London, Edinburgh or Cardiff, must be uniformly adhered to in every detail.

Although this study is concerned with Europe's offshore islands, interaction does not stop at the Channel or the North Sea, or even the Atlantic. Whatever the situation may have been in the past, this whole group of islands is now linked, economically, culturally, and now politically, with various multinational complexes. For the Scots, Welsh or Irish to assimilate to the English pattern of education would solve little in the long run—not even for the English, who are now finding themselves in the situation that the minority nations have known for centuries; they may find the experience of the Scots, Welsh and Irish instructive. However dominant the English pattern was in the British Isles, and even farther afield, the world has been changing. The European Economic Community is the most obvious of the multinational groupings which call the over-riding validity of the uniform national pattern into question.

The Treaty of Rome contains no provision on education as such, but it does include other requirements which make pressure on British education certain. One of these is the provision for 'normalisation and harmonisation' of professional qualifications.[22] So far, after some alarm expressed on the British side, the approach has been cautious. But the process has begun, even if it as yet affects little more than agreement about equivalences, and is unlikely to stop at adjustments of the length of courses, or even their content, to make these equivalences more credible. To expect this process to be confined to a few higher professions runs counter to the experience of the British Isles, or any other multi-systems complex.

The number of individuals involved is small, but this makes little difference; whatever happens to the most prestigious sectors of any educational system tends to affect the rest of it sooner or later. This has been obvious enough in England. Only a small minority have ever proceeded to higher education, yet the expectations of the universities have determined the patterns of courses of far more pupils than were ever likely to attempt to enter them. The controversy over comprehensive education, and the organisation of most comprehensive schools, have given great importance to the place of traditional, i.e. academic sixth-form work, minority concern though it is.[23] Again, by copying many 'public' school practices—sixth forms, prefects, uniforms, 'houses', and so forth—grammar schools, and many comprehensives too, display the same phenomenon.[24] Institutions with less prestige tend to copy the practices of those with more. There is no need to postulate (always) deliberate policy in this; but it happens none the less. Within the British Isles, as we have seen, the most widely copied model has been that of the southern English upper-middle class. The strengthening of even a few international links, however, can put a rather different gloss on this for the future.

Even if 'harmonisation' were confined in the first instance to such professions as medicine, law or engineering, the mechanism is set in motion. All three are high-prestige professions on the Continent, and the first two at least in the United Kingdom, where the relevant faculties exercise considerable influence in the universities. Similarly, non-university institutions of higher education, even now, tend to use the universities as a model—as witness the conversion of the colleges of advanced technology into universities, or the keenness of polytechnics and colleges of education to teach university-style degree courses. The capacity of higher education to influence the secondary schools has already been observed. All the parts of any educational system are interconnected, and it is impossible to change one part without affecting the rest. If pressure is applied at a particularly important point, the effects on the whole system are likely to be wide ranging indeed.

Nor does EEC influence stop there. Another relevant provision of the Treaty of Rome requires free movement of labour, obviously including educational workers at all levels.[25] It is not likely that the UK will experience a large influx of French and Italian teachers, but the Germans, Dutch and Danes at least are linguistically expert enough to treat Britain and Ireland as part of their potential employment area. Also, the possibility of having to seek employment on the Continent is likely to have effects on British and Irish education similar to those caused by the prospect of emigration to England or to North America on schools in Ireland, Wales and Scotland—the demand for recognised qualifications, marketable skills, linguistic competence. How widespread this will be is as yet unclear; but if the balance of political and industrial power continues to shift from London to Brussels and the Ruhr, British and Irish education can expect during the latter part of the twentieth century the same pressures that affected Ireland, Scotland and Wales during the nineteenth and early twentieth. Assimilation to the English system would solve no problems for *any* of the inhabitants of these islands.

Ironically, it is the English system that is 'out of step' with the continental models, rather than those of Scotland or Ireland, particularly on the question of subject specialisation. We have seen how Scottish and Irish secondary school and university curricula have moved closer to the English specialist model, but retain something of the generalist tradition. But on the Continent the position is otherwise. All the European countries permit some degree of specialisation in their secondary schools, but nowhere is there the degree of concentration on allied subjects that is found in Scotland, let alone in England.

Against an international background it is the English system that looks 'odd'; the Scottish and Irish systems, occupying the middle ground, seem rather less so. Of course, being the odd one out may be no bad thing; the objections to distorting one's own system to conform to the patterns of another are as valid for the English as anyone else. But the pressures we have been examining do not always operate according to what is desirable; and if the 'social Darwinism' of educational interaction continues to operate blindly, the English system too is likely to find itself faced with the prospect of assimilation or isolation. The consequences for the smaller systems are as yet a matter of conjecture. Perhaps wider international contact may reinforce the ailing generalist tradition in Scotland and Ireland. Far though they have gone on the road to assimilation, what is left of their native educational idiom could well prove to adjust better to international needs than in the case of England. Alternatively—and this applies more obviously to Scotland than to Ireland—awareness of pressure building up within the European community has already brought out the capacity of the English to assert their own peculiarities. Given the ease with which England, Britain and the United Kingdom are so often equated, this could mean growing pressure on Scotland to conform to an embattled 'British' (that is, English) pattern.

How this will work out may be a matter of timing. We are still some way from being sure how fast and how far the European community moves towards educational co-ordination, or whether the minority nations in Britain will be able to hold off assimilation long enough to forge their own links with the Continent. Both processes are at work; and it is our guess that there is a good chance of educational and cultural pluralism being established as the norm. For, in the long run, total assimilation to a single model is no solution. Let us, just for the sake of the argument, postulate the emergence of a single educational system for the entire EEC, with a unified administration responsible to the European parliament, a common pattern of curriculum, examinations, a common policy on comprehensive schooling, an agreed structure of higher education and an articulate common policy on entrance, a common pattern of teacher training, and so on. Let us suppose that some way has been found to reconcile French centralism with British 'partnership' between central and local government, that consensus on comprehensive education has managed to embrace the Danes and the Germans, we are still faced with some awkward facts—the societies still differ, new needs arise at different rates, the idea of having to route any action on these through some central body in Strasbourg raises fearsome practical problems, to say nothing of sporadic upsurges of national pride on both sides of the Channel, the Rhine, or the Alps. Even if all this could be resolved, the European Economic Community is not the only multinational complex to which the member states belong. Britain and Ireland, for example, are also members of what might be termed the 'North Atlantic Community' in the sense of having a common heritage and a common language, more or less, with the United States and Canada. Politically, the days of Britain's 'special relationship' with the USA may well be over, but educationally the links are close. Indeed, it makes some sense to define a wider anglophone cultural area, including Britain, Ireland, Canada, the United States, Australia and New Zealand and indeed the whole Commonwealth; for all the widening political distance between these countries, there is still considerable cultural and educational interaction, as the constant movement of academic staff and students testifies.

The connections with the 'New Commonwealth' should not be ignored either. Though India and the independent African states are markedly disinclined to see themselves as under British tutelage any more, the educational links are there. There is no need to revive the old anti-Market arguments to doubt whether this intercontinental connection can be replaced completely by identification with a European body rather than with the British Isles, even if integration should proceed much farther than is envisaged at present.

The habit of thinking in pyramidal patterns, whereby smaller units make up larger ones and these make larger ones still, has its uses, but has limitations as well; it can too easily obscure the fact that it is normal to belong to several groupings. Many nation states overlap different groups. Denmark, for instance, is a full member of the EEC, and as such is liable to whatever educational pressures develop within that body. But it is also a member of the Nordic Union, along with Norway, Sweden, Finland and Iceland, none of which is in the EEC, and with all of which she is linked culturally and geographically. The Nordic Union also has provisions for educational 'harmonisation' and exchange.[26] Denmark, it should be remembered, is a small country of about 5 million people, about the same as Scotland. If this is thought too small, and the suggestion has been made, then the further question needs to be asked: if Denmark has to assimilate, to which system can she turn? To Sweden with a population of 9 million, or West Germany with over 60 million? So far, the answer has been neither, though under some pressure from both. The reform plans of 1975 were closely modelled on the Swedish system with some major modifications. On the whole, though, Denmark has managed to keep her own identity, has been able to give influence as well as receive it, and has developed an educational system which is both Scandinavian and quite clearly her own. In so far as Denmark, like Norway, is conscious of being cut off from the outside world by a language spoken by few, she makes her outside links mainly with Britain, not only as a member of the EEC or as a traditional trade-partner, but as the nearest part of the English-speaking world; all Danes study English at school, many use it regularly in their work, students of most subjects read books in it. The question of assimilation does not really arise.

Denmark is the most obvious example of cultural overlap, but there are others. One can identify a German-language area, with the Federal Republic in the EEC, Austria and German-speaking Switzerland outside; but interchange is common, and it is quite possible that *détente* may bring East Germany closer as well, without expecting it to be detached from the Eastern bloc.[27] In recent years, there has been a similar increase in contact between France and other francophone areas, notably Quebec.

As a further complication, some minorities straddle frontiers. The Catalans and Basques live on both sides of the French-Spanish frontier. Attempts to assimilate them into the major cultures have not been conspicuously successful. Until the death of Franco, the Spanish authorities regarded their own Basques and Catalans simply as Spaniards, and insisted that Castilian only be used in the schools. The French policy[28] towards their own Basques, Catalans and others has been the same in principle, if less bloodily enforced. For purely internal minorities, assimilation to the majority culture may be at least feasible, though often resisted; but for shared minorities even that solution is doubtfully viable, with co-nationals across the frontier as a counter-balance. France has consistently reinforced economic and demographic pressures with a rigidly unitary school system; but even there the long-denied right to schooling in the mother tongue is at least being considered. If even France is re-examining the wisdom of a policy of educational uniformity, the tide may be running for pluralism after all.

It is possible to extrapolate from past and present trends, but only up to a point; a number of unknowns—including timing—make firm prediction impossible. What we can do, however, is to indicate a number of possibilities. Obviously, we also have our own preferences of the way things *ought* to go. These should be obvious enough by now, and can be allowed for; but lest some of our observations be dismissed as wishful thinking, it should be borne in mind that one reason for our favouring pluralism, accepting both the characteristics of the smaller nations *and* the international context, is a practical one: the available evidence suggests that assimilation to bigger, homogeneous units, which once looked inevitable, does not really work in a multinational world. If we are rejecting the policies both of backyard nationalism and of uniformity, this is not only by inclination but also out of regard for the facts. Some of these might be thought so obvious as not to require to be stated; but in view of the level of incomprehension of the issues that arose during the discussion of the 1975 White Paper on devolution, it seems that some of them do need spelling out after all.

First of all, the differences between the educational systems exist, reflecting differences between the societies themselves. Those of the smaller countries do not seem insignificant to their inhabitants just because they are small, annoying though this must be to those accustomed to thinking in simplistic metropolitan terms.

Secondly—and this needs to be emphasised, for it has been widely misunderstood—insistence on retaining one's identity, in education or anything else, does not necessarily imply hostility towards any other group. For reasons already examined, substantial numbers in these islands see some form of direct control over their own affairs as the only hope of avoiding the total submergence of their identities in the English pattern—especially as they perceive how little an appeal the idea of multinational 'Britishness' has had to the English in the post-imperial period. Further, in spite of Roger Young's remarks, there is not a great deal of 'ours is better than theirs' sentiment. Few Scots can now believe in the superiority of Scottish education, whatever may have been the case in the past, though resentment does move some to cling to this belief as a defence against metropolitan arrogance. More commonly, all they will claim is that Scottish education has different origins, has developed differently, and should continue to develop with reference to its own society instead of someone else's.

Thirdly, the differences *between* systems seem to over-ride the internal ones, real though these are. Quite a few MPs seem to misunderstand this issue. Eric Heffer, for example, has declared that the economic problems of Tyneside are just as grave as those of Scotland, which is near enough true; but Tyneside is not a nation; Tyneside does not have even the remains of a distinctive educational system, national church, legal code or independent history. If the Tynesiders perceived themselves as anything but English, that would be a different matter; but they do not. There is a powerful case for *decentralisation* within England, in education as in other functions, but that is a different issue. That such basic confusions can still come up so easily shows how little the fundamental issues of identity have been understood.

We have already spent much of this volume deploying arguments against ill-considered assimilation. But digging in one's heels and refusing to have anything to do with ideas of practices of neighbours we feel to be equally undesirable. Since the most obvious threats to the integrity of the smaller systems come from England (so far, at least) it is in many ways an understandable reaction, but we believe it to be a short-sighted one. Policy making by contraries can produce some odd results. When the Czechoslovak authorities in 1968 began to reintroduce early selection for the *gymnasium* (the academic school, hitherto taking pupils from age 15 to 19), they were both yielding to middle-class pressure and making a nationalist gesture, since comprehensive schooling was identified with Soviet influence. Ironically, it was not a particularly Czechoslovak institution that was being revived, but something that the First Republic had inherited from the Austro-Hungarian empire. A genuinely Czech tradition, exemplified in the work of Comenius, would have been more like the comprehensive structure from which (temporarily, as it turned out) the Czechoslovak government was moving.[29] In much the same way, educational opinion in West Germany after the war favoured the reintroduction of the pre-Nazi system, without really considering whether the world might have changed in other ways. Again, this was understandable, but it fixed West German education in a traditionalist mould for decades; and the heated rejection of any kind of comprehensive reform, on the grounds that anything the East Germans were doing could not be right, held up even the most timid plans for reform right up to the present.[30] Indigenous traditions are less easy to identify than is commonly supposed.

There are plenty of examples of this kind of thing in these islands. The wrath of the Gaelic Athletic Association at De Valera's professed liking for the English game of rugby has already been mentioned. In fact, membership of the GAA was long held to be incompatible with playing, or even watching, 'British' games at all. In Wales, the willingness of the National Eisteddfod to admit singing in Italian or German—virtually any language except English—is of the same kind. Again, one sees the reason for this decision—Welsh has never been under threat from Italian or German—but it does have a slightly comical flavour about it. A good Scottish example is the spectacle of a distinguished Scottish historian defending selection at 4-plus in certain English-style Edinburgh schools as part of the authentic Scottish tradition.

But however genuine the existing tradition may be, uncritical resistance to innovation can be as damaging as uncritial assimilation. The fact that the English have been doing something is not, in itself, a very good reason for doing it in Scotland or Ireland; but it is not a very good reason for refusing to do it either, since in both cases it means defining one's own needs in relation to someone else's. To cling to features *just because they are distinctive* is to run the risk of being stuck with characteristics that events in one's own society may render irrelevant or even harmful, and it certainly makes it more difficult to consider on their merits ideas from any source. Permanent stagnation is a high price to pay for the symbols of distinctive identity.

These are difficult times for small nations, but there are opportunities as well as dangers, opportunities to develop educational systems responsive both to their own needs and those of the larger world, a world much wider than appeared during the long period of Britannic self-sufficiency and English dominance. In spite of the dangers, however, the opportunities are real. Internationalism in education and politics is not the same thing as cosmopolitanism, the absence of any national roots at all. On the contrary, the very multiplicity of international links makes a base of one's own, from which to relate to the wider context, all the more important. Similarly, we need not regard concern with national and cultural identity as a divisive force, to be labelled dismissively as nationalistic, but as a way of providing greater security within the complexity of human cultures. We are all several people, and the complexity of modern society is such that identity on several levels is not only possible, but necessary. There is no reason why an individual should not be able to think of himself as human, European, British, Welsh (or whatever), as well as a Presbyterian, a socialist, or a veterinary surgeon; and it is reasonable to expect his education to take account of this multiple identity. There is, therefore, no contradiction in the decision of one major school in Edinburgh to pay particular attention to developing Scottish studies (including Gaelic) *and* planning to introduce the International Baccalaureate, with its emphasis on modern languages as well as the familiar broad-based continual pattern of studies.[31] Both are ways of breaking out of a unitary pattern which has become a barrier to national and international sensitivity alike.

Allowing that the dangers mentioned are still strong, and that the benefits of pluralism will not come automatically, what practical steps can be taken in these islands?

First, it is necessary to pursue devolution of education vigorously with a clearer appreciation of the interdependence of the parts of the educational systems than the 1975 White Paper demonstrated. Both the unitary policy and that of half-hearted administrative devolution have proved ineffective in enabling the Scots and Welsh to run their own systems to suit their own needs.

But, secondly, *internal* pluralism also has to be accorded due recognition. How far this should be translated into regional reorganisations in, say, England depends on how far the people of the various areas feel that their differences are great enough to require special educational arrangements. The differences in Scotland between Gael and Lowlander, though not affecting their identity as Scots, are real enough, and have to be allowed for. In a symbolic sense, Gaelic is now seen as something belonging to Scots in general, but in the Isles and parts of the Highlands it is still the language of everyday life. Its status in the educational system therefore has to be different in the different parts of the country. It would also be worth considering some sort of special provision for Shetland, and possibly Orkney; in the first case at least, the inhabitants are reluctant to be considered Scots at all, having historical links with Norway, and a history of exploitation and neglect after union with Scotland.[32] It would be foolish to insist that they assimilate to a pattern more appropriate for the Scottish Lowlands; there is nothing inherently less valid about the culture of 17,000 people than of 5 million. Cultural and economic repression in the Highlands and the Western and Northern Isles has been the work of Scots as well as English; if the Scots cannot find a way of making acceptable arrangements for *their* minorities, they can hardly be surprised at failure on the part of the English.

There is also an obvious need for machinery to facilitate international contact and interchange. While not accepting the argument of Roger Young, we do take the point that mobility between England and Scotland is made more difficult than it need be by the examination system. By the same token, of course, it is even more difficult between these islands and the rest of Europe as well as North America. Without pretending that uniformity is either desirable or possible, we would suggest two courses of action.

First, having identified those characteristics that help international recognition of qualifications, it should be possible either to adapt one's own system to the required extent (with the advantage of adapting to an international pattern rather than that of *one* other system) or to provide an alternative qualification recognised by one's own system and by sufficient other countries to make it internationally credible. The International Baccalaureate is a good example of what can be done.

Secondly, the several educational systems—*especially* the smaller ones—have to make a particular point of keeping in touch with other countries. When properly organised and taken seriously, there can be great value in school and academic exchanges long or short special courses and conferences. The British Council, the Ministry of Overseas

Development and individual institutions sponsor a fair amount of this already. There is danger of abuse, it can add to the cost of education, and expenditure on this kind of thing is often the first to feel the financial draught. It is important, however, that these links be maintained and extended and that genuine internationalism be used to avoid insularity and at the same time protect identity. It could be fatal to any system to have only one set of ideas to draw on from outside. It seems worth paying a little to secure the alternative.

There is a task here for teachers, administrators, planners and researchers. But this is an area where there is work for educational theorists too. The need for more careful and thoughtful planning at the micro-level is obvious enough in all educational systems. But the macro-level has been relatively neglected, involving as it does the policy of educational systems, their development and their interaction with each other. There is a need to *use* the work of educational historians, for instance, to identify genuine rather than spurious educational traditions and to add to our insight into the working of educational systems. There has been a tendency of late to dismiss educational history as of purely antiquarian interest, perhaps as a reaction to its previous uses as mere cataloguing or, worse, reinforcement of national mythologies with tales of 'past glories', real or imagined. Misunderstanding a system's past has often helped misunderstanding of its present.

Comparative studies, too, have a real contribution to make in the formation of educational policy. They can help disseminate ideas by identifying general trends, and even, to an extent, predict developments under certain conditons. By demonstrating the connections between educational systems and their contexts, they can warn against uncritical transplantation of practices and principles; and, by the same method, may identify some things that *can* be transplanted. The much-maligned educational sociologist has his part to play too, by examining what the social realities of education actually are, not just what anecdotal evidence and 'common-sense expectation', that most unreliable of guides, leads us to believe they should be; he can also remind us of the damaging role of class-based emulation in the British Isles. To introduce some direction and purpose into what has often been the blind interplay of forces in education requires clearer policy making on the part of the authorities in all the countries concerned; and for this an adequate theoretical basis, an understanding of how systems work, is urgently needed.

There is also a need for a shift of attitudes all round if the interplay of forces is not to produce more confusion. Things cannot be allowed to drift unless we are prepared to accept total uniformity (which would be dull and probably unworkable) or, possibly, total fragmentation. If we are to attain a system combining basic unity with diversity, we need—while accepting enough common ground for exchange and mobility, and reasonable degree of shared experience—to accept the fact of human variety, to respect the identity of others, and to understand the importance of context for all systems, majority and minority alike. In a shrinking world, where no man, nation, state—or educational system, or part thereof—is an island, this is a task of the utmost importance. If we cannot get the balance right in the educational systems, if we cannot fashion them to meet the needs of English, Irish, Scots and Welsh alike, if we cannot through the schools teach awareness and respect both for our own identities and those of the other peoples with whom we share these islands, then our prospects for civilised relationships with each other, let alone with the European Community we have joined and the wider world to which we belong unavoidably, must be reckoned bleak indeed.

NOTES AND REFERENCES

1 Robert Burns, 'Such a Parcel of Rogues in a Nation' (*Poetical Works*, London, Collins, 1948), p. 406.

2 See, e.g., John Prebble, *Culloden* (Harmondsworth, Penguin, 1967), and *The Highland Clearances* (Harmondsworth, Penguin, 1969).

3 For background to the strength of the economic motives, see John Prebble, *The Darien Disaster* (Harmondsworth, Penguin, 1970).

4 See, e.g., S. L. Hunter, *The Scottish Educational System* (Oxford, Pergamon 1971), pp. 1-22; Ned Thomas, 'Education in Wales', in Bell, Fowler and Little (eds), *Education in Great Britain and Ireland* (London, Routledge & Kegan Paul, 1973), pp. 14-19; Norman Atkinson, *Irish Education: A History of Irish Institutions* (Dublin, Figgis, 1969); P. J. Dowling, *A History of Irish Education* (Cork, Mercier, 1971), pp. 73-100. For a fuller account of Irish methods of sustaining elements of their own system under penalty, see P. J. Dowling, *The Hedge Schools of Ireland* (Cork, Mercier, 1968).

5 For a general treatment of the development of the separate systems, see Atkinson, op. cit., and R. E. Bell, 'Ireland: a case study', in *Education, Economics and Politics: Case Studies 3 and 4* (Open University Course E352 Block 5, 1973), pp. 7-8.

6 Roger Young, 'Sixteen to twenty-one: the "debatable area"', in R. E. Bell and A. J. Youngson (eds), *Present and Future in Higher Education* (London, Tavistock, 1973), pp. 78-9.

7 ibid., p. 81.

8 It may be a small but significant point, but James VI and VII of Scots were known as I and II respectively, of Britain as of England. But the principle does not apply in reverse. If it did, the monarchs referred to would be known as William II, Edward I, Edward II, and Elizabeth I. (None of the Plantagenets or Tudors was King of Scots, though some claimed to be.) The implication seems to be that size counts for more than history, logic or courtesy. As for the Union flag (*not*, as it is so often incorrectly termed, the Union Jack) it is just what the name suggests, the flag of the Union of

England, Scotland and Ireland; it is not, and never has been, the flag of England only. That is a red cross on a white ground, but since few seem aware of this it is rarely used.

9 *Our Changing Democracy: Devolution to Scotland and Wales* (Cmnd 6348, London, HMSO, 1975).

10 See, e.g., Jack Brand and Donald McCrone, 'The SNP: from protest to nationalism', *New Society*, 20 November 1975, pp. 416-18.

11 Brand and McCrone, loc. cit.

12 Even allowing for sampling errors, only about half the population seemed to favour devolution in a BBC poll (November 1975).

13 For example, Iain Mac Cuinn and Iain Mac Aonguis, 'Gaidhlig air Gallachd Alba', *The Weekend Scotsman*, 6 December 1975, p. 7.

14 The Greek practice of labelling non-Greeks 'barbaroi', or the French habit of imposing French institutions on Africans and Asians, are both in the classic tradition farther afield.

15 There is an extensive literature, mostly European or American, on this theme. For a useful examination of the basic problems, see George W. Parkyn, *Towards a Conceptual Model of Lifelong Learning* (Paris, UNESCO, 1973).

16 See further Oskar Anweiler, *Die Sowjetpädagogik in der Welt von heute* (Heidelberg, Quelle u. Meyer, 1968), pp. 32-66 (A. S. Makarenko und die Pädagogik seiner Zeit); Sheila Fitzpatrick, *The Commissariat of Enlightenment* (Cambirdge, CUP, 1970); and N. Grant, *Soviet Education* (Harmondsworth, Penguin, 1972).

17 'The issues on which Northern Ireland policy would be or is allowed to differ British policy as a whole are few; by far the greater part of Northern Ireland legislation is simply a duplication of Westminster.' Roy Bradford (former NI Minister), *Listener*, 20 July 1972; cit. Bell, op. cit., p. 20.

18 For a penetrating critique of excessive specialisation in the English system see John Hajnal, *The Student Trap* (Harmondsworth, Penguin, 1972).

19 *Report of the Working Party on the Curriculum of the Senior Secondary School, Introduction of the Ordinary Grade of the Scottish Leaving Certificate* (Edinburgh, HMSO, 1959).

20 This point is expanded by J. P. Mackintosh, 'Politics and Citizenship', in J. Lowe, N. Grant and T. D. Williams (eds), *Education and Nation-Building in the Third World* (Scottish Academic Press, 1971), pp. 141-2, and N. Grant, *Society, Schools and Progress in Eastern Europe* (Pergamon, 1969), pp. 59-72.

21 For fuller treatment of this period, see Anweiler, op. cit.; Fitzpatrick, op. cit.; and Janusz Tomiak, *The Soviet Union* (Newton Abbot, David & Charles, 1973).

22 Treaty Establishing the European Economic Community (Rome), 27 March 1957, Article 57.

23 Eric James, *Essay on the Content of Education* (London, Harrap, 1949), makes the alleged difficulty of maintaining a sixth form of viable size one of his main arguments against comprehensive schooling. So, to an extent, does Robin Davis, *The Grammar School* (Harmondsworth, Penguin, 1967), pp. 54-6.

24 For some revealing comments by grammar school headmistresses, see Brian Jackson and Dennis Marsden, *Education and the Working Class* (Harmondsworth, Penguin, 1966), p. 239.
25 Treaty, Article 48.
26 For example, A. C. Vaigo, 'Nordic Council plans joint curriculum programmes', *Times Educational Supplement*, 29 December 1972.
27 For a thorough treatment of this question, see Arthur Hearnden, *Education in the Two Germanies* (Oxford, Blackwell, 1975).
28 Paul Sérant, *La France des minorités* (Paris, Laffont, 1965).
29 Radim Palouš, 'Pädagogische und soziologische Aspekte der Differenzierung im tschechoslowakischen Sekundarschulwesen', in Oskar Anweiler (ed.), *Bildungsreformen in Osteuropa* (Stuttgart, Kohlhammer, 1969), pp. 154-67; and Donald Skinner, 'Secondary school reform in Czechoslovakia' (University of Edinburgh M.Ed thesis, 1970).
30 S. B. Robinsohn and J. K. Kuhlmann, 'Two decades of non-reform in West German education', *Comparative Education Review*, October 1967, XI, pp. 311-30.
31 The Royal High School.
32 Norwegian visitors, generally seamen, are frequent enough to make Norwegian seem to many pupils worth learning. For the depredations of Scottish rule, see Eric Linklater, *Orkney and Shetland* (London, Robert Hale, 1971), pp. 72-84.

Appendix 1

Figures

Educational systems of the British Isles

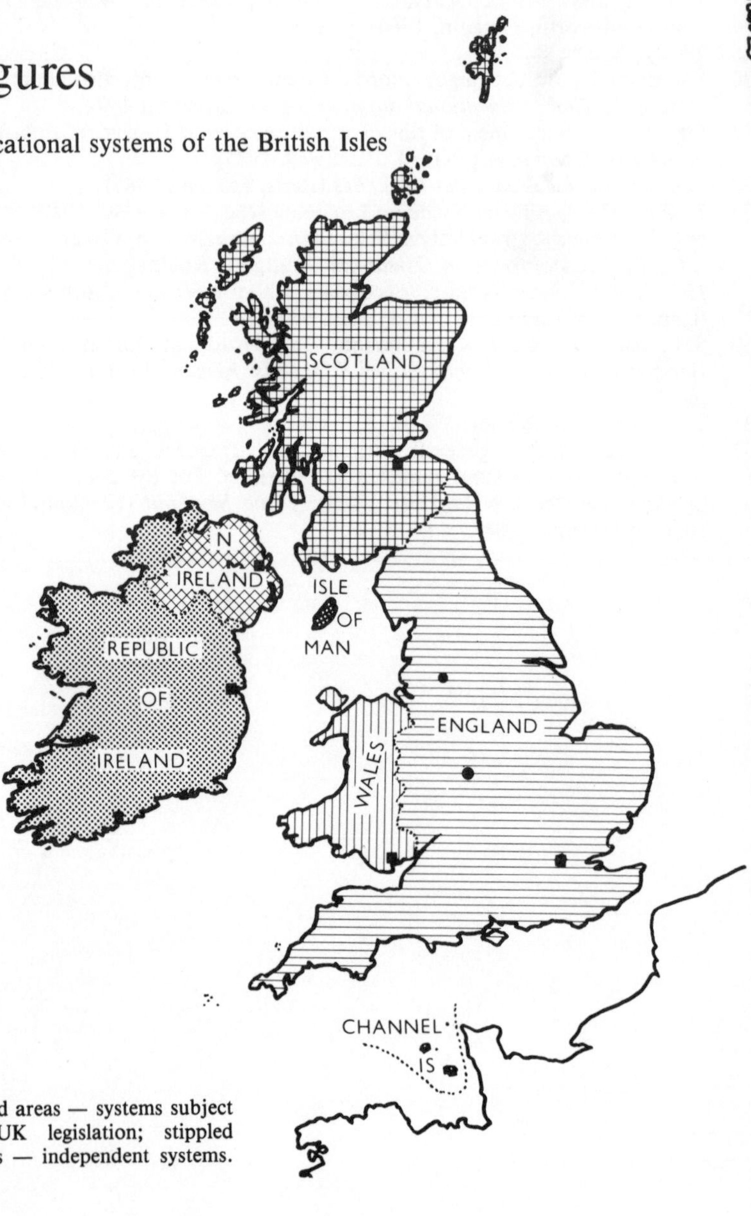

Lined areas — systems subject to UK legislation; stippled areas — independent systems.

Figure 1 *Educational Systems of the British Isles*

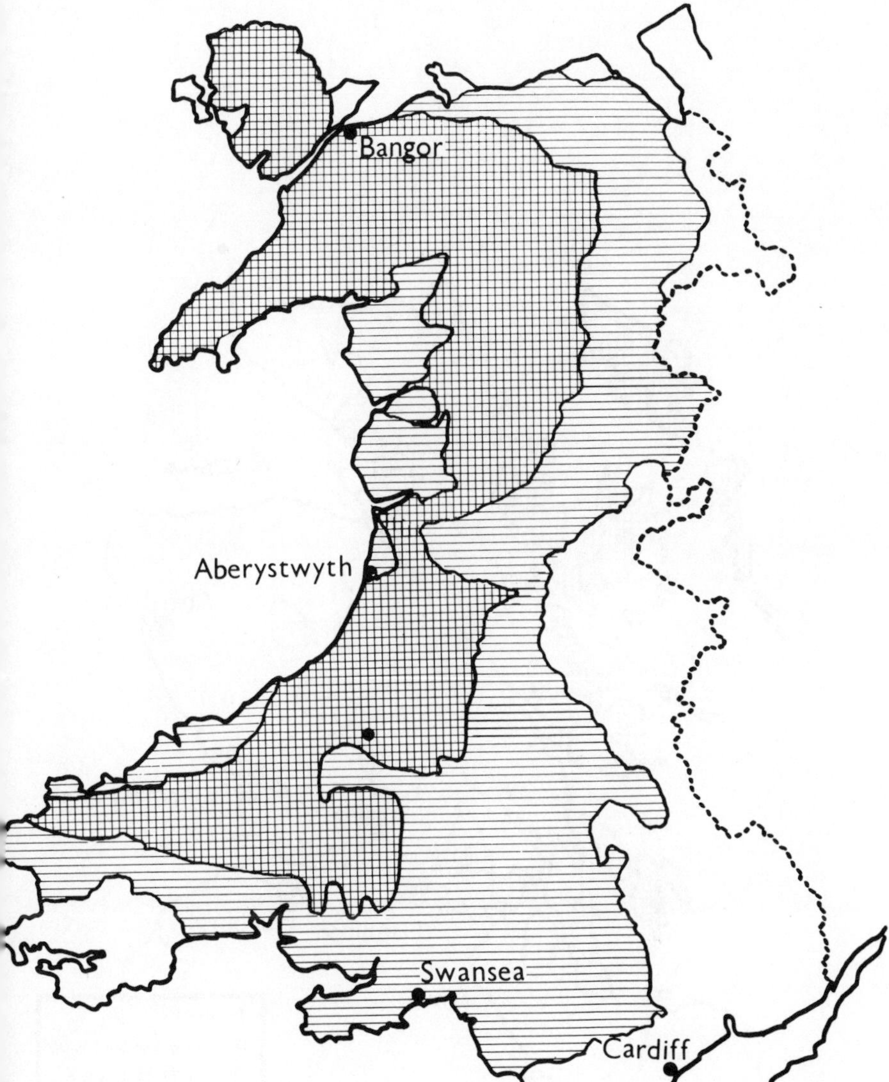

Figure 2 *Wales: Welsh-Speaking Areas and University Colleges*

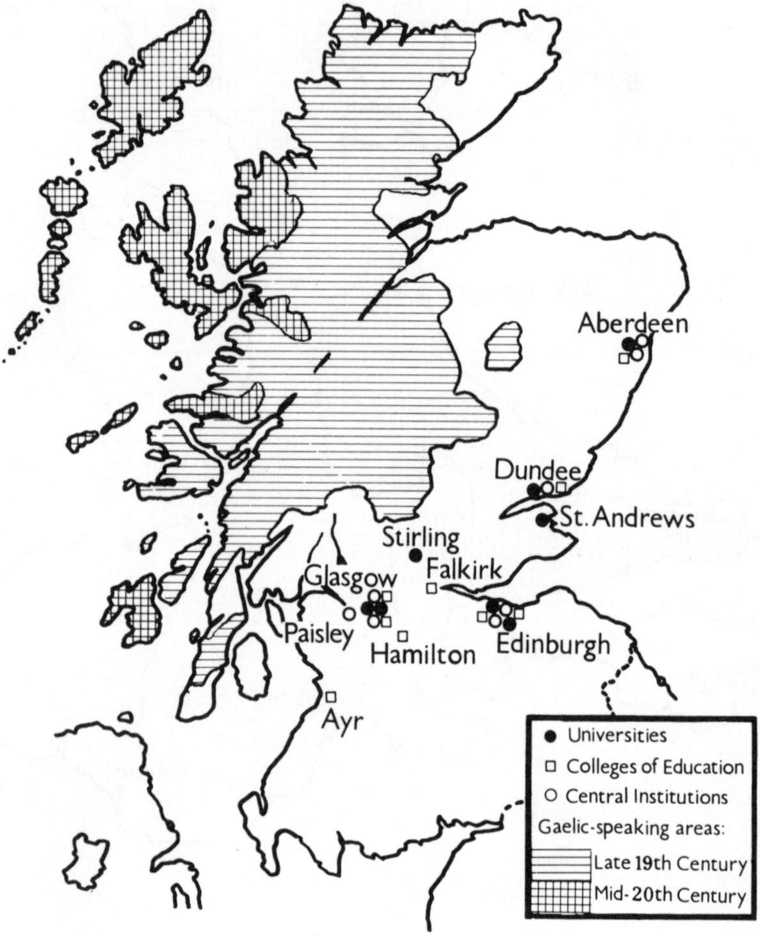

Figure 3 *Scotland: Gaeldom and Higher Education*

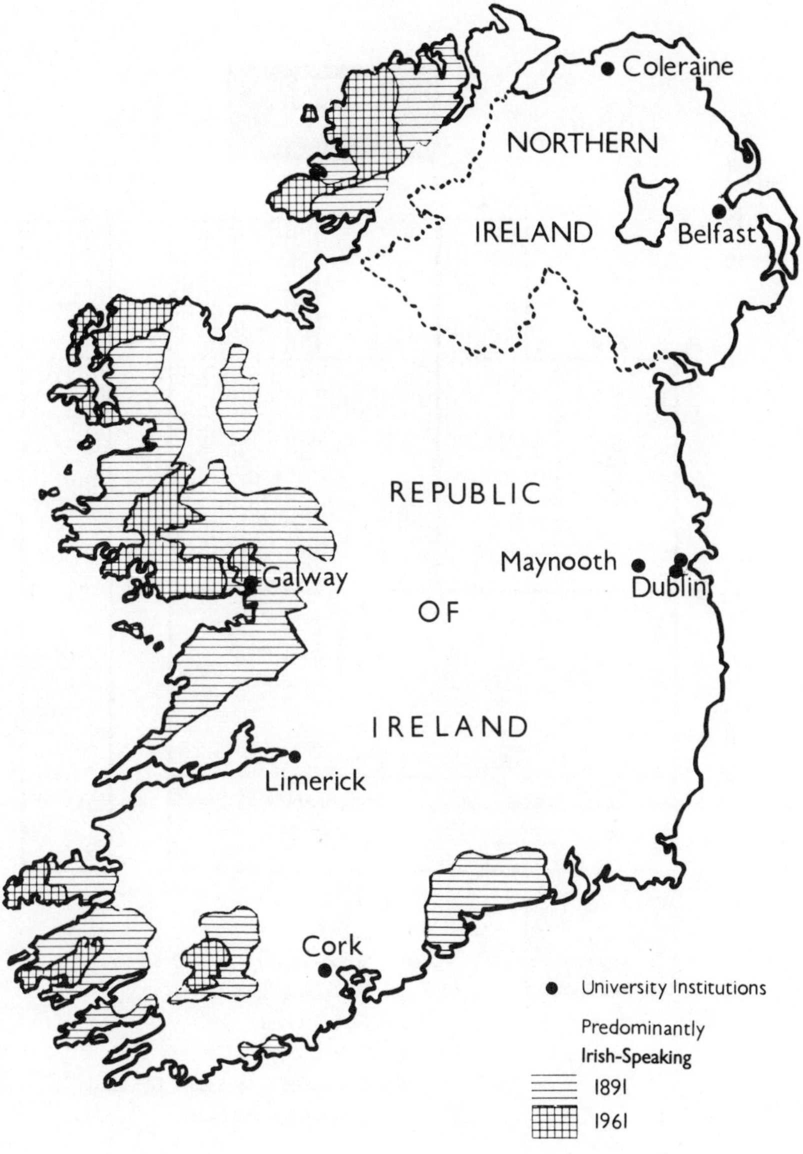

Figure 4 *Ireland: Gaeltacht and University Institutions*

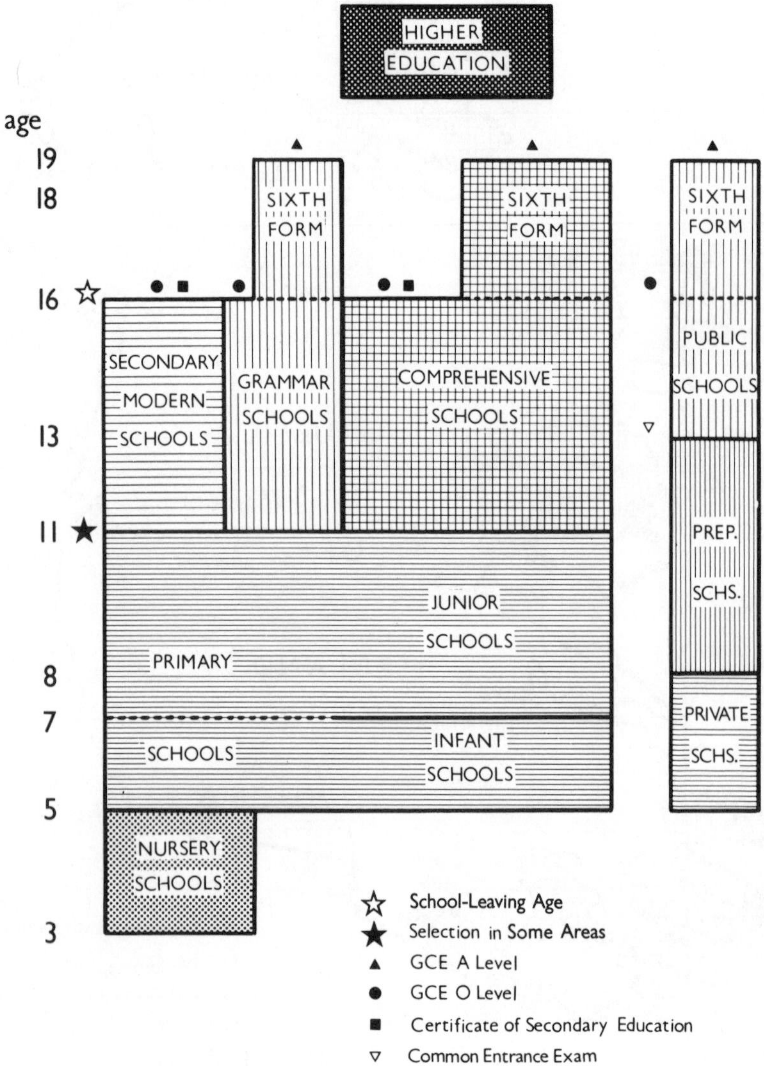

Figure 5 *The School System of England and Wales*

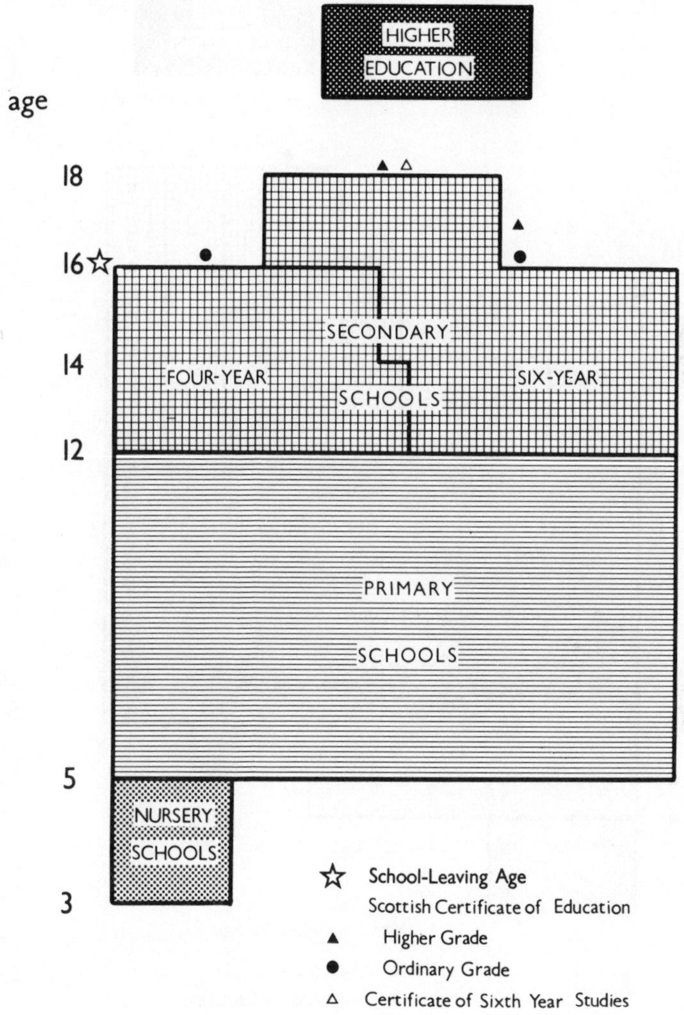

Figure 6 *The Scottish School System*

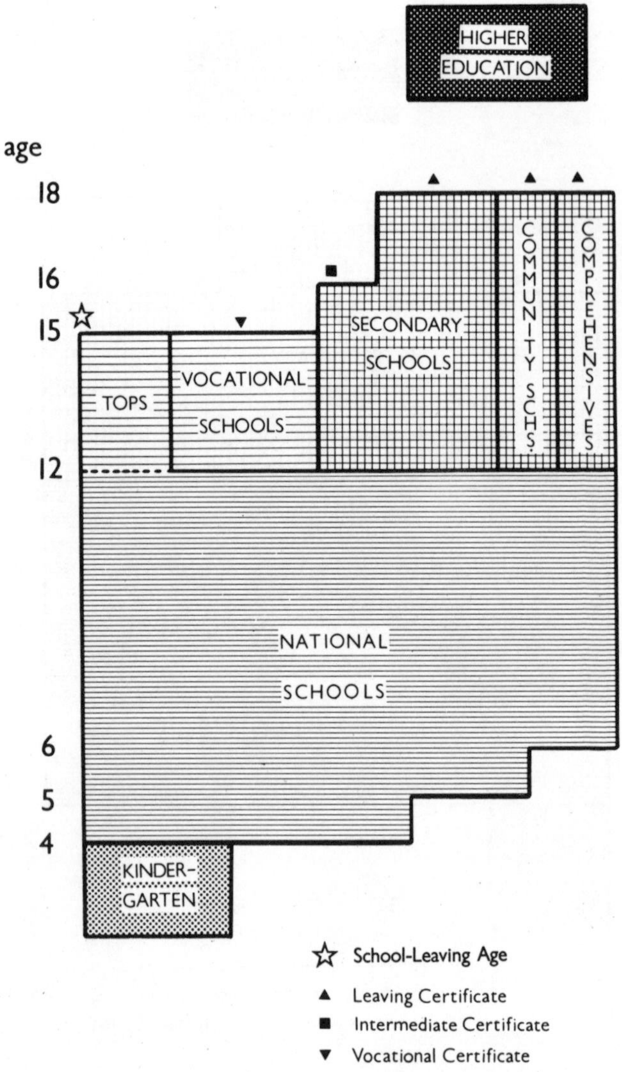

Figure 7 *The School System of the Republic of Ireland*

Appendix 2

Irish Differences in 1970

Those who were broadly 'Catholic' and 'nationalist' would include at least two major groupings (though we must emphasise that these and our other categories are by no means exhaustive).

CN1 The Catholic members of both Sinn Feins (the political wings of the two IRAs)—all those holding a belief that a sovereign, independent, united Ireland should be established by force if necessary, opposing Ireland's membership of the European Economic Community but often far from agreed on whether a sovereign, independent Ireland should be primarily Gaelic or English speaking or on how far its political institutions should be socialist in character.

CN2 The Catholic supporters of all three major political parties in the Republic as well as the Social Democratic and Labour Party (SDLP) and the nationalist parties in the North. All these groups share an ostensible belief in the desirability of establishing a sovereign, united independent Ireland by peaceful means (though they are often split over whether Ireland should join the EEC, often have differing views on how Ireland should relate to the rest of the British Isles, often differ over whether socialism is desirable and often differ over the extent to which the revival of the Irish language should be made compulsory in schools).

But there were also significant groups which can be described as 'Catholic' and 'unionist':

CU1 In Northern Ireland, a growing number of mainly middle-class Catholics who see economic and cultural advantages in union with Britain and have lost all interest in a united Ireland. They might well support 'unionist' political parties, including the Northern Ireland Labour Party which is as committed to maintaining the border as the Ulster Unionist Party proper.

CU2 A growing number of Catholics in the Republic (mainly middle class) who feel a stronger pull towards the values of United Kingdom and American society than to what they would regard as an outdated nationalist ideology. They welcome what their opponents would regard as the disguised surrender of sovereignty provided by the free-trade area agreement with the United Kingdom and entry to the EEC. They may, nevertheless, for sentimental or commercial reasons still pay lip-service to statements of 'national' sentiments (as, indeed, may members of CU1).

CU3 Professional and upper class Catholics all over Ireland who have never abandoned their loyalty to the British imperial concept and see themselves essentially as part of the career and social structure of the United Kingdom whose political withdrawal from most of Ireland they have in fact refused to treat as a reality during the past fifty years.

There are also groups who are both 'nationalist' and 'Protestant' (itself a diffuse and ill-defined term—ranging in its cover from lapsed Seventh Day Adventists to Anglo-Catholic nuns):

PN1 The small number in Northern Ireland who have adhered to a strict nationalist ideology either of the extreme CN1 type or (more probably) of type CN2. Such Protestant membership of nationalist movements has, of course, a long history. While they were nearly always the exception rather than the rule, they did throw up significant figures such as Wolfe Tone, McCracken and Parnell who were accepted as nationalist leaders by Catholics.

PN2 The majority of Protestants in the Republic whose views (particularly of those under the age of fifty) are now broadly similar to those of CN2. Paradoxically, however, many Protestants in the Republic combine a commitment, sometimes even an enthusiastic commitment, to the views of political parties in the Republic with assumptions (similar to those of CU3) that their children still belong to the career structure of the British Isles as a whole. This is, of course, a function of the old British and unionist role of Protestants in the South but the assumption is possibly dying out among the young. Members of this group have tended to be emigration-minded and have been less committed to the promotion of a Gaelic culture, which is often seen as both Catholic and anti-British. They do, nevertheless, think of themselves as Irish rather than British, however alienated they may sometimes feel from Catholic- or Gaelic-dominated groupings.

PN3 Those in Northern Ireland who have no political belief in uniting Ireland and who may even vote for Unionist candidates (in their Conservative capacity) but who primarily regard themselves as Irishmen, read the Dublin *Irish Times*, and would welcome eventual reunion on their own terms. They are the chief cause of continued cultural integration and, until the recent troubles at any rate, saw the border as no real barrier in pursuing their major interests (i.e. cultural, religious and sporting).

The most obvious grouping of all is those who are both 'Protestant' and 'unionist':

PU1 Those in Northern Ireland who see themselves as not being Irish in any sense and indeed regard Ireland as being inhabited by two quite separate nations, the Irish and the British. Until recently they have never represented more than a minority of the Northern Ireland population.

PU2 The vast majority of Protestants in Nothern Ireland along with one or two small groups of Protestants in the Republic (mainly members of the smaller Protestant groupings). They are totally opposed to Northern Ireland's political integration with the Republic but are now in some disarray over the form which any new political arrangement protecting Northern Ireland interests should take — whether it should involve total integration into the United Kingdom (i.e. with the abolition of the Belfast Parliament), a return to the previous status quo (before 1972), unilateral declaration of independence, etc. Most of them would regard themselves as being both British *and* Irish with emphasis on the former. They may or may not be interested in general Irish culture. They may, for example, send their children to Dublin University (Trinity College) or to 'smart' schools in the Republic but have little knowledge of Irish history and literature.

N-CN and N-CU There are, in addition, some non-Christian and/or revolutionary groups who would refuse the Catholic/Protestant label altogether but even they are to be placed at different points of the nationalist/unionist continuum — some hold views broadly similar to CN1 but others, such as the British and Irish Communist Party, fully accept PU1's two-nation theory.

The above material is taken from Robert Bell and Karen Jones, *Education, Economy and Politics: Case Studies,* Parts 3 and 4, which forms part of Block 5 of the Open University course 'Education, Economy and Politics' (Milton Keynes, Open University Press, 1973).

Suggestions for Further Reading

1 THE HISTORICAL AND GEOGRAPHICAL BACKGROUND

Edwards, Ruth Dudley, *An Atlas of Irish History* (London, Methuen, 1973).
Jackson, Kenneth, *Language and History in Early Britain* (Edinburgh University Press, 1953).
Linklater, Eric, *Orkney and Shetland* (London, Robert Hale, 1971).
MacLean, Calum I., *The Highlands* (Inverness, Club Leabhar, 1975).
Morgan, Prys, *Background to Wales* (Llandybie, Davies, 1968).
Murray, W.H., *The Islands of Western Scotland* (London, Eyre Methuen, 1973).
Norman, Edward, *A History of Modern Ireland* (Harmondsworth, Penguin, 1973).
O'Brien, Conor Cruise, *States of Ireland* (St Albans, Panther, 1973).
O'Brien, Conor Cruise and Maire, *Concise History of Ireland* (London, Thames & Hudson, 1972).
Prebble, John, *The Lion in the North* (Penguin 1972).
Raftery, Joseph (ed.), *The Celts* (Cork, Mercier, 1967).
Rees, William, *A Historical Atlas of Wales from Early to Modern Times* (London, Faber & Faber, 1972).
Smout, T. C., *A History of the Scottish People, 1560-1830* (London, Collins, 1969; Fontana 1972).

2 THE POLITICAL BACKGROUND

Brown, Gordon (ed.), *The Red Paper on Scotland* (Edinburgh, EUSPB, 1975).
Clarke, M. G. and Drucker, H. M. (eds), *Our Changing Scotland: A Yearbook of Scottish Government 1976-77* (Edinburgh, EUSPB, 1976).
Edwards, Owen Dudley, Evans, Gwynfor, Rhys, Ioan and MacDiarmid, Hugh, *Celtic Nationalism* (London, Routledge & Kegan Paul, 1968).
Fitzgerald, Garret, *Towards a New Ireland* (Dublin, Gill & Macmillan, 1973).
Gronnenberg, Roy, *Island Governments* (Lerwick, Thuleprint Paperback, 1976).
Kedourie, Elie, *Nationalism* (London, Hutchinson, 1960).
Kellas, James J., *The Scottish Political System* (Cambridge University Press, 1973).
Kennedy, Gavin, *The Radical Approach* (Edinburgh, Palingenesis Press, 1976).
Mackintosh, John P., *The Devolution of Power* (Harmondsworth, Penguin, 1968).
Our Changing Democracy. Devolution to Scotland and Wales (Cmnd 6348). (London, HMSO, 1975). *Supplementary Document* (London, HMSO, 1976).

3 THE EDUCATIONAL SYSTEMS

Atkinson, Norman, *A History of Educational Institutions* (Dublin, Figgis, 1969).

Baron, G., *Society, Schools and Progress in England* (Oxford, Pergamon, 1965).
Bell, R. E. and Youngson, A. J. (eds), *Present and Future in Higher Education* (London, Tavistock, 1973).
Bell, Robert, Fowler, Gerald and Little, Ken (eds), *Education in Great Britain and Ireland: A Source Book* (London, Open University/Routledge & Kegan Paul, 1973).
Bell, Robert and Grant, Nigel, *A Mythology of British Education* (St Albans, Panther, 1974).
Boyle, Edward, Crossland, Anthony and Kegan, Maurice, *The Politics of Education* (Harmondsworth, Penguin, 1971).
Brosan, George *et al.*, *Patterns and Policies in Higher Education* (Harmondsworth, Penguin, 1971).
Burgess, Tyrrell, *A Guide to English Schools* (Harmondsworth, Penguin, 1972).
Davie, George, *The Democratic Intellect; Scotland and her Universities in the Nineteenth Century* (Edinburgh, Edinburgh University Press, 1950).
Davis, Robin, *The Grammar School* (Harmondsworth, Penguin, 1967).
Dowling, P. J., *A History of Irish Education: A study in conflicting loyalties* (Cork, Mercier, 1971).
Green, V. H. H., *The Universities* (Harmondsworth, Penguin, 1969).
Hajnal, John, *The Student Trap. A Critique of University and Sixth-Form Curricula* (Harmondsworth, Penguin, 1972).
Hunter, S. Leslie, *The Scottish Educational System* (Oxford, Pergamon, 1971; 2nd ed.).
Hurt, John, *Education in Evolution* (London, Paladin, 1971).
Jarman, T. L., *Landmarks in the History of Education* (London, Murray, 1963).
Lambert, Royston and Milham, Spencer, *The Hothouse Society* (Harmondsworth, Penguin, 1974).
Layard, Richard, King, John and Moser, Claus, *The Impact of Robbins* (Harmondsworth, Penguin, 1969).
Macgregor, Forbes, *What is Education in Scotland?* (Preston, Akros, 1971).
McPherson, Andrew and Neave, Guy, *The Scottish Sixth* (Slough, NFER, 1976).
Murphy, Michael W., *Education in Ireland: Now and the Future* (Cork, Mercier, 1970).
Musgrave, P. W. (ed.), *Sociology, History and Education* (London, Methuen, 1970).
Osborne, G. S., *Scottish and English Schools* (London, Longmans, 1967).
Parkinson, Michael, *The Labour Party and the Organization of Secondary Education 1918-1965* (London, Routledge & Kegan Paul, 1970).
Pratt, John *et al., Your Local Education* (Harmondsworth, Penguin, 1973).
Robinson, Eric, *The New Polytechnics: The People's Universities* (Harmondsworth, Penguin, 1968).
Scotland, James, *A History of Scottish Education* (London, University of London Press, 1969).
Simon, Brian, *The Radical Tradition in Education in Britain* (London, Lawrence and Wishart, 1972).
Smith, W. O. Lester, *The Government of Education* (Harmondsworth, Penguin, 1965).

4 LANGUAGE PROBLEMS

Aitken, A. J. (ed.), *Lowland Scots* (Edinburgh, Association for Scottish Literary Studies, Occasional Paper No. 2, 1973).
Campbell, J. L., *Gaelic in Scottish Education and Life* (Edinburgh, W. & A. K. Johnston, 1966).
Central Advisory Council for Education (Wales), *Primary Education in Wales* (The Gittins Report (London, HMSO, 1967), chs 11, 12, 13).
Corkery, Daniel, *The Hidden Ireland* (Dublin, Gill & Macmillan, 1967).
Corkery, Daniel, *The Fortunes of the Irish Language* (Cork, Mercier, 1968).
Dodson, C. J., Price, E., and Williams, I. T., *Towards Bilingualism* (*Welsh Studies in Education*, Vol. I) (Cardiff, University of Wales Press, 1968).
Dowling, P. J., *The Hedge Schools of Ireland* (Cork, Mercier, 1968).
Jones, W. R. *Bilingualism in Welsh Education* (Cardiff, University of Wales Press, 1966).
Mac Colla, Fionn, *Ro fhada mar so a tha mi* (*Too Long in This Condition*) (Caithness, John Humphries, 1975).
Mackay, J. R., *Gaelic Is ...* (Inverness, An Comunn Gáidhealach, 1969, 1975).
MacKinnon, Kenneth, *The Lion's Tongue* (Inverness, Club Leabhar, 1974).
MacLeod, Angus (ed.), 'Gaelic: A time to survive', *New Edinburgh Review*, no. 33, 1976).
MacThómais, Ruaraidh/Thomson, Derick (ed.), *Gáidhlig ann an Albainn/ Gaelic in Scotland* (Glaschu, Gairm, 1976).
Ó Cuív, Brian, *A View of the Irish Language* (Dublin, Stationery Office, 1969).
Price, G., *The Present Position of Minority Languages in Western Europe* (Caerdydd, University of Wales Press 1969).
Scottish Council for Research in Education, *Gaelic-speaking Children in Highland Schools* (London, University of London Press 1961).
Scottish Education Department, *Teaching Gaelic in Secondary Schools* (Edinburgh, HMSO, 1961).
Sharp, Derrick, *Language in Bilingual Communities* (London, Edward Arnold, 1973).
Sharp, D. W. H. *et al.*, *Some Aspects of Welsh and English: A Survey in the Schools of Wales* (London, Macmillan, 1973).
Welsh Office, *Legal Status of the Welsh Language* (Hughes-Parry Report) (Cardiff, HMSO, 1965).

5 INTERNATIONAL COMPARISONS AND PERSPECTIVES

Beck, Robert H., *Change and Harmonization in European Education* (Minneapolis, University of Minnesota Press, 1971).
Dakin, Julian, *et al.*, *Language in Education* (Oxford University Press, 1967).
King, E. J., *Education and Development in Western Europe* (Reading, Mass., Addison-Wesley, 1968).
Lowe, J. L., Grant, N. and Williams, T. D., *Education and Nation-Building in the Third World* (Edinburgh, Scottish Academic Press, 1971).
Sérant, Paul, *La France des minorités* (Paris, Laffont, 1965).
UNESCO, *The School and Continuing Education* (Paris, 1972).

Index